Kaye stuck at fashion design, her first career choice, for fourteen years. She caught the writing bug during two years timeout for travel, working as a features assistant on a London magazine. On her return to Australia, she embarked on further study. No one could accuse Kaye of quick career changes – a part-time arts degree took the maximum ten years to complete, as did the Diploma of Professional Writing and Editing which followed. During this time Kaye worked in the family publishing business, most recently as publisher and managing editor on *Your Life* magazine. A life-long learner, she has recently added basketball and bike riding to activities she pursues (albeit badly), but considers the challenges of parenting teenagers the most awesome and captivating experience of all.

how to change the way you live

Sick of work?
Stuck in a rut?
Dreaming of moving?
Don't know what to do next?

kaye fallick

First published in 2004

Copyright © Kaye Fallick 2004

All rights reserved. No part of this book may be reproduced or transmitted in any form or by any means, electronic or mechanical, including photocopying, recording or by any information storage and retrieval system, without prior permission in writing from the publisher. The *Australian Copyright Act 1968* (the Act) allows a maximum of one chapter or 10% of this book, whichever is the greater, to be photocopied by any educational institution for its educational purposes provided that the educational institution (or body that administers it) has given a remuneration notice to Copyright Agency Limited (CAL) under the Act.

A Sue Hines Book
Allen & Unwin
83 Alexander Street
Crows Nest NSW 2065
Australia
Phone: (61 2) 8425 0100
Fax: (61 2) 9906 2218
Email: info@allenandunwin.com
Web: www.allenandunwin.com

National Library of Australia
Cataloguing-in-Publication entry:
    Fallick, Kaye.
    Get a new life.
    Bibliography.
    ISBN 1 86508 962 1.
    1. Conduct of life. 2. Change (Psychology). 3. Goal (Psychology). 4. Self-actualization (Psychology). I. Title.
    158.1

Edited by Karen Ward
Text design and typesetting by Pauline Haas
Printed in Australia by Griffin Press
Author photograph by Simon Greenwood

The extract from *Oh, the Places You'll Go!* by Dr Seuss has been reproduced with permission from HarperCollins Publishers

10 9 8 7 6 5 4 3 2 1

CONTENTS

Foreword — xi

INTRODUCTION — 1
How to use this book — 3
Some questions you might be asking — 5

Part One: WHAT CHANGE MEANS

1. WHAT IS CHANGE? — 12
Endings — 13
    Coping with your endings — 13
The neutral zone — 14
    Handling the neutral zone — 14
New beginnings — 16
    Understanding your beginning phase — 17
How change comes – invited or otherwise — 19
    Your choice — 19
    Unexpected change — 21

2. ARE YOU READY? — 24
Checking your change-readiness — 25
Excuses we use to avoid change — 27
    Twelve reasons why we avoid change — 27

3. PLANNING YOUR CHANGE — 32
Timing and type — 33
Working by yourself — 34
    Taking stock — 34
    Why are values important? — 37
    Finding your passion — 38
    Where have you been, where are you going? — 39
    Making connections – finding your crossover point — 40

Seeking assistance	41
Vocational guidance	41
Self-examination	44

4. GETTING STARTED — 47

A series of small steps	47
Goal-setting	48
What is your main goal?	49
Goal evaluation	49
Acknowledging difficulties	50
Making a commitment to yourself	51
Goal planning	52
Achievable tasks	52
Breaking down your goals	52
Goal pursuit	53

5. AFFORDING YOUR LIFE CHANGE — 56

Getting started	57
Stocktake	58
Projecting your future needs	60
Making the link	61
Seeking independent advice	62
Living on less	63
What is downshifting?	63
How can you try to live on less?	64
When all else fails	64

6. FINDING NEW MEANING IN FAMILIAR PLACES — 66

Having a rethink	67

Part Two:
CHANGING YOURSELF

7. RELATIONSHIPS: THE HEART OF THE MATTER — 78

Looking after number one: Your relationship with yourself	78
Self-esteem	80
Attitude	81
Accountability	82

Self-discipline	83
Significant others	84
Relationship in need of repair	85
Relationship over	87
Losing someone close	89
Being lonely	92
Finding someone	93
Ways of meeting someone new	95
Romance, friendship or more meaningful communication?	95

8. EXPLORING YOUR CREATIVITY 97

What is creativity?	98
Unlocking your potential	98
Ten strategies to get you going	101
Finding a form	102
The creative journey of writing	104

9. THE LEARNING CURVE 108

Creating your life change through education	108
Why are you doing this?	110
What level of education are you seeking?	111
How do you get started?	115
Getting back into study and study habits	116

10. GETTING PHYSICAL 118

Your health questions	119
Finding basic information	120
Your general practitioner	121
Background reading on health change	122
You don't have to go it alone	123
Unexpected health change: The diagnosis	125

11. ASKING THE BIG QUESTIONS 130

What are the big questions?	130
Finding your faith or path	131
Philosophy as a way of life	132
Where do you find out more?	134
The retreat	135
Entering the faith	135
Committing to your faith	136

Part Three: CHANGING YOUR WORKING LIFE

12. YOUR DECISION: YOU JUST CAN'T DO THIS ANY MORE   146
- Timing   149
- Letting go   151

13. THEIR DECISION: DON'T COME MONDAY   153
- The job   154
- How are you likely to feel if you are made redundant?   155
  - How long are these feelings likely to last?   156
- What can you do?   156
  - Do your sums   157
  - Start with the short term. Then the medium term, then long term   159
  - Receiving outplacement   159
  - After the first shock   161
  - Relationships and redundancy   163

14. YOUR WORK OPTIONS   164
- Life/work balance: Getting it right   164
  - Does it have to be a competition?   165
- Portfolio work: Becoming a business of one   168
  - How do you get started?   170
  - Modifying your situation   173
  - Call in the consultants   173
- Small business startup: Doing it for yourself   175
  - What's the big attraction?   175
  - Summary   178
  - Getting started   178
  - Invaluable advice   179
- Buying a business   181
  - Franchises   183

15. NOT THE RETIRING TYPE   186
- How does it all work?   187
  - Research on ageing well: Those who've gone before   187
  - Listing your priorities   190
  - Beware the danger zones   191
  - Recognise the opportunities   191

Getting money in perspective	193
Grab the discounts	194
Consider a club	195
16. LOOKING OUTWARD	**197**
Volunteering	197
Why do people volunteer?	198
When shouldn't you volunteer?	198
How do you get started?	198
Mentoring	201
How do you become a mentor?	202

Part Four: MAKING YOUR SEA-CHANGE

17. HOME	**213**
Reasons for moving	214
Concerns you may have about moving	214
Doing your research	215
About you	216
Your new location	216
The trial run	218
How much does a home-swap cost?	220
How does it work?	221
Decision-making time	223
Understanding your motivation	223
Working out your priorities	224
Costing all aspects	225
Deciding whether to buy or sell first	225
Staying put	226
18. THE JOURNEY: USING TRAVEL AS A TRIGGER	**229**
Life-changing travel	230
What types of experiential travel are available?	232
Learning journeys	234
Through the eyes of a volunteer	234

    Asking for adventure   235
    The activity-based break   236
    Culturally inclined   237
    Wellbeing   238
    Seeking spirituality   239
Going solo   240
    Expectations   242
    Maximising your enjoyment of solo travel   243
A career in travel   244

19. THE EXPATRIATE EXPERIENCE: TRADING NATIONS   248

Getting started   251
    Gather information   251
    Move from the general to the specific   252
    Review your work/activity options   252
    Do a realistic cost projection   253
    Review income expectations   253
    Set a timeline   253
    Emotional checklist   254
    Cultural readiness checklist   255
Happy expats   256
    Characteristics of successful expats   256

ON YOUR WAY   261

Where are you at?   262
So what does it all come down to?   263
In short   268

ENDNOTES   271

RESOURCES   274

CHECKLISTS   307

ACKNOWLEDGEMENTS   324

FOREWORD

To Davy who said *'Of course you can do it ...'*
To SJ who said *'Stick to what you know ...'*
To Lucy who said *'Just don't make it boring ...'*

One doesn't discover new lands without consenting to lose sight of the shore for a very long time

This quote by Andre Gide turned up on my desk calendar one day and I just loved it.

At the time I was out of my depth at work and struggling to earn enough to live on. For a while I had felt as though I was paddling, alone, directionless, with no horizon in sight. Now, through Gide's words, I realised that not knowing might be an exciting state – and a necessary one for an extended period. For the first time I understood that not knowing where I was headed was not only okay, but might signal a period of great personal growth.

Soon after, I heard psychologist Peter O'Connor talking about the value of anxiety. Again I felt relief – it was okay to feel anxious; in fact it could be a valuable stage in your life journey. Rather than fighting it, allowing this feeling to tease out your real concerns could prove to be a critical and positive phase in your life.

Losing sight of the shore and valuing uncertainty are part of the core philosophy underpinning this book. In writing *Get a New Life* I have tried to act as a tour guide to some of life's changes and the many resulting options, rather than telling readers how to live their lives.

Being publisher of *Your Life* magazine has exposed me to many issues which arise when people are told they should retire – as though they had a use-by date. It has taught me to ask a lot of questions about what constitutes life, work, and how you might find fulfilment by mixing the two successfully. Or if you are not enjoying what you do, how you might create something more satisfying and meaningful. This book shares the better questions I have learnt to ask and many of the answers people have offered.

There is no one answer – there are multiple questions, a myriad of possibilities, and many profiles of people who have seized the chance to get a new life.

Hopefully, as instructed by Lucy, I haven't made it boring.

INTRODUCTION

*I want to change my life but
I don't know how, or in what way*

Do you sometimes feel like a fish out of water? Are you wandering through life, feeling vaguely dispirited, but not sure if it's a passing phase or a more serious disconnection with your job, your partner, your community, or your aspirations?

Maybe you read about and encounter people who are vibrant, passionate, and full of energy. They seem to be leading much juicier, more colourful lives while yours is painted in shades of grey. They are full of enthusiasm for their possibilities and you wonder why you don't feel as though you have any.

Maybe it seems as though a vital something is missing: a person, vocation, adventure, or opportunity? And all too often other people seem to get the lucky breaks, or the better deal, while you feel stuck, resentful, and fearful that life is passing you by.

Change is a non-negotiable part of your life. Whether you invite it, plan it, embrace it or deny it, it is on your agenda, and will bite you on the bum at some stage.

The real challenge is to recognise the stages and manage your own change to the best of your ability, at your own pace.

As a society we have been trained to understand life as a linear progress building to a pinnacle of achievement ('making it'), and then a gracious denouement via retirement to death. The popular media reinforce this idea with endless stories of good-looking 'celebs' in dream homes, having 'found love' at last. As we mature into adults we are somehow supposed to be getting wiser and more fulfilled. But this is a misconception. It is just not the way things work for many of us. Maybe you berate yourself that by now things should have 'worked out', and you should be happier than you are. Steady on. You've not only given yourself an arbitrary 'use-by' date, you've also decided you've passed it!

Get a New Life has been written for people grappling with these issues. It is for those thinking of changing the way they live, or needing to manage a change which has been thrust upon them. It is designed to help you work your way through the issues, explore your options, and make sound decisions. Essentially it is about your unfulfilled dreams, your untapped potential and how you might combine the two.

It's also *not* about many other things…

This is not a self-help book. Self-help presumes you need help – with a subtext that there is something wrong which needs to be fixed with the help of a self-appointed expert, full of born-again zeal. If this is what you are seeking, this is not the book for you. You are in control of the type, pace and degree of change. *Get a New Life* is not about telling you what to do or how to live your life – instead it offers strategies, options, examples, information and resources which you can access to create your own plans.

Nor is it about 'success' as defined by glossy magazines which insist you can have it all – great job, house, spouse, designer children, huge investment portfolios and luxury holidays in 'undiscovered' destinations. This book is definitely not about the money. If your idea of 'making it' is based primarily on the size of your bank account, head to the finance section now!

Nor does it suggest that everyone needs to change and if they don't, they're losers. Change for change's sake makes very little sense at all. Sometimes the hardest, and smartest, strategy can be to reappraise a situation and work through the difficulties, perhaps gaining a new appreciation for the familiar.

In short, *Get a New Life* is not about finding answers, but about asking useful questions. It's not about having it all, but about achieving the bits that matter. It's not about wealth, measured in monetary terms, but about personal wealth which only you can evaluate. And it's definitely not about living happily ever after, but about living fully – and all that that entails.

The aim of this book is to share some typical questions being asked by Australians seeking a sea-change, and to highlight a wealth of resources which might allow you to find your own answers. Along the way, we'll meet people who've explored their own individual changes and are prepared to share the highs and lows of their experiences.

How to use this book

Essentially, *Get a New Life* has been written to help you look at the 'big picture' of your life, assess it, and come up with a plan to pursue your long-held dreams, ambitions and goals in an achievable manner. Quite simply it is a plain English guide to managing the different types of life change. Part One, What Change Means, covers the context of change and how you might handle it. It looks at the processes and types of change, so you can create a roadmap of your own possibilities. It assists with your goal-setting, as well as offering realistic strategies for those with time and money constraints. It also helps those seeking the space and encouragement to think, question, and make their own best decisions. Parts Two, Three and Four address the three major aspects of change: yourself, your working life and your location. Part Two, Changing Yourself, looks at the more personal manifestations of change in your relationships, creativity, personal development, wellbeing and spirituality. Part Three, Changing Your Working Life, overviews vocational changes and work options, as well as creative options for the realm of retirement, and looking outward with community engagement. Part Four, Making Your Sea-change, explores the geography of change, from moving home to moving country as well as making significant journeys.

Because we tend to prefer being shown – rather than told – what life is all about, each section has liberal sprinklings of profiles of 'those who have gone before' and what they've learnt.

Perhaps one of the most useful aspects of any contemplated change is the list of resources available so you can do your own research, and reach your own conclusions. All the books, websites, journals, government departments and member associations referred to throughout the chapters are available in the Resources Section at the back of the book, with a brief note evaluating the relevance and usefulness of each particular resource in managing a specific change in your life.

In a nutshell, *Get a New Life* has been written to remove all the excuses which sit between you and your dreams, and to get you on your way. Some readers will want to start at page 1 and read through to the end. Others will just plunge in at the chapter that relates to their current life situation.

Enjoy!

some questions you might be asking

- How do I know if I want to change?
- What are the processes of change – how can I work my way through them?
- How do I evaluate whether it is a good idea?
- What questions do I need to ask?
- What help can I get with this process?
- How can I afford a life change?
- How do I get the courage to make the leap?
- What if I don't want to change, but would like to find a new appreciation of what I already have?
- What if I don't have a passion?
- What if I think I'm too old for this?
- What if my family think I'm an idiot?
- Am I just being self-indulgent?
- What resources are available for my particular form of change?

Part One: WHAT CHANGE MEANS

> Congratulations!
> Today is your day.
> You're off to Great Places!
> You're off and away!
>
> — DR SEUSS,
> *Oh, the Places You'll Go!*

Most human beings are uncomfortable with change, even those who, superficially, seem to seek it out. Although they may continually change themselves with new jobs, new relationships and new horizons, they also may feel the fear of leaving the old and plunging into the new. If we accept the belief that knowledge leads to power, then understanding what change is, and how it can affect your life will enable you to manage your changes more effectively. And life changes are not one-offs. They will occur again and again. The best way to work your way through these changes is to recognise the processes of change, and the specific stage you are currently at. This will give you a far better overview of your situation, enabling you to make more informed decisions with which to travel forward. Just when all seems to be in disarray on the ground, you will manage to climb the ladder, and survey the progress you have made, the new and exciting possibilities which lie ahead, as well as the confusion of the moment. Understanding the middle phase of change, the neutral zone between an ending and a new beginning, also alerts you to the possibilities you may unearth in this confusing and disorienting aspect of your change.

Part One, What Change Means, introduces you to the nature of change, and how you can apply your understanding of the processes to your own situation. It opens with a profile of Nola, a bean counter who became a mosaic artist, and more. Chapter 1, 'What is Change?', explores the nature of change, and how it comes into your life, whether invited or otherwise. Chapter 2, 'Are You Ready?', helps you assess your change readiness, and Chapter 3, 'Planning Your Change', looks at the more practical aspects of planning and managing change. Chapter 4, 'Getting Started', helps you translate these plans into reality by breaking your larger life goals down into manageable steps. Chapter 5, 'Affording Your Life Change', addresses the nitty-gritty of the money – how to afford your goals, and if you haven't got enough, how to get your finances in shape so you can move toward an achievable goal. But change isn't for everyone. Many who feel vaguely discontented are not actually seeking a major life shift, merely a more meaningful connection with what they already have. Chapter 6, 'Finding New Meaning in Familiar Places', highlights the ways we can find more meaning in the familiar places in our lives, rather than implementing change for the sake of it.

Nola Diamantopoulos: Dumping the answer

I became an artist seven years ago. I had not had previous formal artistic training. I was working as a tax manager for an oil and gas exploration company. My role was still enjoyable but the long hours and continual travel were wearing.

About this time I attended a workshop where I heard a statement by satirist Georg Christoph Lichtenberg – *Question everything*. I did this, in particular by asking myself, 'What kind of a person do I wish to be?' That question triggered many insights and within a few weeks I knew that I wanted to do something with a high degree of personal significance, I wanted to express my being, and I wanted to be able to hear the smile in my voice. I realised that I would need to create such a life; it would not be something I would find ready-made.

This coincided with my attempts to create ceramic icons to celebrate the birth of my nephew, Michael. My efforts were disappointing, but I kept working and reworking the patterns. I read books, took classes and worked some more.

Despite my friends' misgivings, I gave up my day job, and attended more classes. I worked in oils, I drew every day.

Soon after I made the very personal decision to describe myself as an artist. In the beginning, as I was learning to draw, my efforts did not produce anything very good. The real point is that I did *not* discover a hidden talent that I was then forced to pursue. On the contrary, I discovered a hidden desire – that I was then forced to pursue. For about the first nine months of studying drawing and the work of other artists, I was very embarrassed about my creative output. So I would throw my initial works away, screw them up and toss them out. When people asked me what I did, I would either say, 'I'm learning about art', or, depending on the venue, I would say, 'I'm an emerging artist'. Emerging from my bad drawings, is what I would quietly think! Anyway, that kind of language was only reinforcing my inner fear. When I realised this I decided to call myself an artist. And everything began to change. Because my thoughts had changed, then my behaviour changed. I stopped throwing out my bad drawings and wow! What happened was that I could now see that I was improving. And then the big thing happened – I began to like what I did, even though it was not very good. I could accept my work. Now I could grow.

But I was still a little uncomfortable. I had yet to hold an exhibition; I hadn't produced anything I liked enough. Yet I was living as an artist – my clothes consisted of art smocks and socks and ankle boots. I read art books, mostly artists' biographies, art movements, art theory and technique. I was honouring my journey. I was not calling myself an artist because my ego liked the sound of it. In fact, the truth is, I don't like that word very much — I prefer being called imaginative or creative.

About this time I rented a studio in Glebe, and decided to run workshops. I chose to teach mosaic techniques because I was creating mosaic tables at the time, and had done a huge amount of research on the art form. What I learnt from these workshops was that I love to teach as much as I love expressing myself through paintings and mosaics. Gradually the classes moved from just being about mosaic techniques, to exploring wider creative processes and possibilities. This led to a class called 'Art for Strictly Beginners', where students are encouraged to still their inner critic and limiting beliefs and free themselves up to enter the world of visual arts. I now hold 'Out of the Question' workshops for those who want to explore the possibilities of thinking, and questioning the questions. This is, in a way, a reaction to the linear form of teaching in schools where we are continually driven to come up with outcomes. I work with stories which are analogies or metaphors to start a process of mental gymnastics where we learn to dump the answer and give power to our own journeys.

> *I believe that if you are not expressing yourself you are acting out a life*

Within five years I managed to set up my own studio in Rozelle. It is here I try to feed the senses with colour, visuals, food, aromatherapy, and inspirational, or hysterical, music. Two years ago I founded the Mosaic Association of Australia (Mos-Oz) to hold exhibitions, and introduce international artists to the local scene. I also run a mosaic shop, called the Madness Shop, from the studio.

I don't earn as much as I used to, but I don't feel as though I am missing out. I have my indulgences — brightly coloured work smocks, special perfume, and good wine. I also enjoy the occasional 'me' day when I spend time in my garden courtyard with books and music. I am seduced by my painting and drawing and mosaics and know I am on the path that I am meant to be travelling. I believe that if you are not expressing yourself you are acting out a life.

I now describe myself as an expressionist. My definition of 'creative' is a desire to express yourself. I have that desire — in whatever I do — hence I am an expressionist, which is also the way I draw and paint.

It's been three years since my last exhibition. I am now preparing for a second one. A trip to Paris last November was to get inspired and I'm definitely that. I have many things I want to say and as to how I will say them — well, that's the mystery of the creative process. I can't wait. So the coming year will be about teaching less and painting, sculpting and mosaicing more. I'm attending a one-week lithography class soon and I have already prepared several models to sit for me. My challenge will be to maintain the balance I have achieved between expressing myself on canvas and in clay and the desire to teach.

What does art give me? Wow — where do I begin? I am continuously learning and that's exciting. Art stimulates me. And in return I am able to stimulate others. Art has not only given me the opportunity to change my life and make it meaningful, art has also let me make a difference in the lives of others. Art fulfils me.

Chapter one
WHAT IS CHANGE?

Whether your change is voluntary or something thrust upon you, the more you understand about the processes of change, the better your chances will be of managing it, rather than merely 'coping'. What do people go through when they experience change? Grief, loss, anger, confusion? A narrowing of their horizons? Or a sense of liberation and excitement and a widening of their possibilities? A feeling that they can meet any challenge thrown at them? The short answer is, usually, both.

Until recently, many 'change experts' found it useful to define the process of change in a similar manner to the stages of grief, as outlined by Elisabeth Kubler Ross in *On Death and Dying* in 1969. In the 1990s, American change management specialist William Bridges reworked the stages of change to assist American corporations that were downsizing as a consequence of economic rationalism. In his book, *Managing Transitions*, Bridges recognised that change is actually a back-to-front experience. Rather than following the popular notion that people make a decision to change, and then go through the Kubler Ross grief model emotions, Bridges' work with organisational change showed him that most change begins with an ending, moves into a neutral zone, and ends with the beginning – the new job, marriage, career, location. The neutral zone, which Bridges also calls 'the wilderness', represents the time between the old reality and the new, often involving emotional struggle, anxiety and/or denial. But it can also be viewed as a time pregnant with creative possibility, 'the night during which we are disengaged from yesterday's concerns and prepared for tomorrow's'.

Endings

Endings don't have to be a purely negative experience. By recognising the range of emotions attached to endings, and trying to resolve them, you can help clear your path in order to progress.

Some of the emotions you may experience include:

- grief
- anger
- desire to bargain
- stress
- anxiety
- sadness
- lethargy
- confusion
- depression
- longing for answers

Coping with your ending

The first step is to admit that an ending has occurred, then to identify related issues. This can be easier said than done. If you have missed out on an opportunity, perhaps a promotion at work, you may have tried to suppress your expectations by telling yourself you were unlikely to be chosen. But when you find out someone else has been selected, the full impact of your loss may affect every part of your life. Perhaps subconsciously you had already 'moved' into the new office and were taking control of the new department, and in not receiving the promotion, your hopes and dreams have taken a battering.

- Say out loud what you feel you have lost with this ending.
- Or say what you might lose or threaten if you choose this ending.
- Recognise the private losses (self-esteem, love, dreams, beliefs) as well as the public (marriage, status, career, house, income).
- Ask yourself if there are things you might gain by this ending.
- Or if there are things you have already gained.

- Talk about your feelings with someone you trust.
- Understand this confusion and anxiety as a necessary part of the re-sorting process. whereby insights gained, albeit painfully, will inform future achievements.

Successful change rarely denies the past. Instead it honours and incorporates it. Write out a list of positive achievements, skills, learning experiences in your past, as foundation stones for building your future.

The neutral zone

The time between your old situation, and that which is to follow may be confusing, stressful, even frightening, but it can also lead to new discoveries about yourself and your situation which greatly enhance your chances of successful change. Many people experience a form of depression, sometimes mild, sometimes more severe, when they feel stuck in a situation from which there is no way out. It doesn't seem to help to be told you'll get over it. But it may be useful to try to see this as a midway point, and as an opportunity to assess as broad a range of options as possible, to go with the flow, and see what emerges. Forcing yourself to come up with answers is likely to lead to a resolution – but not always the best one. It's time to think tortoise rather than hare.

Handling the neutral zone

Write a description of the types of issues which might surface during your neutral zone – the emotions you might encounter, as well as the things you might discover.

If you are fearful about the change that is occurring, or is about to occur, ask yourself what would constitute a successful change, and what your fallback position will be if this fully successful change is not achieved.

For example, you may be going through a separation after many years of marriage. Your idea of 'successful' change may involve re-establishing a better relationship with your departed spouse, and ultimately getting back together. Not achieving this may require admitting that it is possible they are happier without you, and want to move on, and start a relationship with someone else. This will obviously involve a very painful re-evaluation of where your change is heading, but it may be possible to entertain some fall-back positions. These might involve establishing an amicable relationship rather than rekindling the romance, exploring your own vocational needs which may become more possible with the extra time you have as a single, or enjoying long-anticipated travel to destinations your ex-spouse would never have agreed to explore.

> *It is better to have absolutely no idea where one is and to know it, than to believe confidently that one is where one is not*

Confusion during the neutral zone is very common – try to be clear about how you define your change as successful and what period of time is reasonable/bearable before you conclude it has been successful or otherwise. If you have been out of work for six weeks, it is worth remembering that most job-seekers take between three months and a year before finding new employment. Being mentally flexible and not stuck in the 'I want what I had' rut also helps you to understand your change may have brought unexpected gains which outweigh other anticipated, but yet-to-be delivered, benefits.

Some common feelings during the neutral zone:

- less energy
- less motivation
- frightened
- ambiguous
- ambivalent

ASK YOURSELF

- How can I equip myself to manage my transition?
- What resources/skills do I have (for example, am I flexible, eager to learn, courageous)?
- Within my skills audit have I included the personal and creative as well as the purely vocational?

- What resources/skills will I need? (patience, good financial budgeting for trying financial times, languages for a new country?)
- When is it an ideal time to start to acquire these skills?
- Who can help me?

It may be that while you are drifting through this difficult stage, you are surrounded by those who seem to have a very clear idea of where they are going. It is important to have the courage not to follow those who seem to know what you should be doing, those who seem to have the answers. There may be many answers to your dilemma, or none. It also helps to continue to question on your own behalf and to remain dissatisfied if none of the apparent answers dovetail with your question.

While you are working your way through this transitional time, enhance your creative possibilities by challenging yourself with new sights, sounds and patterns. These challenges might be as simple as reading a different magazine, drinking at a different bar, swimming at a new beach, driving to work a different way, or inviting a different group of friends home for dinner.

Don't expect to like it all – expect some of it to 'fail' – and expect rejection. The point is not that every new experience is going to be a positive one, but that in exposing yourself to new places, opportunities and people, you just may find some connections which have very real value during a particularly testing time.

New beginnings

The very word 'beginning' has a freshness and zing to it, a promise of getting on track. Yet this time can be just as fraught as an ending. Part of the reason beginnings can be so frightening is your own, and other people's, expectations that you will 'deliver'. This might mean that, as a new CEO you are expected to turn around a company's bad performance and considerably enhance the share price. It may mean that as a new spouse you should be a constant joy to come home to. Or, at a far simpler level, it may mean that you will expect a 'new you' to emerge – a more restrained, patient, mature, charming you – along with the new relationship, responsibility, and so on. Beginnings also signal that the 'drifting' phase is over and you are (metaphorically) back on the job. Thus you are expected to be accountable, to deliver.

Hopefully the time spent in the neutral zone has assisted you to ask yourself some very tough questions, and to gain a clearer understanding of the type and magnitude of your change, and how you might gain from it. For some, previous 'beginnings' may have led to negative life experiences, so anxieties associated with these memories may be rekindled.

Understanding your beginning phase

A hearty dose of realism can only help, particularly during a time of change. Life is not about 'getting things under control', 'getting it right' or 'getting your act together' for the simple reason that we live in dynamic times and as soon as we work out a solution for one set of circumstances, another will arise which requires new solutions and new strategies. Understand your beginning as your current task or strategy. This attitude will help maintain a flexibility of thought and action which allows for setbacks, discouragements, and all the shades of grey which life will offer.

Remember, beginning is a big word. If you can break down this concept into a series of steps that help you see the formation of this beginning, way back with the original ending, as well as the very diverse places this beginning may take you, it may help reduce some of your fears and concerns into manageable chunks.

CONSIDER

- What are your expectations for yourself and others?
- Are they realistic?
- Having made this change, do you now hope to live happily ever after?
- Have you considered a fall-back position if this new beginning doesn't deliver all you hope for?
- Remember to congratulate yourself on the progress you've made.

TIMING IS EVERYTHING

It is useful to remember that the external perception of your change does not have to match your emotional progress. To the outside world you resigned your job in April, and recommenced work in September. The ending of one experience was April, and the new beginning in September. In between you had a great break with your family. In reality you may have felt insecure in that first job for the previous six months, and your ending was the October before. Your neutral zone may well have stretched beyond the new job's start date of September – it may be something you grabbed out of economic necessity, and not your dream job at all. You may still feel very confused and still be searching for a direction which best suits your talents and dreams, but the rest of the world has ticked the box beside your name: another job change successfully resolved.

Helen Johnson*: I needed to do more

I've learnt that if you're not happy with how your life is going and who you are, you need to accept that your upbringing and personality are a large part of your existence. What you have to work with, the things you can change, are relatively small. But this can be enough.

I didn't realise I was depressed until my marriage started to unravel, but I look back at parts of my life and realise I lived in a black tunnel for a long while. I felt as though my family's happiness depended on me and I could no longer carry the load. I got to the point when getting up, cooking a meal, getting through the day all took a huge effort. I realised I needed to do something.

I finally went to my GP. He suggested a psychiatrist who put me on some medication. After four weeks on one medication he would decide I wasn't improving, and would switch me to something else. The abrupt change in drugs just sent me crashing to the ground. I went into a hole, and decided to kill myself. I carefully prepared all the things I would need and put them in the boot of my car. I drove around like that for a week. Then I told my GP who contacted the psychiatrist, and he convinced me to admit myself to a psychiatric hospital.

I spent three weeks in hospital, before going back home. My husband and I had a few marriage counselling services, but one night we just looked at each other and agreed the marriage was over.

I knew I needed to do more for myself than just talk to a shrink. I attended an outpatients' program and learnt about basic living skills, how to survive whole days. I knew it was up to me to just try harder. I would plan each day down to the last thirty minutes, to make it all more manageable. I wrote a journal, mainly about my moods, but also about understanding different points of view about things that upset me. This helped me see lots of little achievements, small steps I made each day which built into bigger steps. Slowly I crept back into the world.

My relationship with the kids is very good now – we enjoy lots of laughs and fun times together. It's my behaviour that's changed, not theirs. Last year I met someone special, and we're getting married in the near future. I have so much to look forward to.

✶ Name has been changed

How change comes – invited or otherwise

Significant life change can come in one of two ways – we create the change in our lives, or a life event thrusts us into a new situation. The first reason allows us to initiate change and have a degree of control over its form, shape and pace. The latter generally arrives without any warning and, for a short while at least, offers very little sense of control of our own destiny. Understanding the issues behind both types of change can help us navigate our way.

Your choice

For those who have been reluctantly thrown into new and challenging territory by an event such as widowhood, retrenchment or life-threatening disease, initiating change may seem like a forbidden luxury. Yet those who long for change, but can't quite get their act together to make it happen, often secretly wish an external factor would force them down a different path. As always, the grass seems greener.

REASONS FOR WANTING CHANGE

Reasons for wanting change are many and various. Some of the more common ones are:

- *I just can't do this any longer* – My soul is withering, it's bad for my health, and I'm continually in a bad mood. I've spent far too long in this place.

- *Feeling trapped* – Not unlike the feeling commonly described by sufferers of depression – a feeling that it's not worth getting out of bed in the morning, that all life can offer is a sameness of activity and enjoyment levels, and that there is no escape from this drudgery.

- *Mismatch of values* – I don't truly fit in this community, this relationship, this career. It just doesn't feel right. If I have to keep doing this it will actually make me sick.

- *I have another calling* – I was born to achieve something great and what I'm currently doing is not it. This feeling often results in feelings of low self-esteem, as the next question is often, 'Who do I think I am to think I have a calling?' It can take a huge effort of will to not belittle oneself in this situation.

- *The MTL syndrome* – There's got to be More To Life than this. When I'm on my deathbed, if this is all I've ever done, I will be thoroughly disappointed in myself.

- *Curiosity* – I have an idea, a career or a creative calling I am just dying to explore. There is so much more I want to learn/need to know about this. I cannot contain my curiosity any longer.

- *Someone else inside me* – There's another person inside me who is just waiting to burst out. This other person is looking far more attractive than the negative weary self who is currently shuffling through my existence. I cannot keep this stranger locked inside any longer.

Adrian[*]:
Matching values with purpose

For many years I worked in the HR department of a multinational mineral company. I was restless at work, but not entirely unhappy. My wife was not working, and with a young daughter, we both felt we needed my income to maintain a lifestyle we all enjoyed. Sensing my dissatisfaction, a friend loaned me a quiz which highlighted how suited you were to your current employment. It made me think about some of the issues, and told me a lot I already knew about myself, but was too scared to admit. I was actually sick to death of what I was doing — clearly, I should have been planning to make a major change. I wanted to go back to university and get a psychology degree.

My very good luck was that I was able to make a career change without the degree. I took a pay cut to do it — it wasn't even close to a hard decision — it was such a relief to move closer to something I really wanted to do, and further away from yesterday. My friend's questionnaire was the start. But my disillusionment also came from changes my company was undergoing. The value system and culture was changing — there was more encouragement to be dishonest. Towards the end of my time there, the US chairman was visiting and I was encouraged by the managing director to disguise the truth of a certain situation.

Crunch time came. All my friends and peers, my boss, and the director who had asked me to lie, were present. For one split second I hesitated, and then my values kicked in and I told the truth. There were no major repercussions. I had already realised that the job was no longer fun, and didn't suit my ethics. Honesty is important.

Soon after, I was offered a position with a consulting firm and I now have a job which enables me to work honestly and productively with people in need.

[*] Name has been changed

Unexpected change

It may be that your life change was anything but an answer to a growing need. You may have felt perfectly happy with your existence, and through the loss of a loved one, job, home, career or health, your situation has changed irrevocably. If this change is indeed irrevocable, managing it well may be the only degree of choice you have. When a life event becomes the key catalyst for change, one of the few options you might have is to benefit from the experience and wisdom of those who have gone before.

TYPES OF UNEXPECTED CHANGE

Relationship breakup can be one of the most painful, and this doesn't just apply to adult love relationships, but can be a breakup with adult children, with parents, siblings, or very close friends. Often our life patterns have been predicated upon the assumption that a significant other will always be there, and their exit from our lives can cause a total re-evaluation of every other aspect.

The death of a child, sibling, parent or partner/spouse can prove to be the most severe form of relationship dislocation, but the death of a close friend or acquaintance can also set in motion a deep questioning of the meaning of your life, and how you currently express yourself, or how you might like to change that form of expression. Nothing is quite so thought-provoking as the celebration of someone's life, their achievements, and setbacks.

Losing your job through retrenchment or redundancy can sometimes pack as powerful a punch as losing a person — whether others think this should be the case or not, this can be the feeling for those who are asked to go.

Serious accident or illness can rudely interrupt our sometimes arrogant assumptions of ongoing good health, reducing our ability to function physically as well as we previously could. Whilst medical support may be forthcoming, you have also entered a period of intense renegotiation of your hopes and options.

Financial setbacks can also force a major reassessment of your future. Every year more than 20000 Australians file for bankruptcy — many thousands more hover near the brink. Job loss, unwise investments and loss for which we are not insured can all threaten our financial security. Often a previously comfortable existence is wiped out and for some, this is exacerbated by being responsible for a mountain of debt, often through no fault of their own.

This list makes fairly grim reading. Yet many of the profiles in this book are of people who experienced at least one of these forms of change, and altered their existence to incorporate their new reality and move on.

It's all very well for other people, but I'm not very good at making things happen...

WHAT'S STOPPING YOU?

Maybe you have yet to acknowledge that an ending has taken place in your life? It could be that you are going through the motions each day, dissatisfied with your lot, but in a form of denial that your relationship is in crisis, or your current career no longer holds any interest, or that it is time to leave home and fend for yourself. Think back to previous times of change. Try to define the ending, neutral zone, and beginning associated with those different changes. Was the ending buried, unclear until a long time afterward? Use this information to appraise your current dilemma. Have you experienced an ending, but ignored it? Maybe you are now drifting along in the neutral zone. Do any of your current feelings match those listed on page 20? Or have you moved to a beginning, but wonder if you've made the right choice? Thinking about the elements of change and how they overlap may help to clarify your thoughts and encourage you to go easy on yourself.

Chapter two
ARE YOU READY?

How do you recognise if the vague disquiet you are feeling is a need for change in your life, or just a mood that will eventually pass?

The first step is to attempt to see issues clearly and not have your view clouded by emotion, or saddled with guilt over how you should feel on behalf of a spouse, child or parent. It may be that you will ultimately make a decision to delay your own gratification until your family can more easily handle it. But in the first instance, in order to understand the strength of your need for change, it is important to separate your desires from those of others. It is a difficult task to evaluate your degree of disaffection with your current situation, and it can often be easier to sublimate these feelings and stay in the groove than to challenge your status quo and take the hard decisions necessary to move towards a new goal.

There are very few objective ways of measuring whether you are content in your life situation and at which point contentment can slide into complacency, boredom, frustration, or deep-seated unhappiness. It's also very difficult to evaluate whether your dreams of change are based on a realistic and achievable goal or a mirage, fed by visions of easy success. Our culture abounds with stories of people who have enacted dramatic change in their lives, and appear to be happy, wealthy, and good-looking. Sometimes a less superficial analysis of these individuals will often reveal many previously unsuccessful attempts, years of hard work and knockbacks, and a current situation which may be far from absolute happiness.

Checking your change-readiness

In the absence of an objective measure for your 'change-readiness' try these two short reading exercises which may help you measure your desire for change.

The first book, *Oh, the Places You'll Go!*, is 45 pages of fun. Written by Dr Seuss of *Cat in the Hat* fame, it is a rollicking rhyme contemplating life's ups and downs. If you find it describes your yearning for new adventures and if when you put it down the blood is still thrumming in your veins and you see only the possibilities and not the obstacles, the time may well be ripe for you to 'get on your way'.

The other short read, *Who Moved My Cheese?*, is a parable used by American management guru, Dr Spencer Johnson, to assist workers to cope with the concept of corporate change. Subtitled *An Amazing Way to Deal With Change In Your Work and In Your Life,* it describes the reactions of different personality types to a radical life change situation. One type quickly adapts and seeks alternatives; another becomes frustrated, angry, negative and despondent. A third type agonises and fears the change, but eventually works through his fear, gaining energy and enthusiasm for the task of finding some 'new cheese', asking himself, 'What would you do if you weren't afraid?' This simple tale can be very useful in understanding your own likely reaction to change, and to gauge your readiness to 'put on your running shoes'.

Another test is the itch test. Is there a dream or goal or activity in your life which you want more of? Something to which your thoughts just keep returning? An itch that won't go away? If your thoughts keep drifting from your current life situation to greener pastures, perhaps you, too, are ready to move to the next step.

So you are experiencing the common precursors to making significant life changes: nagging doubts about your existence, feelings that you are on a treadmill, and an inability to take a few hours off to consider these thoughts. If you are under great time pressure, it is likely that your decision-making will be hampered by too little information, too little time to evaluate your life situation objectively, and a perception that you are ill equipped to make good decisions.

YOU KNOW YOU ARE READY FOR CHANGE WHEN:

- You actively seek newspaper or magazine articles on people who've implemented change in their lives and then feel dissatisfied that you haven't.
- You go for long periods in your day job without feeling connected or purposeful.
- You read about Peter Mayle or Frances Mayes and their 'new lives' in France and Tuscany and dislike them intensely for being so obviously happy about the changes they've made.
- In fact most successful people really irritate you.
- You can feel yourself spiralling into a negative world view.
- This negative world view seems to be affecting your health and energy levels – you wistfully recall times when you were slimmer, healthier, more active and more positive.
- It seems easier to live vicariously through TV shows and films than to venture out yourself.
- Your family no longer regards you as energetic or interesting – and, worse still, you agree with them.

It is important to break this cycle, and leave your current pressurised situation *if only for a few hours.* Yet few people will take even half a day away from their duties for a whole-of-life planning session. Why do we afford ourselves so little courtesy, and just expect our souls to grind on without contemplative time? What lies behind 'not having enough time'? Why do we consistently avoid a discussion of the big issues? Let's consider some of the factors involved in this avoidance, in order to understand and, if necessary, overcome them.

Excuses we use to avoid change

It is almost impossible to single-handedly raid our subconscious and come up with accurate reasons why we feel stuck in a rut. The very first step is to take an hour out of your life, and put yourself into an unfamiliar environment with no distractions. Take an empty notebook, a pencil and go to a coffee shop in a location where no-one will know you. Switch off your mobile phone, pager, blocking any form of communication with people who may interrupt you. For the first twenty minutes, switch off your mind as well. Drink your coffee and flick through whatever piece of reading matter the café offers. This could be a magazine, the local paper, a brochure for a cinema chain – whatever. Now order a second coffee, open your journal, and write the date, five things you love about your life currently, and five things you'd like to change. Now your focus is sharpened, and you are ready to consider the following list, and whether any of these points apply to your situation.

Twelve reasons why we avoid change

- Parental expectations – *How can I tell them?*
- Lack of planning structure – *I just don't know how to get started.*
- Investment in current situation – *But I've spent years qualifying.*
- Fear of failure – *What will I do if it doesn't work out?*
- Sense of duty – *Life's not meant to be easy; I should just try harder.*
- Giving up long-held goals or beliefs – *I've never really believed in divorce.*
- Sense of being self-indulgent – *Who am I to risk the family savings on a new business?*
- Interferes with a strong self-image – *I've always coped; I'll manage somehow.*
- Threat to perceived status – *What if my friends think I'm going broke?*
- Affordability – real and imagined – *I'd do it if I had the money.*
- Ageism – *It's ridiculous at my age – I'm far too young/old/middle-aged.*
- Accountability – *If it was up to me ...*

Some of these reasons for avoiding an assessment of your situation, and implementing a strategy to change it, are legitimate. Some are just misconceptions which can be recognised and dismissed. Some go to the core of who we are and highlight long-held fears and beliefs which are not easily dismissed, but at least recognising them might add some objectivity to your thought processes.

HOW CAN I TELL THEM?

Avoidance of questioning a career or life path can be due to an inability to disobey fathers and mothers (even those who are now long dead) with very specific goals for us. It can be extremely difficult to challenge years of parental expectations that you should be a lawyer, a housewife, a farmer, heterosexual or physically tough. So sometimes it is just easier to continue along the path already plotted by your family expectations.

I JUST DON'T KNOW HOW TO GET STARTED

A lack of structure can also inhibit effective life planning. Sometimes the shock of being made redundant becomes a really positive experience when outplacement is offered, and an objective planning structure is provided with expert guidance. For those without any structured support, but filled with a vague disquiet that there has to be a better way, it can be very difficult to tackle the planning process on their own. How do you know how fed up you have to be to warrant a life change? How do you judge when the time is right? How do you work out what you really want to do? It's fine for those with a calling or a passion, but what if you just have a sense that you should change and nothing more?

BUT I'VE SPENT YEARS QUALIFYING

Another very real barrier to life change is the sense of investment that you may have already made to a particular field of study, career path, or relationship – a feeling that if you move on from a particular situation you have 'wasted' all the years of education, experience, or intimacy achieved thus far. The critical question to ask here is whether another ten miserable years in your current situation will make you feel as though you have no longer 'wasted' this investment.

WHAT WILL I DO IF IT DOESN'T WORK OUT?

Fear of failure is another very obvious reason why many of us resist our desire for change. It can be seductively easy to stick with well-trodden paths and manageable expectations rather than try something that doesn't come out the way we hope. Yet it might also be useful to test what we really understand by the term 'failure', how we judge failure for others, and ourselves and whether sometimes so-called failure is really just a setback along a far longer path.

LIFE'S NOT MEANT TO BE EASY; I SHOULD JUST TRY HARDER

It is possible that many of us will not deviate from our current life situation, as we feel it is incumbent upon us to just keep plodding, no matter what. Sometimes long-term commitment can work really well to help us hold to goals and dreams we hope one day to achieve. But if the goals and dreams are no longer those you embrace with a passion, it may be that the sense of duty is the only thing propelling you forward. Whose sense of duty is this? Yours or your family's? Or is it just a habit you'd rather not have?

I'VE NEVER REALLY BELIEVED IN DIVORCE

The longer you have held a goal, the harder it may be to release it. Consider the second-generation farmer whose home, career, lifestyle and family expectations all converge to push him into a vocation on the land. It will take an enormous strength of will to recognise another calling, share this with family, create a new career, and relocate from the farm. For many this would be just impossible, yet for some it has meant a new lease of life.

WHO AM I TO RISK THE FAMILY SAVINGS ON A NEW BUSINESS?

Closely linked with the ongoing sense of duty to stay put, is the sense that changing career or life options is a selfish and indulgent exercise. Far better to stay doing what you do unhappily than to consider yourself important enough to spend time planning and executing a major life change. Lurking somewhere beneath this attitude is the great Australian cringe syndrome – I'm just an ordinary Joe or Jane, who am I to deserve such attention from myself?

I'VE ALWAYS COPED, I'LL MANAGE SOMEHOW

Needing a change can also interfere with your self-image as a person who can cope. If you base your self-esteem upon making good decisions, being right, and the ability to see something through to a successful conclusion then changing direction midstream may threaten this self-image to the point where you consider such a change as a sign of weakness.

WHAT IF MY FRIENDS THINK I'M GOING BROKE?

Often changing from a role is most severely threatened by the perception that we will lose status. It may be that you have had a degree of success in a chosen career path, and your home, family and accoutrements all reflect this 'success'. Choosing to change this career may involve selling your home, no longer driving an imported car, moving children from a private school, doing without expensive holidays. Given society's fascination with material manifestations of having 'made it', how can we turn our back on these symbols of success to follow our dreams? Will the family hate you? Will you hate yourself? How important are these symbols to you?

I'D DO IT IF I HAD THE MONEY

I'd love to make a change, but I've got a mortgage, two kids to feed, ailing parents, I haven't paid off my car ... Most of us have experienced these sorts of thoughts at some stage. These are also very valid reasons *not* to make a change. But, equally, they can be rationalisations why we won't look at other life options. Only by gaining a thorough understanding of your financial situation, and projecting this forward, will you be able to realistically gauge your ability to afford this change.

IT'S RIDICULOUS AT MY AGE –
I'M FAR TOO YOUNG/OLD/MIDDLE-AGED

This can work in two ways – most commonly the 'I'm too old' syndrome. The 'I'm too old' excuse has been disproven time and again, most famously by Nelson Mandela when at the age of 71 he left Robben Island prison after seventeen years of imprisonment to take on the task of leading the ANC and running a country that was in immense political turmoil. But the perception of age-appropriateness can also shackle the young – 'at my age it's ridiculous to think I can set up a company and be the managing director', 'at my age I should be settling down and starting a family, so I can't contemplate a career change or extended world travel right now'. Asking yourself 'Where is it written that at age (insert your age) I can't (insert your project)…' may help you shake yourself free of these ageist tendencies.

IF IT WAS UP TO ME …

It's often easier to complain than take responsibility for your situation. We all do it, whether it involves a complaint about a boss (who doesn't recognise your true worth), a spouse (who is boring, and negative and no longer loving), or education (my parents didn't have enough to send me to a decent school). We can easily stay in an unsatisfying situation, blaming others for our predicament. The more rewarding path is to challenge this 'bad luck', stop blaming others, and change yourself.

The above list of reasons why we won't address our life change possibilities is by no means exhaustive. But it may be enough to get your thinking started, and to encourage you to take some time out from your schedule to explore your own possible underlying concerns about changing your situation, as well as strategies to rebut these concerns if your desire for change is strong enough.

Now if it was only up to me …

WHAT'S STOPPING YOU?

Are some of those excuses making you feel uncomfortable? Or do they make you want to retreat into your shell, mumbling about self-help books written by smart-arse Pollyannas? Hang on a minute, remember, you're in charge of this show. If these reasons are truly and necessarily stopping you from reaching for your goals, and you are feeling intensely frustrated by continually denying yourself the opportunity to go for it, let's look at your change-readiness in a different way. Let's suppose you have a combination of circumstances – say, family, financial, and time – which prevent you from doing a more satisfying job or living where you really want. What's to stop you developing a ten-year plan to move toward your goals? What's to stop you from doing the planning, the research, and setting the financial target so you can get there, but just over a longer time frame?

chapter three
PLANNING YOUR CHANGE

For most of us, the question, 'What do I want to do with the rest of my life?' is simply too big to handle.

Yet consider the research and money you would devote to buying your first property. First, you would probably spend some hours reading newspaper classifieds and real estate magazines to get a feel for what's out there. Next the physical search – hours driving around, checking out all the 'maybes'. The choices are then narrowed to the most appropriate, and affordable, and then the real fun of making offers or attending auctions starts. Choosing a lender, negotiating mortgage conditions, finding and briefing a solicitor, reading and signing contracts; it's almost a full-time job. Most people consider this time and money well spent as the purchase of property is often described as the biggest decision you will make in your lifetime.

But this is not necessarily the case. On purely financial grounds alone, the management of your superannuation can involve more dollars. And often, your career choice can have a far larger impact on your finances than a property purchase. But let's go beyond the financial aspect, and talk about decisions which will affect your life happiness. Clearly, choosing or changing your vocation, permanent address and/or relationships (which involve day-to-day contentment as well as income) can have far wider ramifications. How much time are you prepared to devote to these decisions?

Timing and type

This chapter looks at the steps involved in the planning process, beginning with how to tackle these aspects on your own. It then looks at the assistance available, for those who prefer to work with a counsellor, or coach, or within a program. It may be that you choose to do some of the initial planning work on your own, and then take your findings to an objective mentor to seek some further guidance.

There are many paths in the search for meaningful change. Some will suit you, some will not. For the self-starters, the DIY method is the way to go. Others might prefer to do their research in conjunction with counsellors or life coaches. Whichever approach you choose, as with most other important decisions, a little homework can go a long way.

For Maree, the chance to start her life planning began in the hills of Tuscany ...

Maree Goodings: The list-maker

At 55 I was tired, worried and fed up with the long hours involved in running a bric-a-brac business in north-eastern Victoria. Joining a walking tour in Tuscany in 1998 changed my life. Based near Trequanda, central Tuscany, our tour group of fourteen walked 200 kilometres from villa to villa. The change in surroundings sharpened my clarity of thought and I found myself waking at 2 a.m. each day, my head full of poetry and new ideas. Equally unsettled and excited by these strong emotions, it took me a full year to work towards my goals.

I was concerned my desire for change might dissipate when I returned home. On my return, I visited a clairvoyant, who suggested I tape my various ambitions, and break them down into logical, achievable steps. Replaying the tape would remind me of the dreams I held. He also suggested that I should try to adopt a long view of my desire for change – selling my shop would probably take a while, and there was little point in becoming impatient about this. My resulting list included 35 desires – from the major (selling my business, returning to Italy for a longer period) to the minor (cleaning out my wardrobe). It took ten months before a customer walked in and offered to buy my business, but it did happen. I have now ticked off 34 of my wishes, the only one left is to learn Italian. Since then I have tried working on a new list, and can only come up with ten items.

I have also discovered how empowering it can be to travel on my own. When I'm away, I get up at 5.30 a.m. and return about 8 a.m. for breakfast. By then I've already spent time walking in back lanes, meeting little old ladies, storekeepers, the local cats, and seen two hours of real life.

Working by yourself

Planning your change by yourself can be frightening, exhilarating, confusing or very satisfying. Or all of the above. The advantages are that you will probably be less likely to be swayed by the opinions or ambitions of others. Disadvantages are that objectivity may be hard to achieve, and without an external structure, deadline or reporting system your plans may simply wither and die. Your personality will also be likely to inform the nature of the results. If you are a born planner, and relish the opportunity to set goals, and tick them off as they come to fruition, this will seem a very natural process. If you loathe the idea of contemplative time, and list-making seems like a waste of time, if may be that you are better suited to another style of planning. For those who are prepared to spend time with their own thoughts and a blank sheet of paper, the life planning process will involve the following elements:

1. taking stock – why, how, and time out
2. defining your values
3. finding your passions
4. understanding where you have been and where you are going
5. making connections

Taking stock

WHAT IS IT?

Taking stock means allowing yourself a period of reflection in which you can assert your core values, define your strengths and experience. You are attempting to identify what you don't enjoy about your current situation, what you might prefer, and whether this fits with the key values you hold. You can then convert this information into a practical assessment of where you are in your life cycle, where you dream you might be, and make some rational connections between the two. This will help you establish a list of goals, which can then be broken down into manageable tasks to help you progress towards these goals.

WHY DO IT?

When you engage in financial planning, one of the first exercises your accountant or adviser urges you to do is the personal balance sheet, or statement of income, outgoings, assets and liabilities. A personal stocktaking is based on the same premise – that it is not possible to move forward with good decision-making unless a comprehensive understanding of your current status has been achieved. But given our very different reasons for our voluntary or involuntary change, and very different life situations, it can be difficult to come up with a method of taking 'life' stock which is achievable and effective.

HOW DO YOU GO ABOUT IT?

We've all read about the frustrated executive who decides he needs time out, and so rewards himself and his family with a year off in a luxury beachside apartment where he enjoys life balance, contemplates his navel and ultimately emerges with clearer focus. If money is no object, this might be a solution. But most of us need a more affordable and practical way of incorporating some reflective time into an overloaded schedule. Essentially, what you will need is a way of removing yourself from your regular activities and environment for a period of time that is sufficient to allow you to do some hard thinking about yourself, your relationships, your vocation, your aspirations, and how you can emerge with a personal balance sheet which reflects where you are at, as objectively as possibly.

You might choose to devote some annual leave to an extended period of time to think this through. If so, you can build in the luxury of a couple of days' total break from thinking about work before attempting to take personal stock. But whether you incorporate your time out into a holiday, or merely mark out a day or two during a work period, don't confuse this self-assessment with a holiday or long weekend. Your time out needs to be structured so you come away with a much clearer understanding of your options and possibilities – not a suntan. Be clear about this goal, and don't let precious time dwindle away without confronting the key questions you are hoping to resolve. Use a notebook or journal divided into left-hand

TIPS FOR YOUR TIME OUT

- Do things differently — dress, music, reading, exercise, food — this is a great opportunity to broaden your vision by exciting your imagination.
- It's difficult to have whole-of-life vision in your day-to-day environment. If you can't retreat for a few days to the bush, the sea, a different landscape, then take yourself for a few hours to a different part of your neighbourhood.
- Seek advice — apart from the more subjective elements of your planning, seek input from experts and those who've gone before. Contact anyone who knows more about your aspiration than you do — any extra information will be of great value when you need to make hard decisions.
- Entertain the ridiculous — give as much credence to your silly ideas as your sensible ones. Lurking behind these fantasies may be an achievable goal.
- Don't put pressure on yourself to come up with hard decisions — this is time for an exploration of your ideas, not bottom-line outcomes.

pages (ideas, thoughts) and right-hand pages (exercises, assessments, 'to do' lists). Determine to come away with a list of immediate, short-term, long-term and lifelong goals, as well as a resolve to review them within a four-week time span. The Finding Your Crossover Point and Goal Planning: Creating Achievable Tasks checklists in the Resources section will assist.

The confronting part of working out what you want is that the question digs down to the very core of your being, and in this process of self-evaluation, you often discover that you have not achieved many of the things you had hoped to by now, and this can lead to a strong sense of frustration and disappointment. A couple of strategies which may help are to start by listing what you have achieved that brings a smile to your face, and then ask, 'What do I still want to do?'

This may be a short list or, as in the case of Maree Goodings' list of 35, much longer.

It is easy to give up on personal planning because you find it difficult to clearly enunciate goals and ambitions. Other people can look maddeningly secure in their goals while you struggle to find what might suit you. But instead of feeling negative about this struggle, try seeing this time of anxiety as a valuable opportunity for concerns to surface and be addressed. Rather than looking for quick solutions, and feeling inadequate if these aren't immediately forthcoming, recognise the complexity of your search, and take the pressure off yourself. It's okay not to know.

Why are values important?

One of the reasons change can plunge us into turmoil so thoroughly is that it pushes upon us some very difficult 'meaning of life' questions, along the lines of:

- Who am I?
- What am I doing here?
- What's it all about?

Answering these fundamental questions can prove to be one of the most difficult aspects of the planning process. Values are the fundamentals by which you operate, and if your primary activities are at odds with your core beliefs it is unlikely you will feel comfortable. It is this conflict which often drives people to seek a change in their lives. No-one else can tell you your values. No-one can take them away. Sometimes they are obvious, but sometimes it takes a crisis or a new situation before they reveal themselves to you. Although you may still be forming some values, an understanding of what really matters is a good starting point for your planning any changes in your life. Let's say you have been offered a great job in another country. As a career move, this looks both logical and beneficial. But your one unshakeable belief is in the importance of the family unit. You love your parents, your brothers and sisters, and their children. You feel truly at home within this family environment. A recognition of this sense of value and peace should be an important part of your decision-making process. This is not the same as calling it the key factor in your decision, but you need to be clear about what you will forgo if you do make the move, and at least aware of feelings of loneliness and homesickness that are likely to occur.

DEFINING YOUR VALUES

But how do you know what your main values are? Are you born with them or do they change over the years? Helping people define their values has been a growing area of interest in corporate life and there are many programs offered to employers to assess their personal values and how they fit with those of their employer. For individuals, however, there is very little practical structured material available.

Sitting alone with a pencil and blank page will not necessarily be the most conducive start to an examination of your values. You might like to start with some books which cover these issues.

In *How Are We to Live?* Peter Singer explores the possibility of taking an ethical approach to life, and how this may help escape a trap of meaninglessness. Having broadened the discussion, it may help to do some checklists on who you are, and how you rate the different aspects of your life. One place to find such an exercise is in *Life Strategies* by Dr Phil McGraw, the resident counsellor on the *Oprah Winfrey Show* before hosting his own series, *Dr Phil*. The idea of a megastar counsellor may be a turn-off for some, but Chapter 11, 'You Have to Name It to Claim It', and Chapter 12, 'A Guided Tour of Your Life', offer a very useful starting point to identifying what matters most to you. In a similar vein, Martin Seligman, author of *Authentic Happiness*, includes in his book and on his website a Values In Action (VIA) signature strength test. This is not quite the same as a purely value-based assessment, but can be a good thought-starter. In *What Color Is Your Parachute*, author Richard Bolles offers an exercise called the Flower Exercise which includes a section on determining your values, purposes and goals.

Finding your passion

It's all very well to think about finding your passion and creating a meaningful life – but what if you don't know what your passion might be, and you are (in your opinion) totally unqualified for anything but your unsatisfying day job?

Happily, there are strategies from those who have faced this question previously, and it's comforting to remind yourself that on any given day a large proportion of the population has no clue whatsoever as to what they might want.

Another entry point for a 'What I want' checklist is to start with a comprehensive assessment of what you *don't* want. For instance, it may be that you think you might want a new job, but underlying this vague thought is the strong desire to not live with debt. The new job (and related assumption of higher income) may be a smokescreen for the fact that you are not comfortable with your present level of spending, and that you actually enjoy working for your current employer. In this case it is not a job change, but a debt reduction program which may prove the best course.

In *What Should I Do With My Life?* author Po Bronson writes of many people who have struggled with the same question – many made changes which moved them to a happier sphere, but this was not universally the case. Bronson writes about a large number of people, and the diversity of activities they have attempted provides another useful starting point for your own search.

If defining what you want still creates a mental block, try listing occasions and places where you feel most at peace with yourself, as well as activities which truly excite you. Add to this the types of articles you are inclined to head towards in a newspaper, and the section in which you will be found browsing in a bookshop. Is a theme or pattern emerging yet?

Working out what you want is not a one-off process. To assist your search, grab the notebook from your time out session, and turn it into an ideas book/personal journal. It's not a diary, but a record of your best ideas, thoughts, quotes that have relevance and meaning to you. A notebook with pockets is even better, for saving articles and mementos which have resonance. Record in the back ideas for action which come from your musings, and prioritise them as they fit with your change journey.

Reread these notes regularly.

Where have you been, where are you going?

There is one last useful point of reflection which is needed before trying to tie your information together. This involves taking a very long view of what you have been doing, what your current situation is and how, in the past, you made the transition into new roles and responsibilities. It is a way of reminding yourself that you have lived through or created change previously, and it was more than achievable.

This is a particularly comforting analysis for those who fear change, as it usually reveals change has been a major part of your life, and you have coped with it very well. To broaden your thought process you can also include an evaluation of your family, checking whether their plans are complementary to, or at odds with, yours.

The Orientation checklist in the Resources section will assist you to fill in this information, looking at where you were ten years ago, five years ago and now, and how your situation, role and plans have moved during this period. Listing basic skills and experiences associated with these different roles will also help you realise you may already possess many of the attributes needed to move towards your new goals. The Ideas column is to help you start making connections between your past and your future.

Making connections – finding your crossover point

By now you will have a basket of information about yourself:

- your key values – what matters most to you
- your dreams and passions – what you really want (or your best guess)
- past roles and experiences – how you've managed change up until the present

The crossover point refers to the common links which you have identified. Put another way, it's an attempt to extract from these three fundamentals – your values, your passions and where you've been – the vital ingredients needed to signal where you wish to go. It is these ingredients that you will build upon to create or manage the change in your life.

To synthesise your insights and find your crossover point for a new beginning or to add perspective to a change which has already occurred, use the information you have gained from the Orientation checklist, and build upon it with the Finding Your Crossover Point checklist on pages 307–8. Now add your thoughts in the Would Like To ... column.

Seeking assistance

Some of us are self-starters – some are not. It's very impressive to read about someone who has reinvented themselves, through sheer hard work and a belief in their own ability or calling. One such example is J.K. Rowling, author of the Harry Potter books. For many, the author's struggle against the odds is even more fantastic than those of her characters. But it doesn't suit everyone to work alone. Many of us prefer externally imposed pressures, deadlines, and an objective sounding board to work our way through the issues. Now might be a good time to enlist the aid of others.

External assistance for life change falls into one of two broad categories: vocational guidance or personal self-examination.

Vocational guidance

For those exploring a change of career, there are a number of resources available. Doing a course is one option, or working on a one-to-one basis with a life coach or career counsellor is another way. A question that arises when you seek such assistance is whether the person, or organisation, you are working with has accreditation, and measurable experience in this field. This is extremely difficult to define. What you are really asking for here is a measure of the immeasurable. What equips someone to be a life coach? Are they truly versed in the skills of helping you achieve your goals – or are they a failed gym instructor trying something different themselves?

One of the difficulties in locating vocational assistance in particular is that both career counselling and life coaching are relatively new fields, and, as with many such growth areas, the 'rules of engagement' are still being worked out. It is difficult for consumers to get answers to questions such as:

- What is the difference between a counsellor and coach?
- What are the qualifications for a life counsellor/coach?
- Is there a system of accreditation?
- Is there a professional association?
- How much training/experience/knowledge do people need before claiming they can help others?
- How do these professionals assist you?
- What are reasonable expectations?

The following is an overview of different types of assistance you might seek, but is not a substitute for careful selection and reference checking before engaging any professional services.

CAREER COUNSELLORS

It is very difficult to measure the efficacy of the services of a career counsellor. Even getting a job is not proof that the counselling process has worked – no-one in career transitioning finds a client a job. They can't. What they can try to do is give the candidate practical ideas on how to think through what their realistic alternatives are – helping them to think broadly about options such as more corporate work, buying a business, starting a business, becoming a franchisee, or portfolio work.

The best place to locate a 'retail' (i.e. non-corporate) career counsellor is via the Australian Association of Career Counsellors (AACC). The AACC is a national organisation of practitioners who provide careers services for people seeking to enter the workforce or change life/work direction. Professional members of this organisation must apply to the registration board with proof of either a tertiary degree combined with at least twelve months' current experience in career counselling, or no degree, but at least five years' current experience. Some members of the AACC are also life coaches.

LIFE COACHES

Life coaching is a relatively new vocation. The idea started in America and grew out of a need for middle and senior managers to work with someone who could assist them to stick to a plan, and be accountable. The idea evolved into a broader role whereby the coaches have moved away from the purely vocational and will work on a broad range of ambitions and goals – losing weight, keeping fit, running a small business are just a few. Anyone can call himself or herself a life coach, and there is no Australian regulatory body watching the content of their work, the prices they charge, nor the training they might offer other would-be coaches. As with any emerging industry, when choosing a life coach it is very much a case of buyer beware. Life coaches differ from therapists or career counsellors, as they do not deal with resolving the past, or the purely vocational. Instead they work from the present forward to help clients recognise their potential and set and meet related objectives. In other words, they are attempting to take clients from where they are now to where they want to be. They usually seek a client commitment of at least twelve weeks from engagement, and offer weekly scheduled coaching sessions (varying from 30 minutes to 1.5 hours) via the telephone. Some Australian coaches operate within the guidelines of the International Coach Federation based in America; others are linked with the Life Coaching Academy in the United Kingdom. One such company offers a self-coaching program for clients to do at their own pace, alone. For a try-before-you-buy sample of life coaching, you may enjoy interacting with top British life coach, Fiona Harrold, via her book *Be Your Own Life Coach*.

COURSES AND PROGRAMS

At this stage there are very few specifically tailored courses to help you set and achieve life goals through change. No doubt as the industry matures such programs will move from Internet-based quizzes to the classroom or seminar environment. Many financial services companies do offer planning sessions, but most of these start from the premise that you are most interested in growing your money wealth as opposed to your personal fulfilment stakes. One company which does provide a rich cache of resources for life planning is the Centre of Worklife Counselling based in Sydney, New South Wales. The centre also offers support through affiliates based in other states.

PROFESSIONAL ETHICS

The more rigorous coaching companies tend to support the philosophy and ethics as set out by the International Coach Federation on its website at: <www.internationalcoachfederation.com>

Self-examination

For those wishing to gain a better understanding of themselves, or to learn to modify their behaviour, working with a suitably trained and qualified professional is often the right strategy.

The changes you wish to make in your life could involve long-held habits, attitudes, beliefs or fears. These may stem back to early childhood and might be of a deeply personal nature. If you have tried addressing such issues previously, but are now ready to confront them with some professional assistance, it is useful to understand the different types of help that are available. You could be seeking a psychiatrist, a psychologist, a psychotherapist or a particular type of counsellor. How can they assist you? How do you know which professional to start with?

PSYCHIATRISTS AND PSYCHOLOGISTS

Psychologists and psychiatrists work with mental health, attempting to equip people with skills to function better and to manage or prevent problems.

Psychiatrists are doctors who have specialised in psychiatric medicine through postgraduate study. They can further specialise into certain fields such as treating children, adolescents, adults, or geriatrics. Psychiatrists traditionally spend the majority of their professional time in providing diagnostic and prescriptive services. They can prescribe medication to alleviate psychological complaints and behavioural symptoms. Some psychiatrists also provide psychotherapeutic services.

Registered psychologists have completed a university bachelor degree that includes four years of approved training in psychology, accompanied by either an accredited postgraduate course or two years of supervised experience in professional practice. Psychologists treat issues from a variety of perspectives that encompass environmental, social, cognitive and behavioural factors. Psychologists are required to register with the psychologists' registration board in their state or territory, and observe a code of ethics. Nationally they are represented by the Australian Psychological Society.

PSYCHOTHERAPISTS AND COUNSELLORS

Psychotherapists and counsellors work with people to help them understand themselves better, and make changes if they so desire. Counselling is often associated with specific, short-term problems or adjustments, whilst psychotherapy is related to the restructuring of the personality or the self, at a more intensive level, over a longer period of time.

Psychotherapists and counsellors may hold a professional qualification and/or registration from many fields including (but not limited to) psychiatry, psychology, social work and nursing. Counsellors will also work in specialist areas including relationship, bereavement, adolescent and addiction counselling. There are many different sources of training for these professionals, and an overview of training standards and professional practices can be obtained from the website of the Psychotherapy & Counselling Federation of Australia, Inc. (PACFA). Another association representing psychotherapists and counsellors is the Australian Counselling Association.

To decide the form of professional help from which you will benefit the most, first work out what your expectations are. What is the nature of the issue that you are trying to address? If it's as broad as 'to be happier', you might need to spend some time defining what this really means for you. Are you wrestling to resolve a long-held hurt, change a tendency toward negativity or increase your self-esteem?

When you have an idea of which aspect of your personality or behaviour you would like to tackle, then look at the information on the websites for the different professional bodies mentioned above. These websites have clear definitions of what their members can offer in the way of methods and treatments. Discuss these methods with your GP. Having a clear understanding of different approaches will help you to select the most appropriate and well-qualified partner for behavioural change or increased understanding.

Before engaging any professional services, always check qualifications, registration, and experience, and whether you may be entitled to claim a rebate from Medicare or a private health insurance company. Also make sure that you have a rapport with the professional — do you feel secure in their care, do they seem to understand you, do you feel that they will be able to meet your needs?

☞ *I'd like time out to take stock, but my boss, my family and my friends will think I've gone soft in the head.*

WHAT'S STOPPING YOU?

A 'me' day: totally structured to allow you the freedom, space and time to think through some of your more important issues; the luxury of listing wild ideas, hopes, fantasies and working out how you might make them happen . . . and then you come down to earth with a thud. There's that report due in, that basket of washing to do, that meal to cook, that car to get serviced, that plane to catch, that contact to phone. It's not about your opportunities, sadly, it's more about your truckload of responsibilities. And they just seem to get more complex. Taking a 'me' day now would be a seriously selfish thing to do.

Correct!

That's the whole point. Because as you head into overload and finally burn out, you won't be worrying about washing, cooking or phone calls anyway. The 'me' day is your chance to better understand your priorities and direction. Ultimately it will help you to respond in a more meaningful way to your current responsibilities by clarifying which really matter and which simply don't. Your day out to think may not deliver any earth-shattering conclusions or encourage a radical change, but if it helps you to understand where you are at, and where you might wish to be this time next year, it will have worked well.

One day out of 365. Is that a big ask?

Chapter four
GETTING STARTED

Great things are not done by impulse, but by a series of small things brought together

– VINCENT VAN GOGH

In Chapter 2 we looked at the excuses we make which hold us back from creating or going with the changes in our lives. Getting over the *It's all very well for them – they are richer, smarter, better-looking, younger, better-educated* syndrome. Now it's time to look at some practical tools to get you going, to move from your overview (dreams, goals, life ambitions) and flesh out your change with some actual detail. In preceding chapters you have explored your values, listed your dreams, and audited your skills. These ingredients have been allowed to percolate, marinate and have produced a strong indication of the type of change you are seeking. Now is the time to move from dreaming to doing it.

A series of small steps

This chapter will look at the steps involved in converting your broad ambition into concrete, achievable steps and setting them into a time frame. Most of our bigger life ambitions seem remote and unachievable if we view them as one huge goal. The key strategy is to define this big task and then break it down, element by element, into a hierarchy of smaller, achievable steps. As with most successful planning it starts with goals; goal-setting, goal planning and goal pursuit.

Your Change Toolkit

Breaking the big picture into smaller steps becomes much easier when you appreciate the rich supply of resources available to you today. Managing change successfully is all about mustering these resources and applying them to the challenge in front of you. Consider the following 'toolkit' and how these elements can be utilised to get your change program (or acceptance) under way. In defining these strengths, you will remind yourself of how very well placed you are to handle change. You will also answer the question, 'What other tools do I need to complete my plan of attack?'

- your attitude
- your personality
- your value system
- your personal experience
- your educational qualifications
- your vocational experience
- your family
- your friends
- your work colleagues
- your financial assets
- your ability to access finance

Goal-setting

The major steps in goal-setting are a clear enunciation of your goal or objective, an evaluation of what will be involved, an acknowledgment of the associated difficulties, and a commitment to yourself to see the project through.

What is your main goal?

A clear definition is essential. To state that you wish to change your life by setting up your own business is a start, but too vague to take you any further. On the other hand, to define that you wish to start up your own business as a landscape gardener in the north-eastern suburbs of Brisbane with a specialty in indigenous palms will give you a wonderful starting point. Why? Because this goal includes a specific vocation, a desired location, and a niche focus for the business. All it lacks is a timeline. If you find that you are still fuzzy about detail, rather than trying to get started, consider this an indication that more research about your new path is needed.

Goal evaluation

What is actually involved in your goal? What are the difficulties, stresses, efforts, and expected pleasures? Are they worth it? If this is the first time you've specifically addressed the challenges of your goal, it may be that you're not really ready to move ahead, until you have an idea of how you might cope with these issues. This might mean spending some time with people who know more about the subject matter than you, or researching books or websites to gauge the issues associated with your project. If your plan is to move to a coastal town, there is a wealth of material available which canvasses the negatives as well as the positives of such a move. It may be that your current proximity to family, services, and a neighbourhood full of good friends and positive memories are aspects of this move that you have been subconsciously discounting. Now is the time to evaluate the strength of these attachments so you can progress towards your goal with a full understanding of the potential downside.

Beware the well-meaning friend. Sometimes it is our nearest and dearest who are most threatened by changes we are contemplating. They may be comfortable with us just as we are, and the notion of us moving interstate, changing career or travelling for an extended period of time may strike them with horror. Be careful of their negative assessment of your chances of successful change. By all means listen to the criticism, but be sure to balance it with advice from those who have nothing to lose or gain by your adventure.

Acknowledging difficulties

The list on page 27 explores some of the common limiting beliefs which may surface when you contemplate your future plans. This is the hard part, as only you can deal with these, and decide whether they are of such strength that you cannot comfortably contemplate the proposed change. Perhaps the best way of gaining some clarity of thought regarding these factors is to write out a list of the most powerful thoughts which might prevent you from tackling your project, and then to rate this reason out of ten as to its likely success in derailing you. If the resulting list and score is lower than you anticipated, you may be using these reasons as excuses for just not doing the hard work.

External difficulties will also abound. Any major change is bound to reveal them. Again, enunciating them, acknowledging them, and deciding if they are going to divert you from your purpose is an integral part of your goal-setting. It may be that after years of trying to make a marriage work, you have decided it's no longer worth the effort. On a scale of 1 to 10, this is a 10. And if you contemplate the accompanying tasks (telling partner, family, friends, finding somewhere to live, rearranging financial affairs, dividing possessions) you may quickly feel trapped into staying as it's all too hard. Yet others have successfully made this transition, it must be possible, so acknowledging the difficulty will be your starting point before moving into an action phase.

CHALLENGING YOUR FEARS

Sometimes in the goal-setting process dormant fears can be activated. They may be closely linked to the limiting beliefs outlined above, but they may also be totally unrelated. The most important step here is to define whether the fear is rationally or irrationally based, and then take the necessary steps to address it. Many useful books on this aspect of our behaviour are available. Try reading *Positively Fearless* by Vera Peiffer for some strategies which may help.

CHANGING YOUR THINKING

Are you concerned that your thought patterns are the major obstacle between your current situation and your goals? If this is the case, you might wish to consider researching cognitive behavioural therapy (CBT) and how it might help you clarify your responses to situations and challenges. Again, there is a wealth of useful material on this therapy, but the simplest starting point is the explanation (Introduction) and exercises in Dr Antony Kidman's book, *From Thought to Action*. Another very accessible book that explains CBT is *Change Your Thinking* by Sarah Edelman.

Making a commitment to yourself

This is perhaps the most important aspect of your goal-setting. Having worked through the detail of your goal and acknowledged the attendant difficulties, you are now at the stage of deciding whether to move forward, or whether you need to maintain the status quo a little longer. If you are going to go ahead, your commitment to yourself is the core of the persistence and dedication you will bring to the tasks involved. You do not need to formalise this by placing your hand over your heart and swearing to look after yourself. You will, however, be supported by acknowledging to yourself that you have made a decision, and that you will be using all your acumen and resources to try to bring your project to fruition. Telling a close friend may also make your decision more concrete. They are bound to ask you about your progress, and may keep you going when, on your own, you could well falter. Keeping a journal in which you record your progress is an enormous help. In your diary you might consider marking a weekly three-hour appointment which you set aside for more information-gathering, meetings with like-minded people, and time to re-evaluate your goals and steps and to chart your progress.

Goal planning

This involves breaking your key goal into smaller, achievable tasks, as well as noting means by which your goal might be achieved, necessary actions, information required, resources available, and possible obstacles.

Achievable tasks

Breaking down your change into manageable steps is the task most likely to help you achieve your aims. Yet sometimes it seems the most difficult. One of the most helpful books on this subject is *Feeling Better: A Guide to Mood Management* by Dr Antony Kidman. Ostensibly a guide to overcoming depression and negative feelings, it contains a chapter on Goals and Priorities, with checklists showing how even a relatively simple exercise such as learning to swim can be reduced to more minor tasks which will get you started.

Breaking down your goals

Now it's time to break your goals down into achievable tasks. Use the Goal Planning checklist in the Resources section to record your major goal.

1. In the first column, list your life goal.

2. In the second column, list the component tasks.

3. In the third you can prioritise, numbering from one upwards the urgency or importance of the various tasks.

4. In the fourth column, note the actions you need to take in order to fulfil these tasks.

5. In the fifth column, break down the information you need, relating it to each specific task.

6. In the sixth column, beside 'information needed', note possible resources.

7. In the seventh column, note any possible obstacles, with comments if you have ideas on how to overcome them.

8. In the eighth column, set a deadline for the task.

9. The final column is for a tick when the task has been successfully completed.

Reviewing this map of your intentions on a weekly basis will have two benefits. First, you will be able to tick off the tasks you have achieved, deriving no small satisfaction from the fact that you are 'on your way'. Second, you may notice a task which you seem to be systematically avoiding, doing anything rather than confronting it. Perhaps it's a difficult phone call to a former workmate, where you feel you are asking for help, and are not sure how they will react.

The best strategy? Just do it. But before you pick up the phone, rehearse in your mind how you will react if the worst happens and they are unhelpful, or totally uninterested. Then do it. The worst rarely happens, the information will or will not be forthcoming, and you can now keep going with the rest of your list.

Goal pursuit

Easier said than done. It's fine to come up with great ideas, and often the planning and research stage of the process can be full of fun and anticipation. But doggedly pursuing your goals can often prove to be the lonely, unsatisfying part of the journey. People you thought would be helpful may not be forthcoming, ideas you thought unique may have been more fully developed by someone else, the new location may prove to be

---

Linking your weekly planning to a favourite café, library, desk, or verandah can be a very positive strategy. In *The Road From Coorain*, academic Jill Ker Conway recounts how a lifelong love of learning started when she was eight with her mother making homework into a treat by setting her up at a desk on the verandah with her very own pot of tea.

less than ideal when you do more research. Yet something inside you wants to keep going. This is the stage where you may need some help in sticking to your purpose, evaluating your progress, and making necessary adjustments.

A good starting point for strategies about how you might stick at your project is outlined by Dr John Lang is his book *Re: Life*. In Chapter 2, 'Managing Change', he explains the stages and processes of change, as defined by behavioural psychologist James Prochaska, and how to manage these for successful transitions.

Hopefully you are already reviewing your progress on a weekly basis. For major goals such as moving the family overseas for five years, this may seem a little too frequent, yet it is this weekly session which will probably cement your commitment when the going gets tough. And when the going gets really tough, and your original plan proves impossible, it will be clear you need to make some adjustments. At this stage, rewriting the achievable tasks list makes the most sense. Start with your original, detailed goal, and change the aspects which cannot work. Much of the work you have already done will still be valid – insert these steps as before, and then add the different steps you need to achieve your amended goal.

I've reached a certain point in my planning and seem to have hit a wall ...

WHAT'S STOPPING YOU?

Well-planned change involves:

- including the wishes of other members of the family — not dragging them reluctantly into a new sphere they are bound to resent.
- at least a five-year framework (hopefully longer), which shows how this change will look projecting forward.
- an appreciation of the skills and resources you have as much as an understanding of those you might require.
- a substantial amount of research into the new project.
- many discussions with those who have already traversed this terrain
- an understanding of the value of persistence
- flexibility in changing the method of your approach, whilst maintaining the goal.
- a belief in the project and commitment to yourself which will withstand the inevitable criticism of those less able, less willing, or just plain envious.

Are these elements present in your planning? Are you satisfied with the research you've done? Are your significant others demonstrably less than enthusiastic? Are you in denial about some of these issues? What does your gut feeling tell you?

chapter five
AFFORDING YOUR LIFE CHANGE

When you have defined that you have an 'itch' and you're keen to implement a change, nothing, but nothing, is more galling than to read about the stockbroker or Internet startup guru who has cashed in their shares for many millions of dollars and is now trying something different – redecorating a boutique hotel, buying a vineyard, building a beach resort. Their reality is so far removed from yours, it is tempting to think that making life changes is only for the rich.

Happily, this is not the case, but there are often some very hard decisions which must be faced if you are to move beyond the media dream of 'having it all' and redefining your vision to 'having what really matters'. If you are clear in your focus that you wish to make a change in your life, be it locational, vocational, whatever, it is essential that you fully understand the financial ramifications before plunging in. Why?

- Because there may be very strong reasons not to go ahead now, ever, or in the manner you first envisaged.
- Because you may be risking your income for the latter half of your life.
- Because you may be risking money on behalf of your partner, family, friends, and/or colleagues, and may damage these relationships irreparably.
- Because there may be better strategies available – strategies of which you are currently unaware.

Financial planning is often viewed as medicine we need to take, and therefore, like estate planning, it becomes something most of us delay until we stand in danger of losing money because of our negligence. This may be because we have been told so many times that we 'should' see a financial planner, we rebel against what seems like a straitjacket. There are, however, a few aspects of the financial planning process that may make it seem more palatable:

- Doing your own research first then supplementing it with professional advice will give you the best of both worlds.
- There is a wealth of free information available which will enable you to get started without being obligated to any organisation.
- Reviewing your finances is not a once-in-a-lifetime, pre-retirement planning exercise. It is an important, ongoing necessity. Once you have faced the music and created a plan based on your current situation, you will have done the hard work. Now it will be a relatively easy task to update this template on a regular basis.
- Financial planning is not just for the rich – although they may well have increased their wealth by increasing their financial know-how. Sound financial strategies are even more important for the less well off who, relatively, have even more to lose if things go pear-shaped.

Getting started

Like many other seemingly complex tasks, sound financial planning can be broken down into a few basic steps:

1. a stocktake, or financial audit (Where am I at?)
2. a projection of future needs (What are my hopes/dreams/obligations?)
3. making the link (What steps do I need to put in place to achieve my goals?)

These steps can be further broken down as follows:

A. Stocktake

1. DO SOME BASIC RESEARCH

Ensuring that you understand a basic financial structure should not cost anything except your time. An excellent starting point is a free service offered by the Commonwealth Government through Centrelink. It's called the Financial Information Service (FIS), and the seminars offered introduce the issues and terminology you need to understand in order to assess your own financial structure. There are also some excellent books to borrow or buy which explain the basics. In particular, the 'how-to' books by Noel Whittaker, Suze Orman, and Paul Clitheroe listed in the Resources section are very accessible. Many financial service companies, including banks, also offer helpful information so consumers can understand the steps involved in thorough financial planning. It is not necessary to be a customer to access this information, and much of it is extremely detailed and helpful. The Financial Planning Association (FPA) is a good source of introductory material to enable consumers to understand the issues involved in planning, as is the Australian Securities & Investments Commission (ASIC), particularly their free publication (produced jointly by ASIC and the FPA), *Don't Kiss Your Money Goodbye*. Other options for objective information are the Australian Consumers' Association (directly via the association or their magazine, *Choice*) and NICRI (National Information Centre on Retirement Investments Inc.). Some financial sector websites offer introductory material, although not many offer as full an overview as the organisations listed above.

David: In denial

For years the number one item on my most hated jobs list was tax. When I was married to my first wife, I diligently did our tax early every year. We had so little money, we always got a refund and I wanted that money in our bank account and not the taxman's. When we broke up my motivation dwindled, and I just shoved all my financial records in a suitcase in the top of the wardrobe. By this stage I was earning a better salary, and we'd sold the family home because of our divorce, so getting a refund on time wasn't such a big deal. Then I met someone new, we lived together for five years, and decided to get married. One year off to travel the world would be our honeymoon. The day of reckoning had arrived. No, not the wedding day, but the fact that ten years of denial over tax returns meant I couldn't get a passport. Down came the suitcase, out came the pile of papers, and off to a long-suffering accountant who not only helped sort out this mess, but came up with a really handy refund which financed the first leg of our trip. I'm over denial now – I use a tax accountant and file on time, every year. It's so much simpler.

THE FINANCIAL PLANNING ASSOCIATION

The Financial Planning Association (FPA) is a professional body dedicated to regulating the financial planning industry, by certifying the practitioners, as well as educating the public about reasonable expectations for planners. By contacting the FPA you can receive detailed information about how planners are remunerated, as well as the Advisory Services Guide they are obliged to give you on your first visit. This guide covers all you need to know about how planners work, and how the company which your planner represents operates.

2. COLLECT INFORMATION

The idea of collecting information often elicits an inward groan – it sounds like having to do your tax all over again. But if you are currently filing a tax return, most of the work has already been done. The main information you need to compile is a listing of assets and liabilities, and income and expenditure which will come from the following sources:

- tax return
- personal bills
- credit card statements
- bank statements
- superannuation fund statements
- current investments information
- a realistic understanding of market values of assets you may own (including the family home).

3. LIST ASSETS AND LIABILITIES

Try filling in the Assets and Liabilities checklist in the Resources section. Remember it is important to understand the difference between an asset which may cost you money, and an income-earning asset. To further complicate matters, there are assets which do not earn income, but which cost you money (rates, maintenance, insurance, etc.) that you cannot claim on your tax. These assets, however, may make you more money than any others. An example is your family home with significant capital appreciation over the long term. In most cases this is exempt from capital gains tax, thus likely to increase your wealth more than any other single contributor. Your valuation of assets and liabilities is usually best confirmed by a qualified adviser.

4. LIST INCOME AND EXPENDITURE

Use the Income and Expenditure checklist in the Resources section. For those in a stable job, eliciting this income information from a current tax return should be a relatively simple task. It is when you are working for yourself, or as a consultant, or recently redundant that the task becomes more difficult. At this stage your best educated guess, reviewed regularly, is the only way to go. Expenditure can also be tricky to detail, as so many of us use a mix of credit cards, cash and cheques to pay our way. The easiest method is to assemble your credit card statements, cheque butts, and invoices for the past three months, and use a system of coloured highlighter pens to classify the different expenses you face. You might consider, as well as dividing into the suggested headings in the checklist, using a pink highlighter for 'extravagances' – so if some budget trimming becomes necessary, you have already indicated non-essential expenses.

B. Projecting your future needs

How long is a piece of string, you ask?

You may have a clear idea of the type of change you wish to pursue. You may find it easy to list your hopes and goals and dreams. You may also have had a dream shattered, due to accident, death, relationship breakdown or economic misfortune. For whatever reason, it is still a useful exercise to try to define and project your future needs.

It is only by defining your new reality that you will be able to attempt to cost it. One of the easiest starting points might be to commence with the familiar, and work from there. For argument's sake, you may wish to cut back your work commitments to four days a week in order to spend the extra free time writing a novel in your home study. This change will obviously affect your income, your household and transport expenses, as well as some others. Your starting point might be to calculate 80 per cent of current income, as well as a 30 per cent increase in some household expenses (heating, lighting assuming you are adding a day to your previous two-day weekend), whilst decreasing transport to work costs by 20 per cent, and factoring in costs of writing such as printer cartridges, telecommunications expenses, book purchases and any courses you might undertake, or associations you may wish to join. Working from known expenses, you are now able to plan the unknown. Your best guess might not be very accurate, but it will enable you to anticipate whether you and your family can seriously contemplate this change, or whether other changes will need to occur to facilitate this plan.

Don't forget to consider the period of time over which you need to project. Instead of committing to one such projection, it is often a good idea to use the information gathered to create a one-year, five-year and ten-year plan.

C. Making the link

What steps do you now need to take to achieve your plans? It's a similar process to finding the crossover points with your goal-setting. By now you should have a clearer idea of your financial situation, and a ballpark figure of how much you will need to support your planned lifestyle. How do you make these figures match? You may feel fully qualified to work this out on your own – and more power to you if you can. However, at this stage of your planning, it is usually more than useful (and cost effective) to align yourself with an objective adviser to review your plans and projected expenditure. A qualified financial planner will probably be your best resource. Why? You might ask – planners have recently received very negative press about their practices, and some seem to be living off their clients via cleverly devised trailing commissions that aren't always revealed.

Seeking independent advice

How do you go about securing truly objective advice from a financial planner and not just have in-house products sold to you?

There are four main requirements to consider before choosing a planner who will suit your needs:

1. Understanding what a financial planner actually does, and what you can reasonably expect from them.
2. Understanding the different ways a financial planner might be remunerated.
3. Asking the right questions before setting foot in their office.
4. Letting them know your expectations of your meetings and proposed relationship so they can inform you if they are unwilling/unable to participate in such a partnership.

Go to the Resources section for the 50 Useful Questions to Ask a Financial Adviser checklist.

Charles Brass: Choosing to live on less

My background is photography, education and human resources.

Nine years ago I made a decision to leave my well-remunerated role as HR manager in a multinational company and to set up the not-for-profit Future of Work Foundation (FOWF). My children were young, and my salary was the only income, but I had no trouble convincing my wife about the wisdom of this move. She hated the company more than I did. I didn't feel particularly brave. I felt that the consequences of not going ahead would have been greater than the consequences of trying and failing. Had I continued in my former role, I would have worked longer hours and consumed more to justify my existence.

One of the key problems at work was my total lack of empathy with the values of the management. I was also convinced I had a far larger contribution to make to society. The genesis for FOWF came from a forum convened in 1992 by the Australian Human Resource Institute to canvass opinions about how work might look in the year 2020. I was so excited about the possibilities that I wanted the chance to explore how work could evolve for the betterment of all. My new role has brought a degree of fulfilment, but all sorts of things have happened during the past nine years. Setting up *Diversity@Work* where we place employees and assist employers to create a sustainable diverse workforce, is tangible proof of the foundation in action.

Over the years since I left the corporate environment, I have realised it is critical for men to learn to be true to themselves. I am still learning how to do this. My vocational decision has resulted in a much lower level of income. This has significantly changed our family interaction, and how we view the world. My kids have now tasted reality and my wife has confronted how she connects herself to income and wealth.

Living on less

A result of your stocktake, and information you have learnt from a planner, may mean you will decide to live on a lower income. Your reasons for this may be because circumstances have now forced reduced income upon you, or because it will enable you to afford to do something different, or because you have felt trapped into a lifestyle which is beyond your income. Or it may be that you simply wish to try to minimise your expenditure in order to increase your options for a future time. By gaining a clear understanding of what you have, what you earn after tax, and where your money goes, you are now able to decide if you can live comfortably on a lower income. But if what you have on paper is unconvincing, you may choose to practise by living on a restricted income for a month or two to see if it is feasible for a longer stretch of time. Welcome to the life of a downshifter.

What is downshifting?

Downshifting has been documented by Dr Clive Hamilton of the Australia Institute in his book *Growth Fetish*, as well as in research findings on the institute's website. This phenomenon is described as a choice to opt out of excessive consumerism and create a life with more time, balance and meaningful work, aligned with the downshifter's values. A survey undertaken by the Institute revealed that, during the previous decade, 23 per cent of 30–60-year-old Australians had made such a choice. The respondents came from a variety of economic backgrounds, and their changes involved reducing working hours, taking a lower-paid job, changing careers and stopping work altogether.

How can you try to live on less?

There is no magic formula here. It seems easy to spend a salary increase but extremely difficult to cope with a salary cut or, worse, a retrenchment. So how do you trim your expenses? Back to the list. Hopefully by now you will have a clear idea of where your money goes. You will also have marked on your expense lists some items which are non-essentials. The task now is to come up with an annual sum by which you would like to reduce expenditure, divide it by twelve months, and go looking to see if this amount matches the more frivolous expenditure on your statements. To help with some concrete examples of this type of reduction, use the How Can I Reduce My Spending? checklist in the Resources section.

LACK OF CHOICE

We don't always have a choice about living off a lower income. Sometimes a death, retrenchment, illness or lack of insurance may have plunged us into severely restricted financial circumstances. This is more reason to seek professional assistance early. Depending upon your circumstances, the advice you seek may involve paying fees. But it may also assist to minimise your losses. Start by talking to the Financial Information Service (FIS) people at Centrelink for some objective cost-free guidance.

When all else fails

It may be that decades of impulse purchasing have formed a habit which feels impossible to break. If this is your situation, there are two strategies which may help.

WHY BEFORE YOU BUY
Ask yourself if you really need an item, be it a book, magazine, CD, holiday, or jacket *before* you commit to the purchase. If the answer is yes, then ask yourself, 'Why?' This answer may be more revealing – if it is 'Because I

deserve it', you may wish to place the item on hold with the sales assistant for 24 hours, and return after this 'cooling-off' period to purchase if need be. Four times out of five, you probably won't.

CREDIT CARD HOLIDAY

No, don't put a holiday on your card; give your card one instead. Try one day a week leaving the house without access to instant credit. It is interesting how vulnerable you may feel without a stream of finance on call. But whose money is it anyway? If you are having difficulty meeting your credit card commitments, it may be the bank's you are living off, at exorbitant interest rates. If one day of cold turkey works for you, try two per week. This may assist you to start planning your purchases in a more rational way and reduce the impulse buying which is creating the difference between financial control and mayhem.

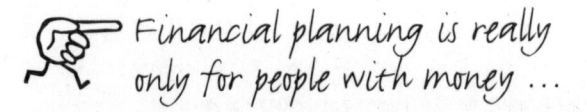

Financial planning is really only for people with money ...

WHAT'S STOPPING YOU?

Three major reasons why people shy away from taking control of their finances are the misconception that planning is only for the rich, guilt that they spend too much, and ignorance of the basic elements of sound money management. Is one of these issues hampering you? If you feel your income and/or savings are too paltry to worry about, try to imagine an extra 10 per cent spending power per year. If this idea appeals, this is probably the low end of what you might achieve with a plan in place. An accountant is the first port of call. If guilt about your previous extravagance is causing some kind of denial, you have two choices. Get over it, and develop some structure to see where all that money might be going, or continue with your head in the sand, and deny yourself the extra income which might help you afford the type of life you really want. If it is a lack of understanding about how money works and how it can be made to work for you, then you are a prime candidate for one of the many seminars or short courses on this subject.

chapter six
FINDING NEW MEANING IN FAMILIAR PLACES

The real voyage of discovery is not in seeking new landscapes but in having new eyes

— MARCEL PROUST

You've felt the discontent and explored the options for change. But somehow it just doesn't feel right. Never underestimate the value of your gut reaction. It may be that instead of making a change, your best course of action is to renew your acquaintance with your existing situation.

Because this book is about change, it does not mean it advocates a change in location, career, or relationship as the best solution for everyone. Quite the reverse. In many cases you may be entering a time during which, rather than stepping away from the aspect of your life which is causing you the most grief, it could be more appropriate to reassess your situation and work out if there might be a fresh approach to this current impasse, a way of reawakening the passion for your possibilities.

Wendy F: Commitment to the now

Fifteen years ago I felt really stuck. Working as a nurse, married to Richard, with three adolescent sons, I felt I was barely keeping up with the day-to-day let alone making any headway in my life. Our boys were attending a private school and every spare penny we earned went to pay the fees. My passion in life was gardening, but all spare time went to running the house, and working shift work at the local hospital. It felt as though this would be the case forever.

It was for the next ten years. I did need to continue working long hours, but somehow managed to incorporate a gardening course. This gave me the balance I needed, and eventually led to a new role as a landscape gardener — a role I grew into over a decade or more. When my last son left school, I was finally able to give up the nursing for good and concentrate on my landscaping business. Today I run this business from a house on the Mornington Peninsula, surrounded by 7 acres of beautifully manicured gardens. I'm often busy, but rarely stressed.

Not everyone wants change. Indeed, many people feel intensely threatened by it. If you belong to this group, it may be possible to enhance your life situation without unsettling yourself by a radical change. Even small improvements may deliver a happier outcome. Wendy's solution was to add a hobby, not change her entire life. The hobby eventually led to bigger things, but it started as a stress-buster.

Having a rethink

Consider your current situation — let's assume it's vocational, although, equally, it could be a relationship, or geographical issue which is disturbing you. Find your crossover point (see Chapter 3, page 40 and use the Finding Your Crossover Point checklist in the Resources section). But rather than using this knowledge to move towards a different career path or radical lifestyle change, bring it back to your current situation and see how it can be applied.

Start by writing a list of the positives and negatives in your life. If you are seriously fed up, don't be surprised if your perceived negatives far outweigh the list of positives. Just let them spill out. Review the positives, and note if there is a recurring theme with these (family, creative?), then go to the negatives and concentrate on each point, asking yourself what strategies you might employ to improve them, or at least neutralise their impact on your daily contentment levels.

Having considered the list of negatives, evaluate whether your current situation is as 'hopeless' as you have been telling yourself. From your list of strategies, is it possible to instigate a series of small changes which might ameliorate the gloom? For instance, you may feel relatively happy in your career, but find that your home life is full of tension due to boredom with your long-term relationship, and the ensuing friction with your partner. This, in turn, may be affecting children living in the same house. Your list of positives and negatives might go something like this:

POSITIVES	NEGATIVES
Bike-riding at the weekend	Bored with marriage
A new project at work	Fight with spouse all the time
Children are healthy	This usually turns into a full family argument
	Can't remember last time we enjoyed time spent together
	Working hours are too long
	Overall sense of hopelessness
	Other women starting to look attractive

From what seems like a long list of insurmountable negatives, some positives could be derived by asking yourself some basic questions:

- Have I taken time out from this busy schedule to ask my spouse, honestly, and in a non-confrontational manner, if she is feeling the same way?
- Have I written a list of truly positive experiences I would like to include in my life during the next decade?
- Have I showed this positive list to my spouse, and are there dreams and goals that we share?
- Do we still take time away from the other commitments we have for a regular date?

- Have we considered relationship counselling?
- Are we aware of the resources available to couples in this situation?
- Am I thinking a short-term slump in our relationship is the beginning of the end? Is it possible this could be an opportunity to build on our history together, and create a stronger union?
- I love bike-riding – have I asked my spouse to join me?
- Are there other activities, new hobbies, entertainment we might like to explore together?
- Are my long working hours set in concrete, or just attached to a current project?
- Is it possible I am taking refuge at work rather than coming home and confronting the inevitable disagreement?
- Can I negotiate shorter working hours? Will this necessarily involve lower income? And if it does is there some aspect of our current expenditure I would be happy to forgo if it contributes to a more harmonious home life?

This list of questions will obviously vary from situation to situation, but it is an attempt to encourage a thorough examination of what *seems* to be a dead-end situation. It also starts with the premise that the subject does not actually want to move away from the marriage, but rather to work towards improving it. The questions are based on an optimistic attitude that fundamentals such as a lack of communication, time, and opportunity are getting in the way. The questions also assume that the participant(s) are willing to bring some positive thinking and habit-changing behaviours to bear.

These principles can be applied equally to other work and lifestyle issues. Could it be that you lust for life in a coastal town as it seems much less complicated that the rushed existence you now endure? But your innermost feeling is one of fear when you consider taking the leap to a new location and trying to join a new community? It may be that the simple existence you envisage is available in your current home. A new way of viewing it might be just what is required. Again, a list of the negatives you currently see in your life, as well as the positives, might reveal being time-poor as the real pressure in your life. A thorough evaluation of this aspect may reveal activities and expenditure you are willing to forgo in order to simplify your existence, and allow for free time spent at the coast, in various different locations, on frequent short breaks, rather than the wholesale move away from your existing community base.

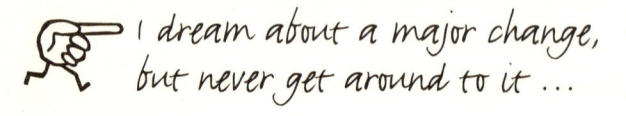

☞ *I dream about a major change, but never get around to it...*

WHAT'S STOPPING YOU?

Maybe you're just burnt out. Try a three-day weekend with your favourite person doing lots of fun things you'd almost forgotten how to do – walking in the rain, bike-riding, eating scones, skimming pebbles at the beach, lying on the grass and staring at the sky.

On your list of positives and negatives, try giving each point a score out of ten. Are the positives coming up really strongly, and the negatives looking more like niggle?

Pick one of the positives, and try to push it further. If it's time spent with family, see if you can increase this aspect of your life, and reduce one of the negatives (maybe a plan to leave work at 5 p.m. sharp on a Friday will enable an early pizza night at home?).

For one week, take a break between your daily chores and the evening meal, and spend ten minutes outdoors, contemplating a tree. Try not to think, just to breathe. At the end of the week, see if this has aided your perspective.

What Nola did

Remember Nola from page 9? How did she manage her change?

Stages of change

- Taking the time and having the courage to ask significant questions.
- Understanding she would need to create this life in order to be creative.
- Persisting – despite early frustrating attempts to make icons – by seeking resources such as classes and books to help her with the difficulties.
- Giving up the day job.
- Adopting the title of artist, and meaning it.
- Taking more and more classes, continuing to draw and experiment with different media.
- Living as an artist, reading about artists.
- Expanding activities from the creative to teaching creativity.
- Feeding her senses, rewarding herself with 'me' days.
- Starting the mosaic association to gather together like-minded people.

ON MONEY:
I don't earn as much as I used to, but I don't feel as though I am missing out.

ON LIFE/WORK BALANCE:
My challenge will be to maintain the balance I have achieved between expressing myself on canvas and in clay and the desire to teach.

ON THE BENEFITS OF HER CHANGE:
What does art give me? Wow – where do I begin? I am continuously learning and that's exciting.

some questions you may wish to explore

- Am I worried how my change will look to other people?
- Do I think I can't change because it will look like I failed?
- Do I sometimes wish an external event/disaster would force me to change?
- Am I measuring myself against my peers?
- Am I prepared to take one day off from my job, family, and commitments to indulge my dreams and see if I want to push my goals further?
- Do I want to challenge myself to find renewed meaning in my current job?
- Would I rather commence a series of small steps to somewhere new?
- Am I trying to earn more money because I am measuring myself against other people's ideas of success?
- In doing this am I spending more than I can afford to maintain what is essentially a 'false' lifestyle?
- In fact, what is my idea of 'success' and 'wealth'?

Part Two:
CHANGING YOURSELF

Every individual has more control over their life than they think they have

— RICHARD BOLLES

We generally expect to be happy. A few generations ago, aspirations were geared towards economic survival and raising enough children so that some, at least, would survive. Loving your day job and having a fulfilling relationship weren't guaranteed, and if you chose your life partner unwisely, this was just bad luck as divorce wasn't an option for decent people.

Things have loosened up a little. In most developed nations, rigid class distinctions, religious imperatives, gender roles and the 'job for life' mentality have weakened and now, with a good chance of not only owning your own home but also earning enough for the occasional holiday and night out, we are looking harder at our feelings, our relationships and how we can heighten our sense of wellbeing. Our expectations of contentment are now very high, and if they fail to be delivered a whole industry has arisen to support our quest for happiness.

Part Two, Changing Yourself, looks at the main ways you might undergo change at a personal level. It starts with Rebecca's story of how you can wake up one day and have your life changed for you, and, with the help of those who love you, recreate a life of hope and accomplishment.

Chapter 7, 'Relationships', gets to the heart of the matter. How do you feel about yourself, your family, your partner, your friends and colleagues? What is your interaction with the world, and those around you? You might wish to do some work on yourself to fit your new life. In fact if you start with yourself, your attitude and your sense of possibility, you may find the other changes a whole lot easier.

Chapter 8, 'Exploring Your Creativity', encourages you to take yourself and your creative urges much more seriously. You may have had some impulses towards a more creative expression but pushed these thoughts away because 'I never was good at drawing' or similar self-defeating statements. Or maybe it just felt too self-indulgent to explore this part of your psyche while there were bills to pay and mouths to feed. Maybe now is the time to silence those negative inner voices and just get going. Or maybe it's a second or third bite at the educational cherry which will really thrill your soul. Chapter 9, 'The Learning Curve', looks at lifelong learning as a better way of understanding your possibilities, as opposed to the old 'I trained as a nurse, so I have to stay one' paradigm. Your renewed commitment to learning might be a way of creating career change, but it is just as valid as a way of maintaining an intellectually stimulating existence. Chapter 10, 'Getting Physical', looks at some of the options for maximising your fitness and health at any age, as well as the more complex requirements of handling unexpected health setbacks. Perhaps your main direction is gaining a deeper understanding of your existence, and how it fits into a bigger scheme of things. This often translates into a spiritual quest. Chapter 11, 'Asking the Big Questions', looks at how this search might be undertaken.

Rebecca Doyle Walker: At least I don't dribble any more

At 29 Rebecca Doyle Walker was running her own business: selling, installing and networking computers. Then she had a stroke.

I don't remember a lot. My husband Darren and I were walking our dog. I said I wasn't feeling well. I felt weak, and was losing peripheral vision. When we got home I sat in an armchair – Darren thought I had fallen asleep. But I kept asking for Mum, who is a nurse. She came over and took one look at me and thought to herself, 'why hasn't an ambulance been called?'

I have no recollection of the first three days – I had slurred speech, my right side was immobile, my face had dropped. But I have no memory of this.

What I do remember is becoming conscious of being in hospital in a four-bed ward, with a lot of older people. I thought, you've got to be kidding, guys. I couldn't go to the toilet without help. There was no feeling at all in the right side of my body. No movement. This was scary, very traumatic.

I don't remember what the staff were saying to me, but they told my husband I had had a stroke. After one week, they gave me a choice of rehabilitation facilities. In hindsight I chose the wrong one, because it was close to home, and I didn't want to join the public health waiting list. My health insurance covered me in rehabilitation fully for fourteen days, then they literally told me in the morning I was going home that day as my cover had run out. I was still needing assistance from two people to get to the toilet, but that was it, I had to go. They graciously lent me a wheelchair, but said I really needed to organise my own. My family were shocked. As a nurse, my mother just couldn't believe it.

I fought and argued and convinced the doctors to get me into rehabilitation at Parkville (Melbourne Extended Care and Rehabilitation). These were the people who got me walking. The physiotherapists there challenged me from the first day. I had not managed to stand much at all, and they made me stand for 45 minutes from the very start. From the ladies at the front desk, to the therapists, they were all great. The social workers found me a handful. I was not an obedient patient — I kept challenging what they were saying and asking more questions. If I was obedient I would still be sitting in a wheelchair.

My daughter Jessica was inconsolable when this first happened — she had just turned seven, and saw me at my worst during the stroke when I was slumped to the ground. My mum tells me she sat with my head on her lap saying, 'Don't die, Mummy'. My stroke forced her to grow up fast. She had to go and live with my parents, as the school she had just moved to had no before- or after-school care, and until we knew what was happening, my husband and I couldn't look after her.

I found this so very hard. I wasn't mobile and couldn't get to see her enough. I also had to deal with who the chief decision maker in her life would be, and if she was living with my parents, it was best for her if they took that role.

Within two years I have recovered the full use of my right arm. It took me eighteen months of hard work to get most of the function back — I worked hard on a surprise for my family for that Christmas — to give them a two-armed hug. My daughter still says it is the best present she's ever received.

I was very conscious of not succumbing. I had a good friend who passed away from cancer — she told me no matter how bad she felt, she would always say she was okay. Even when I had a really bad day, I would keep talking, and push myself. The last thing I wanted was pity.

Now I don't dribble any more. Occasionally I get stuck on a word. I still use aids to walk, and wear a brace on my leg, or use crutches. When I am really tired, I will use my wheelchair. My arm is pretty good, but I am using my back muscles to drag my leg around, it's just swinging, and I can't feel my foot.

> Challenge everything in order to challenge yourself — if you just accept things, where will this leave you?

I joined the Country Fire Authority as a volunteer in February 2000, and had nearly finished my recruit training when I had the stroke. I didn't know any of the people there that well, so I just dropped out, but was paranoid about having them think I just hadn't turned up to training. My husband told them what had happened, and the other members would drop in and say hello. Then one of the firemen said he would take me down to the fire station. I was very uncomfortable going in a wheelchair, but they were so welcoming. They never treated me any differently. A lot of people will ignore you when you are in a wheelchair, but they didn't.

I wouldn't have got through the whole thing without my family: my parents, my older brother who flew straight back from London when he heard, my husband Darren who has been my rock and who saw me at my very worst, my daughter Jessica, and the fire brigade.

I sat down with our then Captain, John, and he encouraged me to continue with any training I could manage, and to start helping there again. I asked him what I could do, and he said, 'What do you want to do?' He realised and understood how very important this was. It was an important part of my rehabilitation to stay involved, to have something worthwhile to do.

At first I would just enter a fire report, then as I got stronger, just over one year ago I joined the critical incident stress peer group which supports and chats to those involved in a traumatic situation. We don't counsel, just listen. I also do work with the Junior Brigade.

Since the stroke my perceptions have changed completely. Things that were important no longer seem so. I don't take people for granted now. Being able to walk the dog with my daughter is such a gift. So are all the things that, by rights, I shouldn't be able to do.

There is always someone worse off. I don't want people to be focused on me – I have never been comfortable being the centre of attention. Some friends couldn't handle me being in a wheelchair – they drifted away. When I reflected upon it, they weren't such good friends after all. The good ones never treated me any differently.

My life is not worse. It is different. It is not bad, I just have a different way of living. Needing people to help with your personal care takes your control away – it was only a few months ago that I took that control back. I used to organise my day around when a nurse would arrive to help me shower. I got sick of working around everyone else, so I now manage my own shower. Getting my licence back was also a big deal.

My advice to anyone undergoing medical trauma is: don't believe everything you're told – the so-called specialists are not always right. Ask questions – always ask questions. Challenge everything in order to challenge yourself – if you just accept things, where will this leave you?

I know now I have the ability to overcome adversity. Every day was a battle, but you just have to get on with it. Every day is still a challenge; the heat saps my energy, it is extremely physically demanding to even appear 'normal'. I work very hard at being 'normal' in other people's eyes. People who haven't seen me often during my recovery ask me if it feels good to be back to 'normal'. My response to them is usually 'What is normal?' They seem to forget that this *is* my normal and that every different stage I have been through with my recovery has been my normal.

chapter seven
RELATIONSHIPS: THE HEART OF THE MATTER

Relationships lie at the very core of our existence. When they are going well, life seems easy. When they go badly, most other aspects of our lives are affected. Experiencing change in our relationships is one of the most traumatic events of all. This chapter explores different aspects of the relationships in our lives, starting with your relationship with yourself, based on the belief that when you are comfortable in your own skin is when you will be best equipped to deal with the other facets of your life.

Looking after number one: Your relationship with yourself

When it comes to change, you can be your own worst enemy. Happily, the reverse is also true, and you can be your own most supportive friend.

You know the script by heart. Until you have strong self-esteem and lay to rest the negative thoughts or self-limiting beliefs which hamper your courage, you won't be able to implement the changes you truly desire.

It is so easy to be disenchanted with ourselves, and want to change an aspect of our lives, and struggle to try to make a change, but blame ourselves if we can't. There is no lack of resources available to help you improve your relationship with yourself. A visit to any bookstore reveals an ever-expanding 'self-help' section with books with titles in large type and numerals, shouting at you. Titles like:

10 WAYS TO STOP MOANING AND START LIVING
ACHIEVING THE PERFECT LIFE IN 60 DAYS
12 TESTED STRATEGIES FOR LIFELONG CALM

and so on. Others have large type headlines telling you that you can do anything:

YOU CAN DO IT – If you only want it badly enough

and the subtext is that if you don't become rich, thin and famous very quickly, it's probably because you weren't *committed* enough, didn't *persist* long enough, and didn't *believe in yourself* sufficiently.

Resources such as these, with copious strategies to support your self-discipline and efforts to incorporate or initiate change, can be helpful. The problem occurs when the suggested program refuses to allow for bad days, backsliding and the general shades of grey which life reveals. They can then have the opposite effect, leading the reader to give up in frustration, with a lower sense of self-esteem than when they first started reading. The best of the self-development books allow for different personality types, and offer more gradual attempts at change rather than a complete metamorphosis in a prescribed period of time. *Your Best Year Yet* by Jinny Ditzler recommends a few hours out of your normal schedule to review your past year, both achievements and disappointments, to allow you to see a more balanced (that is, less negative) picture, and then to move forward slowly with achievable goals for the next twelve months and beyond. This is not rocket science, but solid commonsense, allowing you to recognise your failings, balance the picture with your strengths, and deal with them all in order to move on. Ditzler also recommends that out of the seven or eight 'roles' in your life, you choose one, and only one, on which to focus for the next twelve months. This is not to underestimate the importance of

> We love our limitations – we must – because we certainly don't want to let them go
> – JINNY DITZLER

the other roles, but to recognise the reality that one major goal in a year may be all you can hope to handle. Another very useful book for those wishing to understand their relationship with their selves is *The Successful Self* by psychologist Dorothy Rowe. Dr Rowe doesn't rant or rave at you to 'improve' yourself, but rather looks at the ways we develop as social human beings, and how in understanding this, we can learn to value and accept our true selves.

Self-esteem

If you do believe that you are limiting your own potential, it is useful to ask yourself why this might be the case. Are you doing this by your attitude, mood, or aspirations or by succumbing to others' expectations? Some of these reasons will sound similar to those which can cause you to get stuck in a particular career path. Maybe you find yourself circling an issue, not advancing, but just harbouring a desire to break out of your current situation. Is a particular pattern of behaviour holding you back? Could it be that you are worried that you will be 'getting above yourself' if you have a go at something different? That you will disappoint friends and family? You will look foolish? The reasons you are not proceeding are many and various, but the residual concern may be that your self-esteem is not robust enough to allow you to take a bet on your chances of succeeding at something new.

How do you measure something as elusive and fragile as self-esteem? Australians often worry they are getting above themselves if they have a healthy respect for their skills, abilities and traits. So often one man's healthy ego is another's over-confidence. And even if you believe that healthy self-esteem is a good thing to have – how do you go about building your own? In recent years affirmations have received very good press, and many authors will exhort their readers to place sticky notes all over their houses with positive 'I will succeed' style messages on them. This is fine for those who feel comfortable doing this, but many won't. If you're someone who feels horribly self-conscious at the very thought of affirmations, what do you do?

There are no easy answers, but it may be time to do some work on why you think your self-esteem is low, and then to find an area of your life where it's not too bad, and build on those small successes. Try taking small risks and learning you won't fall off the planet if they don't work. Deliberately surrounding yourself with giving people who genuinely like you and applaud your efforts is another good strategy and one which encourages you to try ever more challenging things. Forcing yourself to go somewhere different, try something different, meet someone different is another way of removing yourself from your comfort zone. Let's face it, if you were 100 per cent happy with that comfort zone, you wouldn't still be reading this book.

Attitude

You've looked at the toolkit (page 48) in Chapter 4, and are still evaluating the resources you have for a potential life change. One which niggles is attitude. Are there aspects of your attitude or personality which you just don't like? Characteristics you would really prefer to change? And no, 'everything' is not a useful answer. Let's assume you suspect an inclination towards negativity is colouring your thinking and your life.

How do you go about changing this? The best start can often be the most obvious, but least utilised. Consider the attitude issue which is bothering you. Ask your nearest and dearest if they have detected the same shortcoming. Request total honesty and be prepared for just that. And if the answer is, 'Yes, you're right, you do tend to be like that', then ask them when this problem occurs the most. When you are under pressure, facing a new challenge, or is it so entrenched that it happens on a daily basis? If their answer confirms your fears, *do not* let this become one more negative. See it as a real opportunity to turn this knowledge into a part of your change program. Go and browse the self-development section of a large bookstore for material on this particular trait. See if you can pick up some thoughts on how to modify or eradicate the issue which is bothering you. Check classified ads in newspapers for classes which may help (such as anger management, assertiveness training, overcoming shyness, dealing with stress). Try a search of the Internet for more information on the subject. Visit the PACFA website outlined in Chapter 3 (page 45) for a counsellor or psychologist who deals with this subject. If you are genuinely dissatisfied with this trait, feel

> *Invite your fears in, then tell them to sit down and shut up!*
>
> — SARK

free to fix it. No, it probably won't be easy, but surely it's better to try to resolve it than to dislike yourself?

Warning – Be careful, when selecting a nearest and dearest to discuss an attitude issue, that you do not choose someone who has a vested interest in keeping you in your place!

Accountability

In Part One we looked at a list of factors which may prevent you from embracing significant change, and one was accountability, or complaining about all the external factors which prevent you from taking responsibility for your own destiny. Another way of thinking about this might be to ask yourself, whose life is it anyway? Does your life belong to the people or the situations which have formed you so far, or is it time to view it as totally under your own control? Is your continuing discontent really going to add to the good of mankind? This is not in any sense to deny the awful things you may have endured up to now, nor the very very hard work it may take to reassess your situation and move forward. Author Richard Bolles talks of a checklist of forces which people perceive to be holding them back, leading to a victim mentality, and loss of control over their futures. These include:

> History, social class, education, genes, upbringing, parents, teachers, partners, friends, bosses, managers, co-workers, lack of skills, lack of experience, lack of opportunities, taxes, the system, the government, the state, large corporations, a conspiracy, or the devil.

As you can see, it just about covers every aspect of life! And if you add a few to your particular list, you will easily become discouraged and believe there is little hope for change. But Bolles also suggests that even those with the most disabling personal circumstances can climb out of their entrapment by working on *what they can* rather than dwelling on those things they *cannot* change. If you feel that accountability is an area you need to work on, try listing those forces which are shackling your attempts to move ahead, and put a percentage on those you absolutely cannot change. Now consider the remaining percentage of aspects of your life that you can do something about. This is what you can work on, and in making a difference here, ultimately affect or nullify that which appears immutable.

Self-discipline

Don't you just hate it? It's just so hard to keep something going. It can be really exciting starting a new program, but slogging away at it when the going gets tough is sometimes just plain boring. Is your self-discipline and hope for instant gratification a factor in previous aborted attempts to get a new life, or way of living? If this is the case, maybe the first strategy is to get off your own back – you're far too heavy. Yes, you may have disappointed yourself previously but where is it written that this will happen again and again? Maybe your expectations were unrealistic, or you didn't put in sufficient planning time? Maybe your timing was just wrong. Maybe now you can reapproach your goals with renewed vigour and increased knowledge. Whether you are working on changing yourself or some other aspect of your existence, use the Goal Planning checklist in the resources section to define specific goals, break them into manageable (and measurable) steps, and set realistic deadlines so you can review your progress. Detailed planning can help cement your commitment. Regular (weekly) reviews of your progress will also help you keep on track.

For those interested in a thorough and detailed approach to increasing your self discipline, and capacity to make effective personal change, Stephen Covey's *The 7 Habits of Highly Effective People* is an inspiring read.

WHEN ALL ELSE FAILS ... LIGHTEN UP!

Take some advice from American author Richard Carlson's *Don't Sweat the Small Stuff* series of books. These compilations of commonsense are directed at those caught up in the rush of life who are missing the bigger picture. His best advice is to stay playful. He suggests you start by cuddling your children, tickling someone or walking barefoot. Try it – it might just put a smile on your face.

Significant others

In the early seventeenth century John Donne declared that 'No man is an island', and 400 years later, little seems to have changed. Most people still derive maximum pleasure when in the company of others. But when we put our hearts on the line and truly love others, we know we are ultimately very vulnerable if the relationship ruptures due to death, misunderstanding, or another form of intervention. It is also true that many may try to advise you when you encounter a time of loss or breakup, but all the words in the world won't prepare you for the personal impact of this event.

Popular images around us seem to reinforce the notion that unless you are in a relationship, you are not realising life's full potential. This is plainly incorrect in many cases, as well as unfair to those who are not in a relationship, but that doesn't stop advertising image-makers churning out pictures of cuddly couples on the beach at sunset.

As well as divorce or bereavement, other life changes may also initiate a re-evaluation of your primary relationships – a retrenchment may place such pressure on your marriage that you decide you are better off without it. The death of a close friend may encourage you to question the joy in your own existence, and this could result in the questioning of the value of continuing with a current relationship. Menopause may affect you or your partner to such an extent that your emotional and sexual life is severely compromised.

> *Happiness is having a large, loving, caring close-knit family in another city*
>
> – GEORGE BURNS

This chapter is not about counselling to help you achieve a new or better relationship. In fact, it is not about counselling at all. It is about recognising the types of relationship changes you might encounter, brought about by either a relationship breakdown or the death of a partner, and the resources available should this happen.

If a relationship breakdown is the issue, you will need to pinpoint whereabouts on the scale you are at – beginnings of feelings of disquiet, and thoughts that the relationship won't last, extremely fed up with the relationship, or positive that it is over and that a formal dissolution is the next logical step.

Relationship in need of repair

There is nothing so isolating as being in an unhappy relationship when all those around you seem to be functioning well. This is when the 'good old days' do seem good – positive thoughts of times when the community and church would provide confidantes who could absorb your concerns, offer a shoulder to cry on, and make you feel less alone. Society is now different, and can prove less supportive – the service you seek will often involve people you don't know, and you will be required to pay for that willing ear.

There is no generic relationship breakdown advice. Conditions can vary dramatically. You might be the partner chafing at the bit to take off and discover life on the wild side. If this is the case, relief could well be the dominant emotion as you walk out the door. Conversely, you may be the one left behind when your partner finds someone else. Grief, pain and anger may be the feelings jostling for attention at this stage. Or it could be a long, slow and sullen process of relationship disintegration – in this case an inability to act, and fear could guide your thoughts.

When trying to repair or revitalise such relationships there are many different ways (some complementary) of working through the issues:

- by yourself
- with your partner
- with a trusted other (relative, friend, work colleague?)
- with a professional counsellor
- with a spiritual or religious adviser

Perhaps the most difficult question as you examine a problematic relationship is to define the type of help you want. If you feel there is absolutely zero chance of staying with your partner – you actually loathe them – then marriage guidance chats are perhaps past the point. It may be mediation you require, to assist with a fair and dignified exit from the relationship.

One of the best books for those who are not sure what the next step might be, or even if there needs to be a next step, is *Side by Side: How to Think Differently about Your Relationship* by clinical psychologists Jo Lamble and Sue Morris. This is a very practical guide to the difficulties those in relationships can encounter, and how some clarity of thought and realistic expectations of relationships can greatly assist in times of tension.

The five conclusions offered are:

- A relationship without commitment is doomed.
- A relationship is about walking side by side along the same path.
- Thinking clearly is everything.
- It's up to you.
- There is no perfect relationship.

In *Side by Side* the authors demonstrate how these guiding principles can be applied to fragile, tempestuous and worn-out relationships to help couples reappraise the possibilities which may be left to them. Another book which looks at couple issues and offers strategies to reignite the passion is *Passionate Marriage* by David Schnarch, Ph.D. Dr Schnarch believes couples can work together towards genuine intimacy, regardless of how much ill harmony has gone before. His book is full of case studies from his clinical practice as a psychologist and sex therapist.

RELATIONSHIPS AUSTRALIA
What is it? How does it work? Is it free?

Relationships Australia is a partly federal government funded national organisation with offices around the country. It offers services including relationship counselling, parenting strategies and mediation.

Appointments can be made through your local office. If you are seeking a relationship counselling meeting, you will be charged on a sliding scale, according to your income. This fee will be advised when you make your appointment. Should the income no longer be joint, two fees will be advised, one for each different set of circumstances.

Appointments for couples receiving counselling will be made in agreement with the counsellor — they may be weekly or fortnightly, of about 45 minutes' duration, and could continue for some weeks or months. It may be that one party will cease, but the other will continue. Mediation appointments are offered for situations when the breakdown is considered final, and a separation or divorce is planned.

In the best of all possible worlds you will be able to deal with your relationship issues both honestly and productively with your partner. You may decide to do so without external assistance, or you may prefer to use an objective adjudicator such as a counsellor from Relationships Australia.

Relationship over

When you or you and your partner have decided that the relationship is over, apart from the emotional issues which you will need to deal with, the financial and legal aspects also need to be addressed. Mediation with Relationships Australia is likely to be your best first call, in order to try to avoid the need to engage in an expensive and stressful legal process. These meetings normally run for about two hours, and a minimum of three or four appointments are often required, although there is no set number. Mediation is the process of sharing information, options and strategies for as successful a separation as possible, and both parties must be present with a mediator for this to occur.

Finding out your rights is critical. These rights may be custodial, financial, or to do with jointly held assets such as a business, superannuation fund, farm or property. A good starting point is the Family Law Court, by phone, in person, or the Internet. The website offers downloadable divorce kits, enabling you to understand the type of information you will at some stage need to supply.

Lottie & D: We redefined everything

After six years of marriage we were having problems. Our children were not quite two and four, and we had moved from Sydney to the Yarra Valley, in Victoria. It was a brave attempt to live out a dream of a place in the country. But, despite good qualifications, my husband couldn't hold down a job. I was finding the parenting was increasingly left to me.

There was always the sense that this wasn't going to work — even when things were pretty good. My sudden decision to end it and ask him to move out came after he lost his licence for six months for drink-driving. This again focused all the parenting/shopping/arranging of our life on me. I thought, I'm doing it all by myself with him here; the only thing that's going to change if he goes is that there might be a little less stress.

D was very upset and confused about the breakup, much more than me. I suggested he organise counselling with the Marriage Guidance Council of Victoria (now called Relationships Australia), which he did. We both attended. D constantly reiterated that he wanted everything to just go back to being as it was. This statement invariably made me cry — a lot of crying went on in that counsellor's office! The thought of going back to a marriage where I did everything: bills, cooking, shopping, housework, parenting, organising social events, all major decision-making (all minor-decision making, for that matter), was just so appalling. Hearing my husband's wish — his dedicated lack of insight and understanding — made me realise I'd made the right move. I attended counselling alone, too. It helped me clarify my needs, which weren't great. I just wanted to get on with bringing up the children the best way I could. And separately from my husband seemed to be the best way.

Going from a professional income to a supporting parent's pension meant that the cost of a divorce was prohibitive. I couldn't work without forking out vast amounts for childcare. And I felt that I needed to just be at home with the kids, anyway. If I'd been able to afford a divorce, I would have done so.

We spent a total of two and a half years apart. I was alone all of that time. I had no interest in going out with anyone else. It seemed impossible to parent and conduct a new relationship, so hopelessly difficult. And I found I loved the aloneness. I had married at 21, and lived in student houses before that. I really had had no experience whatever of living alone until that time. It made me resourceful, independent and capable. I can still really value the lessons I learned in that two-year period. But the separation made me realise how much I grieved for our lost marriage.

There was no joint custody. D was in a bad emotional state, unable to hold a job or take the children.

I also went to a psychologist who helped me realise that my husband's problem was addiction and he put me onto a twelve-step program for the families of addicts. Believe it or not, before the psychologist named the problem, I was still unsure, in spite of all the evidence, and all the clear pointers. The program for families of addicts, Al-Anon, saved my life. It was where I found understanding, acceptance, and real empathy. No-one I spoke to, not even my very sympathetic and helpful family (my sister was always there — paid bills I couldn't meet, bought the children new shoes, paid for haircuts), was able to give me the support and strength I found through Al-Anon. I would recommend that anyone with addiction in their families should seek out Al-Anon or Nar-Anon through the phone book. There are meetings everywhere.

Then the reconciliation just happened — probably six months sooner than it should have. D started getting help. Within a few weeks he was interacting, talking, being a lovely person to have around, and taking an interest in the children. He was very scared, very tentative — it was touching. If anything, it seduced me all over again. It was like falling in love.

Our daughter, then seven, had difficulty with her father returning, and this has taken some years to resolve. Our son has been okay, and the children are now in their twenties. Looking back, I wish I'd addressed their emotional needs more. In hindsight I wish someone had made it clear to me at the time that I was in an emotionally fragile state. I was so busy Coping Brilliantly that I didn't realise that I was grieving and, to some extent, protecting my emotions. I should have been more honest, emotionally, with my children. I think, in my attempt to appear strong, I may have been brittle. I regret that most of all.

Overall, the separation has definitely been a good thing for our relationship. We redefined everything. We came back together as adults, committed. In the early years of marriage, D was there for sex and I had friends with whom I socialised. Now D represents sex and friendship and love. I feel very lucky.

Losing someone close

Grief is a small word which encompasses huge emotions. It is the reaction to the loss in your life. This loss can range from the death of a loved one, to the loss of a relationship, job, health, home or dream. The experience of losing someone you love is one of the biggest life changes you are likely to encounter, and one which will always be totally outside your control, making a mockery of attempts at life planning and achieving goals. Particularly for those who consider themselves to be in an ideal relationship with their perfect partner, the experience of losing that partner can seem to sweep all else away.

During the course of the past century, death has become a very private matter, and much more medicalised. Previously most people would die in their own homes, surrounded by loved ones and extended family. There was an intimacy and familiarity in the final hours. Now most people die in hospital, in sterile rooms, with beeping machines and tubes. Most of us know little about death, and so the shock of losing someone close is compounded by our own lack of knowledge or experience of this momentous occasion.

It may be that you have no warning about your loved one's demise, and are deeply shocked and aggrieved at your lack of ability to say goodbye. Or it may be that you have lived with a terminally ill partner for a long period of time, and had many opportunities to discuss their wishes. Whichever is the case, there is still no real preparation for the impact their death will have on you, and the way your emotions are likely to seesaw for a long time to come. You will also have to work hard to maintain equilibrium at this time. There are many resources and support services available for those who are grieving – the problem is that you usually don't know about them at the time you most need them.

Some resources which may be helpful cover the three main aspects of losing a loved one; the immediate and practical, longer term emotional support, and the more pragmatic financial concerns.

Living with grief is a lifelong process of incorporating our experiences into our lives. Grief is a part of life.
– NATIONAL ASSOCIATION FOR LOSS & GRIEF

PRACTICAL

The Australian Funeral Directors Association (AFDA) is a funeral service organisation with a national network, and code of ethics. They will supply advice about what happens immediately following someone's death, including:

- what to do when someone dies
- when the coroner becomes involved
- who is responsible for organising a funeral
- funeral costs

The AFDA website also contains frequently asked questions on funerals and grief. Centrelink also produce a booklet entitled *What to do when someone dies* which covers all the key information you might need to know.

EMOTIONAL SUPPORT

When you lose a loved one you may be surrounded by a great deal of loving support – or you may feel as though you are stranded in an emotional desert where no living soul understands what you are going through. Some sources of support are:

Your family doctor – Try booking an extended appointment to allow you the time for a full checkup, as well as discussion of how you are managing, and any strategies the doctor might have for you.

The Solace Association, Inc. provides grief support for those who have lost a partner. They provide meetings or telephone counselling with trained support workers who have also lost a partner. The organisation is national, with branches in every state.

The National Association for Loss & Grief is another very helpful organisation, providing access to counsellors, information about how you may be feeling, and strategies for working on these feelings.

It may be difficult to ask for help if you are not coping. You might feel you are supposed to be coping 'by now' (whenever that mythical moment is). The best time to ask for help is immediately.

FINANCIAL CONCERNS

It is possible you have absolutely no desire to even think about money issues at this stage, and in most cases, major decisions can be delayed, but you will need to gain an understanding of your immediate financial obligations if you don't already know them. If this is difficult, ask a trusted relative or friend to help you work this through with the family accountant. It is helpful to have on hand the following information about the deceased:

- birth certificate
- marriage certificate
- insurance policies
- leases
- trust documents
- employment contract
- will
- bank and shareholding details
- other investment information
- superannuation statements
- tax returns

There are many many books on the grieving process, from classic texts, to more personal memoirs. Your funeral director and doctor may have some suggestions.

Some books which may be useful at this time include *When Bad Things Happen to Good People* by Harold Kushner, and *When Things Fall Apart* by Pema Chödrön. For those women who have been widowed, Marion Halligan has written a fictionalised version of her experience of losing her dearly loved husband in *The Fog Garden*.

Being lonely

Being lonely is different from being alone. You can be lonely within a relationship which is not working. You can feel happy and fulfilled when living alone. Being lonely occurs when you do not have sufficient quality relationships and communication with other people. This may be a temporary stage which occurs when you change location, or after a relationship breakup. It could also be a long-term situation you wish to change. If this is the case, you may benefit from the chance to evaluate what you expect from relationships. Are you hoping partners and friends will be there for you always, no matter what? Are you hoping they will meet all of your needs, as well as your expectations? Are you really expecting too much from fallible human beings? It also may be the case that being in the lonely 'groove' too long has blunted your skills at social interaction, and encouraged you to dwell on your own thoughts, rather than those of others. Shyness may also be a contributing factor. If this is the case for you, a double-pronged attack could help. Firstly, develop some strategies for really enjoying your 'alone' time – this is the time you designate as a valuable opportunity to pursue those activities pleasurable without company – reading, writing, creative pursuits, and so on. Secondly, decide to work on a program of 'people connection' by attempting conversations, or light social interaction without great expectations. In other

> *Each friend represents a world in us, a world possible not born until they arrive, and it is only by meeting that a new world is born*
>
> — ANAÏS NIN

words, prepare yourself for disappointment, but don't expect it. You can do this via a structured environment, such as a special interest group, community organisations (volunteering is a great start), or with acquaintances with whom you would like to develop a friendship. For specific strategies on meeting new people, try reading the chapter on 'Overcoming Loneliness' in *From Thought to Action* by Antony Kidman, or the section on loneliness in *The Beginner's Guide to Retirement* by Michael Longhurst. Both books take a thoughtful and proactive approach to simple ways you can significantly increase your chances of feeling less isolated.

Liz Broome*: I thought this was for desperates

At 45 I had never been married. I had experienced a couple of half-satisfying long-term relationships but still felt I hadn't connected with 'Mr. Right'. I toyed with the idea of placing an ad in the classifieds, but felt this was for desperates. But after two years of no relationships, a serious drought, I decided to give it a try.

I didn't realise I would have to record a message. It was really embarrassing – my voice kept squeaking, but if I tried to speak low, I sounded like someone in drag. After a couple of drinks I started to sound reasonable. Anyway, it worked really well – I had so many calls, and my second date was really nice. I enjoyed having dinner with him, learning about his passion for fishing, and the vibes were really good. It was only when he drove me home, and opened the car door for me – our hands touched – and sparks literally flew. We've been together ever since and I can't imagine life without him. I'm so glad I finally screwed up my courage to place the ad.

✶ Name has been changed

Finding someone

After a prolonged relationship, getting back on the dating scene is one of the most frightening things most adults can attempt. From years of safe assumptions of company and intimacy, giving up cosy coupledom and meeting loneliness and possible rejection is a very challenging thought.

For those out of the habit of being in a relationship, the idea of dating again can be equally daunting. The dating scene has probably changed dramatically from when you were last out there. Maybe you grew up in a more sexually repressive era, when men earned more, paid for dinner, opened car doors and women felt no need to look at the wine list. Perhaps there was no such thing as an answering machine, let alone the Internet where you can flirt online, without having a clue whether the other party is the girl or boy of your dreams, or a sumo wrestler. The whole notion of loving again may seem too emotionally unsettling – you may have carved out a calm and predictable existence, and adolescent surges of feeling may seem more upsetting than fun. For others, this is the ultimate high. The new rules are hard to work out, particularly in regard to meeting people safely, guarding your privacy, and financial issues. Using introduction agencies or Internet dating services have become increasingly popular as a way of widening the pool of prospective partners. Whereas once they seemed slightly dodgy or dangerous, now people from all walks of life happily discuss their successes using such agencies. And whilst not everyone does meet the man or woman of their dreams using this method, many have formed ongoing friendships in this way. If you do agree to a date using an introduction agency, or Internet service, there are a few simple guidelines:

- Acting yourself is probably the quickest way to impress. If you are trying to impress, it will probably show.
- Not every date will bring romance, but there may be a very good long-term friendship to be gained from this meeting.
- Paying for yourself is fair and will allow you to leave early without obligation.
- Meeting somewhere neutral is a good security measure.
- Don't give out your surname or mobile phone number to a stranger.
- Nor your address unless you are prepared to handle an unexpected visit.
- Tell someone where you are going and with whom.
- Don't divulge information you don't need to, including your financial affairs.
- Follow your instincts.
- Looking or acting provocatively may give a false impression.

Ways of meeting someone new

Associations, clubs and courses are an excellent starting point, be they for golf, line dancing or politics. If you follow your passion, you'll have a good time whether you meet someone or not. Some ways of connecting with like-minded people include:

- dancing classes
- bridge
- wine appreciation
- languages
- walking tours
- festivals – film, writing
- political parties
- causes – conservation, animal welfare
- *Yellow Pages* – introduction agencies
- classified advertisements (try metropolitan and regional dailies)
- Internet
- volunteering activities (see page 197)

Romance, friendship or more meaningful communication?

One of the most difficult aspects of reviewing the health of our relationships is knowing exactly what we are searching for. What do you hope to get, and what you are prepared to give? Are you describing yourself as lonely because you do not currently have a partner, yet you enjoy a strong friendship group and relish the occasional moments of solitude in your life? Maybe this isn't really living the lonely life at all, but just noticing that, at certain times, a meaningful romantic relationship is something you would still like to achieve. Knowing this difference will help you work out the extent of your discontent, and whether you want to take it to the next stage and start to more actively seek a partner. Thinking about how you view relationships can only add to the way you decide to progress. Two good books on this subject are *The Five Love Languages* by Gary Chapman and *The Road Less Traveled* by M. Scott Peck. Chapman talks specifically about what we give and what we want to receive in a relationship, while Scott Peck's book is a manual on how to grow up emotionally.

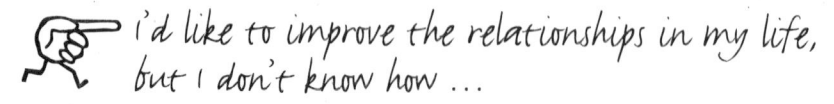

> *I'd like to improve the relationships in my life, but I don't know how ...*

WHAT'S STOPPING YOU?

Often we don't know how to solve a problem until we have a clear idea of the nature and extent of the problem. It may be that you live in a busy household and find the frenetic pace and lack of personal space totally maddening and conducive to explosive fits of temper. Conversely, you might spend most of your waking hours alone and this is causing feelings of depression and frustration. Too many relationships, too few?

Defining and resolving your specific relationship problems may be the hardest work you will ever do, but it also may lead to the greatest leap forward. Start by writing down the types of feelings you have for other people in your life, how you think they are reciprocated, and how you feel about this. Include your relationship with yourself as well. Armed with this snapshot, make an appointment with your doctor, letting them know that this appointment is for a chat. During the appointment, ask them whether some relationship counselling might be useful or if there are other resources they can suggest for the issues you have highlighted. See page 44, Chapter 3, for an outline of the professional services available.

chapter eight
EXPLORING YOUR CREATIVITY

Creativity is our true nature ... No matter what your age or your life path, whether making art is your career or your hobby or your dream, it is not too late or too egotistical or too selfish or too silly to work on your creativity.

— JULIA CAMERON

Exploring your creativity surely has to be one of the most rewarding things you can ever do – one of the greatest gifts you can give yourself. Yet so many people will spend a lifetime using excuses which prevent them from having a strong creative component in their lives. A wonderful visualisation of these excuses is in *Oh, the Places You'll Go*, in the verse, 'The Waiting Place', where people wait for 'the phone to ring, the snow to snow, a yes or no, or their hair to grow ...'

Are you also in waiting mode? Waiting for when you have more time, sufficient money, more opportunity, enough inspiration, before you can unleash your creative soul? It could be that these conditions will never occur, and *now* is the time to put the cart *before* the horse, honouring your creativity first, allowing the time, money and inspiration to flow in afterwards.

What is creativity?

The act of creation is to bring into being, to cause to exist, the product having evolved from your thought or imagination. The creation may be as awe-inspiring as a cathedral, as spontaneous as a batch of scones on a cold winter's day, or as pragmatic as a brick path. Many people will declare that they are not creative at all, that they are driven by right-brain impulses or that, as much as they appreciate looking at other people's artistic creations, they are themselves incapable of producing such work. Yet many artists, and those who nurture artistic spirits, believe that we are all creative but that many of us prevent ourselves from expressing this creativity by refusing to acknowledge this aspect of ourselves. A combination of negative beliefs, preoccupation with other, sometimes more pressing, priorities, and a history of being told they were not creative, can sometimes hold people back for a lifetime. Many also consider that pursuing an artistic endeavour is a self-indulgent or egotistical act. 'Who am I to think I can paint, dance, act?' they ask themselves. Yet, 'Who are you not to?' could be just as logical a response. Where do you fit in this scenario? Is there a creative pursuit you have often hankered to explore, but, for one reason or another, you keep putting it off, losing the thread, failing to take up the challenge?

Unlocking your potential

If you have creative impulses lying latent beneath layers of negative beliefs, and an upbringing which may not have valued the creative, how can you get started? First, by acknowledging that *any* work you produce is of value. It is not about other people's work and how yours compares. It is about the sense of self you capture in producing the work and the joy of the exploration.

For those serious about introducing more creative pursuits in their lives, there are two excellent resources. The first, *The Artist's Way: A Spiritual Path to Higher Creativity* by Julia Cameron, offers a twelve-week program of unlocking your creative potential. This book is a compilation of notes from Cameron's creative workshops in New York, where she has worked for many years encouraging students to develop their talents in screen-writing, dance, and pottery. Cameron asks her readers to follow through the entire twelve-week program in the book, working through at least half of the exercises. Those activities she considers non-negotiable are daily 'morning pages' (stream of consciousness writings to begin the day, and unblock the creative flow), and a weekly 'artist date' where you fill your artistic well with fun, images, and alternative activities. If you are longing to tap into your own creative possibilities, making a 7–10 hours per week commitment to the program in this book could be an excellent start.

Another approach, somewhat more light-hearted, but just as committed to the importance of creative expression, is to be found in the books of SARK (Susan Ariel Rainbow Kennedy). An author and artist, SARK's books are full of fun strategies to get your creative juices flowing. She offers many ideas to encourage you to re-see yourself, as well as the world around you. Try starting with *The Creative Companion*, subtitled *How to free your creative spirit*. Or *Inspiration Sandwich,* to be swung back into your childhood. For the full list of her twelve published titles, visit the website named after her company, Camp SARK.

FILLING THE WELL

In *The Artist's Way*, Julia Cameron suggests that the act of creation can quickly deplete your creative resources. She urges readers to replenish these resources, by regularly 'filling the well' by actively pursuing images. She exhorts readers to 'think magic, think delight, think fun, *do not think duty. Do not do what you should do.* Do what intrigues you, explore what interests you; think mystery, not mastery.'

How do you fill your well? If you find it difficult enough to carve out time for your own artistic endeavours, how will you get the extra time to replenish your imagination? The answer may be easier than you think. Instead of attempting to create extra time to expose yourself to different sights and sounds, how about converting the time you currently have? What if you make it your task to get to your day job by a different mode of transport once a week (walking, cycling, train)? What if you give up reading the newspaper one day a week, and use the 30 minutes gained to look at a book of photographic images instead? What if one weekly visit to the gym was converted into a 45-minute slow jog around the local parks or down country lanes?

Professor Jacques Miller:
The joy of drawing

As a small child, I used to love watching my father paint trees in the Impressionist style. He had been head of the Franco Chinese bank in Shanghai, but took the family back to Switzerland to live when one of my sisters was diagnosed with tuberculosis. In 1939 when the Second World War broke out, we moved to Italy, and caught the last boat out, back to China. It was in China that my sister died. After a year and a half, fearful of a Japanese invasion, our family moved on to Sydney. My father's credentials as a banker were not recognised in Australia, so he started the nucleus of the French Consulate. However his Japanese language skills were soon in demand for translating key intelligence documents. My other sister and I were schooled in Sydney, and I continued on to the University of Sydney to study medicine. I had two main reasons. One was the lack of knowledge about conquering infectious diseases, a direct result of the death of my sister. Secondly my exposure at an early age to war — and a determination to patch people up rather than kill them. For eight years after this I was overseas, working directly on research on T cells and their relationship to immunity and disease. In 1966 I was invited by Sir Gustav Nossel to join the research team at the Walter and Eliza Hall Institute in Melbourne. For years I was totally consumed by my work here — there was so much knowledge to gain, I had no time for anything else. Then about twenty years ago, one of my laboratory technicians showed me some drawings she had done at a Council of Adult Education course. I loved them. 'Why don't you try?' she challenged me. So I went, and enrolled in life drawing. I had no idea what to do, but after four once-a-week courses, lasting about fifteen weeks each, I really began to improve. At first I was shy about my work and about taking a risk, but my teachers noticed my improvement and my wife was very interested and supportive. And it introduced to my life a time when I could stop thinking about work. Before, I used to worry about the next experiment, how we would go about it, but with drawing I forgot work completely, it was so relaxing. I think anyone can find their creativity — it's up to them to try something. I then joined the Victorian Artists Society, nominated by two colleagues from my CAE courses. I have expanded my work from line drawings to oil painting. I love Australian scenery, particularly the seascapes of Victoria and New South Wales. I take my oils and paint on the spot. I don't work from photographs, as I love the atmosphere. Some people have remarked on the resemblance between my oils and those of my father.

Recently I have had two solo exhibitions of my ink paintings — these are very brief, two-minute action poses of nudes. I was told I would never be able to draw lines with ink, it would be too difficult as you can't erase bad lines, but these have proved my most popular works. Persistence has paid off though – the first work I presented for exhibition was rejected, so was the second. At long last it was included, later some works started to sell, and finally the solo exhibition was suggested.

It is interesting how the persistence of science has informed my art, and the creative processes of art have enriched my science. My art has added such joy to my life; it gives me complete relaxation, a larger circle of friends, and an enhanced recognition of life.

Ten strategies to get you going

But it's not just about books. To really kick-start your creative potential, try fuelling the fire with scheduled activities which encourage your transition from thinking about becoming an artist, to producing work which proves that you are.

1. Take yourself seriously.
2. Take your work seriously.
3. Set up a program for yourself. Treat it as though you were designing a course for a night class. Incorporate the work and artist dates into your current schedule. Record in your diary.
4. Expose yourself to as many forms of artistic expression as you can.
5. Pick a course – if you fumble, waiting for your left-brain to find the right course, get over it and start with the 'wrong' one. See how much fun you can have. Picked the wrong one? Find another. Nothing you have learnt will be wasted.
6. Meditate to empty your mind.
7. Take a sketchpad on your walks and draw what you see.
8. Experience solitude.
9. Travel to explore your art – you will be rewarded by a less-distracted mind, and some truly memorable images.
10. Use a digital camera to take photos just because. They need never be printed, but will help concentrate your eye.

Finding a form

If you are finding it difficult to get started, the simple, most practical thing you can do is commit your energy to a weekly class within a ten- or fifteen-week course on something, anything which appeals to your artist's instinct. It may be that you have always wanted to try watercolour painting. A short course, such as those offered by the Council of Adult Education, or University of the Third Age, summer schools within university campuses, and some TAFE institutes, will allow you to explore the materials and techniques of watercolour painting in an atmosphere which is both encouraging and informed. At the end of your first course, you may wish to progress to a more advanced technical level.

> *We learn to do something by doing it. There is no other way.*
>
> — JOHN HOLT

It can be difficult to decide in which artistic form your creativity will find its best expression. For some artists, it may be within a variety of media. For others, only one form will truly satisfy. For those who are searching, the trick is to try to remain as open-minded as possible and allow yourself the fun of experimentation. If you feel textile collages are going to be your thing, then by all means leap in and try this medium. But don't let this rule out the fun of exploring African drumming or landscape gardening when and how you can. Why pre-empt your artistic journey by locking out wonderful possibilities? Again books, films, short courses and one-day workshops will allow you to sample some of the possibilities.

SOME COURSES ON OFFER INCLUDE:

- life drawing
- botanical drawing & painting
- graphic design
- painting
- sculpture
- pottery
- pattern drafting
- photography
- patchwork & quilting

- acting
- scriptwriting
- songwriting
- dance
- woodturning
- leadlighting
- mosaics
- embroidery
- Chinese brush painting
- silk painting
- bookbinding

STRATEGIES FOR MAINTAINING THE FLOW

It is all too easy for dreams and good intentions to disappear beneath the detritus of everyday obligations. Assuming you have committed to introducing creative activity into your life, and have been realistic about the amount of time you can reasonably spend on your creative pursuits, the next challenge will be actually prioritising these pursuits above those which seem to be more pressing or easier to achieve. This is where planning journals and ideas books can be really helpful. If you are keeping such a journal, and using it to plan your activities, large and small, broken into manageable steps, frequent re-reading of these lists and ideas will refresh your resolve, and remind you of the achievability of some of the smaller steps. If you are pursuing your creativity in a group environment (class or workshop) the pre-commitment of time and money will probably keep you going long enough until the enjoyment of the activity kicks in. By this stage your creative pursuit will have assumed a larger status in your life, and will be part of a regular schedule. Committing to creative endeavours on your own is often much more difficult – there's always a friend to phone, a load of washing to do. But this is where your determination and self-discipline will reward you well. If you say out loud, 'Yes, I *know* that call/washing will only take ten minutes, so after I've sketched, sculpted or written for ten minutes, *then* I'll do it', chances are you'll be far too absorbed in your task to want to stop. Try it – it actually works.

The creative journey of writing

The reasons people put pen to paper, or fingers to keyboard, are as numerous as the genres in which they might write. Some are writing purely for personal satisfaction, some to recover a lost childhood, or to resolve a long-held hurt. Others may wish to highlight injustices, the achievements of others or to change the world in large or small ways. For others it may be the first step towards a change of career, or a way of making a lot of money (beware of this one!). For others still, it could be to record history which is in danger of being lost to the world, or celebrating a place or time which is unlike any other. And then there are those who are simply having a love affair with words, phrases, stanzas or fragments of verse. Those who simply cannot *not* write.

REAL WRITERS:
- write
- read widely
- rewrite – six, seven or eight drafts are not uncommon
- know their market
- keep on writing
- call themselves writers without squirming with embarrassment
- respect deadlines
- try their hands at different genres – writing is writing is writing
- discard second-rate writing, no matter how long it took them to achieve it
- take paid writing assignments to supplement their (usually) meagre income
- write some more

What is your motivation? If you are in love with words, and just enjoy the journey of writing with no particularly strong need to see your name on the title page of a published work, your own sense of commitment to the task will probably be strong enough to fuel satisfying bouts of writing activity. For those for whom the endgame is a published book, more structure and focus will be required.

WHO IS YOUR AUDIENCE?

By now you will hopefully have defined who your target audience will be. If it is yourself, then you may write as subjectively as you like, and are sure to please. If it is your family, perhaps with a family history, be aware that most family members will not see the 'facts' through your personal prism, and lower your expectations for unmitigated admiration when you unveil your masterpiece. For those wishing to appeal to a wider audience, a very clear idea of your chosen genre, and current best-selling works within this genre is essential.

WHICH GENRE DO YOU PREFER?

Your chosen genre might be:

- biography
- history
- contemporary novel
- romance
- crime
- fantasy
- poetry
- specialist subject area
- academic
- reportage

LEARNING BY EXAMPLE

From early days at school we have all been taught not to copy. But in searching for your creative self, sometimes a helping hand from a master is just the encouragement you need. One of the strategies used by writer Elizabeth Jolley to develop her style was to regularly copy the words of a classic writer, such as Tolstoy or Turgenev, in longhand in her journal. Jolley maintained that the act of transcribing beautiful prose helped her writer's consciousness to appreciate the rhythm of well-crafted phrases, and informed her own fledgling attempts.

DO YOU TAKE YOUR OWN WRITING SERIOUSLY?

This may seem a stupid question, with an obvious answer. But how seriously are you taking it? How many hours per week are you currently spending writing? Do you talk and dream about it more than actually doing it? How often do you write? If you are planning to be a published novelist, and are aware that the shortest such works usually start at manuscripts of 90 000 edited words, if you are working for just an hour or two a week, achieving first drafts of 600–1000 words or fewer, it will take years to reach your goal. In fact, do you actually have a delivery date in mind for your manuscript? Or is your project less formal than that? And what happens when you get stuck? We've all heard about writer's block, but how do you unblock? Do you retreat from your desk to complain to friends, read other writers' books, do some research on the Internet, or put out the garbage? Getting stuck has only one solution – writing. Real writers write, and writing your way through the block is the only answer to this dilemma.

GETTING STARTED AND KEEPING GOING

Apart from drawing upon your own resources, there are many useful resources to inspire your writer's journey. One of the best is *The Writing Book* by Kate Grenville, a practical guide to fiction writing, full of inspiring exercises and tricks of the trade to keep the words flowing. Try also American writer Annie Dillard, *The Writing Life* and author Stephen King, in *On Writing: A memoir of the craft*. Australian John Marsden shares his ideas in *Everything I Know About Writing*. For those interested in journalism, the classic text is *New Journalism* by E.W. Johnson and Tom Wolfe, an anthology of the best of literary non-fiction from the 1960s and 1970s.

Apart from writing books such as these, reading as wide a repertoire as possible will help refill your creative well. If you are a crime fiction junkie, mess it up with a biography of a gardener. If you love self-development books, throw in a fantasy. Try joining a book club – you'll be forced to change your reading habits, and will be richly rewarded by the diverse texts 'forced' upon you by your club members.

Workshopping with other writers is also an invaluable benchmark for your efforts. The first time you rise to your feet to read out your work will feel like mounting the steps to the gallows, but as you develop as a writer, and provided you are working with those whose opinions you trust, you will find it absolutely exhilarating when you hit the right buttons with your prose.

Objective feedback on your work is also available via manuscript appraisal by writers' associations such as the Australian Society of Authors, and the Fellowship of Australian Writers. Local TAFE colleges also usually offer short and full-length courses covering most aspects of writing and editing.

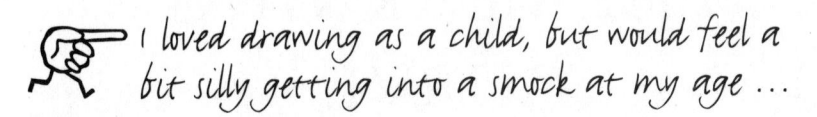

I loved drawing as a child, but would feel a bit silly getting into a smock at my age ...

WHAT'S STOPPING YOU?

Do you have a preconceived notion that everyone who creates is an 'Artiste', capital A? Talented, qualified, and confident? Maybe it's time to drag out the video of Kirk Douglas portraying Van Gogh in *Lust for Life* just to remind yourself that this is not the case. But being creative is not about being an artist anyway. Being creative is about producing from your own mind, or with your own hands or voice something which is pleasing. It's not such a big deal. Many of us have been shaped by our careers to seek immediate solutions, concrete outcomes, finished work. Being creative is more about time out. It is an exploration of possibilities in an atmosphere of freedom and potentiality. Get over 'silly', and get into the smock.

chapter nine
THE LEARNING CURVE

> *Education is not a product: mark, diploma, job, money — in that order. It is a process, a never-ending one.*
> — BEN KAUFMAN

The once-expected linear progress from early childhood to education, to adulthood where very few undertook lifelong learning has been blown apart. In recent years an increasingly flexible workplace has resulted in a similar freeing up of education and learning. A variety of opportunities are now available for people of all ages to modify careers, skills and interests through a course of study, be it short, long or medium. No longer is it mandatory to live in or move to a city or large regional centre to access the best brains in the world in universities, colleges or libraries. Changes in technology mean this content is now available 24 hours a day, wherever you may be.

Creating your life change through education

There is no end to the reasons why adults wish to get back to the books and incorporate learning into their day-to-day lives. Some are born learners, and have never stopped since they left school, moving from short courses to first and second degrees and diplomas with ease and enthusiasm. Others hated school, and have suffered from poor learning self-esteem for decades. Revisiting educational options is an opportunity to redress this hurt. For others, the commencement of mature-age study will be the starting point of a major vocational change. This might involve years of full or part time study to achieve a qualification in a new field. Or it might be defined units as part of ongoing professional development. For others the joy of learning means an opportunity to learn and socialise with other like-minded people. For some, the rewards of continuing education will combine many of these features. There will also have to be an acknowledgment, and agreement if

BUT I CAN'T AFFORD TO STUDY

AUSTUDY

For those wishing to study full-time, the federal government offers assistance in the form of Austudy payments. You may qualify for such assistance if:

- you are over 25
- you are doing an approved course at an approved institution (most master's and all doctorate degrees are excluded)
- you meet residency requirements
- you meet the personal and partner income and assets test

The current payment for a single adult, no children, is $318.15 per fortnight. Advances to get you started and fare allowances also may apply. Abstudy is available for Indigenous students who wish to stay at school or move on to further studies. Check with Centrelink for an application and income and assets test guidelines for both Austudy and Abstudy.

DISCOUNTS

For those considering short courses, or single units, ask for seniors' card discounts, if applicable, or a student discount if already enrolled in another course.

others are affected, of the financial investment you will be required to make. Some courses are very expensive, as well as necessitating forgoing regular income, and it may be difficult to justify such a commitment if it seems a selfish waste of family income. How much does this course of study really mean to you? Can you convince those around you how important this is? Are there ways of ameliorating the financial burden by taking longer to complete the course or supplementing it with extra income?

Whatever is motivating you to take up the books again, it is useful to overview a roadmap of how to approach your learning. The three key stages to place yourself in the right educational environment are assessing your requirements of further education, understanding the different types of options available, and checking your eligibility.

Why are you doing this?

Understanding the reasons why you are keen to start will help refine the questions you need to ask as you seek out the study path best suited to your purpose. If your reason for further education is vocational, then the decision becomes somewhat easier, as required qualifications will generally narrow your choices to a specific provider, such as a university or institute of technical and further education (TAFE). The choice will then be between different providers, depending on location, recognition of qualifications, and ease of entry. If you are seeking to learn a new skill, then it may be that a short course from one of the councils of adult education or TAFEs will suffice. Short courses are also excellent ways of learning a little more about a discipline, testing the water, before committing to a longer and/or more expensive course of study. If your interest is triggered by a desire to keep mentally active, again short courses, or the University of the Third Age (U3A) may best suit your needs.

Perhaps the most critical factor in your decision-making, apart from your passion for the subject matter, is how much time you feel you will realistically be able to devote to your learning. It is sometimes easy to look at a course guide for part-time study and decide that you might as well do two subjects per semester, rather than one. However what is listed as four contact hours per week usually means eight (attached) study hours. One 12-hour subject fitted around a busy day job may work – two may prove a challenge.

What level of education are you seeking?

What is available? The following brief outline of the educational providers may assist your planning.

UNIVERSITIES

Most Australian universities offer both degree courses and single subjects. Degree courses generally take from three years full-time to ten years part-time, with many variations in between. A full listing of Australian universities can be accessed from the Department of Education, Training and Youth Affairs (DETYA). New Hobsons Press also provides a directory of higher education courses. The 'Good Guides' are a popular way of choosing university courses. These guides are comprehensive and independent listings of university courses nationally. The guides are supported by a website which allows an online search by course subject for the most appropriate institution. The printed guides include application forms, and the website allows for online applications.

Higher education in Australia is subject to the HECS fee (Higher Education Contribution Scheme). This can be paid up-front, for which a discount applies, or will be removed from your post-study salary via income tax. The fee will vary according to your chosen course and institution, but, as a benchmark, a three-year full-time Arts degree will require a HECS payment of approximately $3768 per annum, to be repaid when you start earning more than $25 347 a year. If you pay HECS upfront, there is a 25 per cent discount. All HECS fees are likely to increase substantially in 2005.

Most universities also allow students to enrol for a single subject in selected courses. These classes usually involve a six-month or one-year commitment, and cost approximately $600 for eight 3-hour sessions.

TAFE COURSES

Courses offered by TAFE institutes around the country are often the most effective way of starting a career change. TAFE courses not only offer very practical, vocationally based education, but they also work in partnership with industry providing work experience and job opportunities along the way. Some courses are as short as one-year certificates, and the delivery of subjects is usually highly flexible, allowing a combination of work and study in the chosen field.

DISTANCE EDUCATION

With the increasing use of Internet facilities for information delivery, it was only a matter of time before educational institutes would avail themselves of the technology required to deliver courses to those unable to attend in person. For many students, the collaboration and workshopping with other students, lecturers, and tutors face-to-face cannot be substituted by an online class. For others, the freedom and increase in opportunity brought about by distance education has been phenomenal, as courses previously unavailable in remote areas of the country became a real possibility. Some distance courses will try to address the concern of student isolation by organising frequent 'in-house' sessions where students who study via the Internet are required to attend for coursework twice a year for long weekends or week courses. Two such universities are Charles Sturt University and the University of New England in New South Wales.

Open Learning Australia is a consortium of eight universities which offer distance education with universities and TAFEs for a single unit or a degree or diploma or certificate. The vocational, undergraduate and postgraduate qualifications awarded are the same as those achieved on campus, and are currently offered in arts, business, general studies, health and science and technology.

SHORT COURSES

Non-diploma or non-degree courses are often a great way to test your enthusiasm for a subject. A good way to start is with the many councils of adult education in the different states. These organisations offer an amazing variety of courses, mainly short, which allow the student to sample subject areas, and then build on them if the subject proves of interest. Most adult education centres also offer resources to join or start up a book group for those wishing to stretch their brains by discussing their reading. Costs for courses vary according to the different providers, but usually $17 per hour is a good guide for courses which may range from two 3-hour sessions to fifteen 2-hour classes.

U3A

The University of the Third Age started in 1972 in Toulouse, France. Its aims were to improve the quality of life for older people by offering academic programs from universities. Third Age refers to the age after youth and work. Whilst most older individuals now believe they are retaining the youth and work aspects in their lives, the U3A network in Australia is growing rapidly as a source of ongoing intellectual stimulation. Since its inception in 1972, some 172 Australian U3As have been formed. All are autonomous, with no entry requirements for membership or assessment of learning or credentials. Activities vary from group to group, from participatory to conventional lecture style. Annual membership fees range from about $15 to $40, and normally negate the need for individual course fees. A full listing of all Australian U3As is available from the national website.

OTHER LEARNING OPTIONS

Just because your area of interest doesn't seem to be neatly fitting into the area covered by mainstream education providers, it doesn't mean it's not legitimate, or available. It probably just means you'll have to search harder, and be more innovative within your search to find the right course. Circus performer? There are now a few courses available within Australia for aspiring performers. A search via the Internet search engine Google using the words 'circus performer training' came up with many options, including the National Circus and Physical Theatre Association, with ten links to training options. If access to the Internet is difficult, or doesn't bear fruit, remember that not *everyone* is on the Internet – get out the *Yellow Pages* and let your fingers do the walking. Consider also asking those who are already enjoying the subject you wish to explore – not only can they tell you how they did it, but will also share how *not* to get started.

HOW DO I FIND IT?

The Resources section lists all contacts mentioned in this chapter. This is no substitute for talking to the people in the institution itself. Nearly all universities and TAFEs offer open days, usually around August to coincide with September cut-off dates for applications for the following year. If you think you are interested in applying, do yourself a favour and visit the institution to take advantage of the opportunity to talk to staff and students in the course of your choice.

Bill Underwood: Seizing the challenge

I grew up on a farm in Barham in the Riverina region of New South Wales. At age fourteen I left school to work with my dad. This was the done thing; I guess it was pre-ordained in everyone's mind including mine. My father worked so hard, he was doing the work of two men. I really felt a moral obligation to help him out, especially as my brother and sister had moved away from the farm.

When I was 21 my father died of a heart attack. Over the next five years I developed the property to its full potential. It was profitable, but there came a point where, for it to remain viable, I had to either 'get big, or get out'. Buying additional property would have involved incurring a substantial debt. Also, while I still ran the home property, my brother and sister couldn't access their inheritance. The 'economics' of my situation didn't add up!

I started to think there must be other things I could do with my life, but the trigger for my change was totally unexpected. Through Apex I got to meet a variety of people with professional backgrounds, and I started to realise that I was as bright as everyone else, even if I wasn't as well educated. One evening, the principal of the local high school addressed an Apex meeting about the educational opportunities available in our region. He finished his presentation by issuing a challenge that anyone who wanted to could get an education through his school regardless of age or educational history.

I spent days out in the paddock thinking about this and then went to see him. I'd assumed I would have to plod my way through senior secondary school and then spend three or four years at university. To my surprise he explained that the system of mature-age entry made it possible to skip high school, and head straight for a degree course. I found this amazing – he hadn't just challenged me, he'd also shown me the path forward.

I was granted a conditional entry to the Riverina College (now Charles Sturt University). By the end of first semester, if I passed, I got to stay in. If I failed, I was out. I talked the idea over with my mother, brother and sister. They were really supportive. My mother had watched my dad work himself to death at 65 and didn't want that to happen to me. In 1975 we put the property up for auction, and I confirmed my enrolment for a four-year Bachelor of Education (economics major), and moved into the halls of residence on campus. The farm didn't sell so I paid a workman to look after the property while I studied. I was still involved with the farm, helping pick the crops, but I didn't know how long I could maintain both the farm and the study. Finally, after many months, an offer came through and the farm was sold. My mother was able to build a house in town, my brother and sister could both access their inheritance, and I was able to complete my degree.

After I graduated I got a teaching position at Geelong College, where I taught for four years. After this I taught in Canada, spent some time travelling, then returned to teach in Melbourne. In 1998 I won a teaching fellowship at Monash University for a year and then joined the Department of Natural Resources. I delivered a program called FarmSmart, which helped farming families view their businesses and lives more holistically, and make better business decisions. I'm now working for the Department of Primary Industries doing project planning and evaluation work. Along the way I also picked up a Graduate Diploma in Human Resources Management, and discovered a love for sailing.

Where I come from there is limited exposure to different people and ideas, and people tend not to look at things laterally. So many opportunities are missed. Leaving the farm meant I gained an education as well as the opportunity to travel, to work overseas, and to try new things. For example, if I'd stayed in the Riverina I'd never have discovered a love for sailing – I've now participated in six Sydney- and Melbourne-to-Hobart Yacht Races. I'd also have missed out on living in different locations and enjoying the financial stability and holidays associated with salaried employment.

After completing my tertiary education and working professionally I've realised that 'the system' is set up to deal with the average person – you don't have to be Einstein to succeed. It is so easy to become intimidated by the unknown and not to have faith in your own abilities. The really important thing is to share your dreams with those around you. You may be pleasantly surprised by their reactions and the support they provide.

How do you get started?

An extremely helpful guide to returning to study can be located on the Victorian Tertiary Admissions Centre website, under the library section. Titled *Back to the Books*, it explores all major issues relevant to recommencing your education. This information is helpful for students in all states.

Work out also how you are approaching your course decision – are you starting with the subject, reviewing available courses, and arriving at your choice of institution? This may be fine, but if your learning is vocationally motivated, consider talking to a careers counsellor, and working backwards to find the course most suited for that career qualification. The core subject may be the same, but the course suggested may well vary.

More assistance is available from the 'Ten Fields' tab on the Which Course, Which University section of the Department of Education, Training and Youth Affairs website. Here students can access what's on offer,

> **IF YOU'VE ALREADY LEARNT IT, GRAB THE PASS**
>
> ALWAYS ask about RPLs (Recognition for Prior Learning). Particularly within the TAFE environment, many skills you take for granted (word processing, database management, technical knowledge) are subjects with points which can be accredited merely by applying and proving you already have the skills or experience in the specific discipline. In some cases you may acquire two or three subject passes simply by filling in the application.

as well as how previous graduates graded the course content and delivery, and what their job success rate was.

Having chosen your preferred program of study, and hopefully attended an open day to confirm whether the institution is suitable, you will need to check your eligibility. This can be done directly with the chosen institution. If you find your qualifications are not sufficient for your desired course, don't despair. Talk to someone in the registrar's office or the faculty, and see if it is possible to gain entry using a mature-age or discretionary clause. If not, find out specifically the subjects/qualifications you are lacking, and compare these requirements with a similar course elsewhere.

Getting back into study and study habits

It's all very well to enrol for a course; choosing subjects, getting the textbooks and even the stationery can be really exciting and tangible evidence that you are, at last, *on your way!* But sometimes after three or four weeks of study the *merde* hits the fan, and you find your initial enthusiasm waning as the assignments pile up, and your attitude sinks like the sun in the west. Hopefully this is just a reality check, and you really are in the right course. Your workload might be too high, your self-discipline may need some tweaking, or you are just taking time to readjust. At this stage you might benefit from some assistance with your study habits. Planning is the key – along with the removal of distractions. It may be time for the awful reality of giving up something you love doing. You might also need to hone your time management skills – it is quite likely such skills are taught within the learning centre you are attending. If you are really struggling, it's time to seek assistance from the student counselling service. This is not an admission of defeat or a particularly nerdy thing to do. It's just commonsense to attack these problems before you lose momentum.

> *Try not to be a try-hard – high distinctions are very nice, but not if, in striving for the top marks, you miss all the scenery along the way. Are you there to learn, or do well?*

☞ *I'd like to change direction, but I hated school and just don't think I could head back to the books ...*

WHAT'S STOPPING YOU?

What exactly did you hate about school? Was it the school, the teachers, fellow students, or were you just angry with everyone at the time? Did you feel like a low achiever? Were you stuck with subjects that didn't appeal? Was it a repressive environment, or too liberal? Get over it. That was then, this is now. You've changed, but so has 'school'. If it's a few years since you visited a school, TAFE, college or university, do yourself a favour and go to an open day or, better still, make an appointment with the bursar or dean. Have an area of interest or subject in mind, and ask about how the institution delivers the study program. You might be in for a big surprise. You might even apply.

Chapter ten
GETTING PHYSICAL

Changes to your health can be the most substantial changes you experience during your life. Sometimes you can initiate health changes through new exercise or nutritional programs. If you choose the right program, and stick at it, the benefit will often be a new sense of vitality and zest for life.

At other times health changes may be forced upon you, in the form of an unwelcome diagnosis such as diabetes, cancer, multiple sclerosis, or some other type of life-changing condition. Whilst these diagnoses are never welcome, it is often the case that the patient will make significant changes to their lives to manage the new condition, and in doing so may achieve a better life balance and, ultimately, an improved health outlook.

We all strive for a healthy lifestyle, but rarely define what constitutes good health. Is this the same as fitness? We are also, as medical consumers, confronted by a bewildering array of 'solutions', with many of the providers claiming that their way is the only possible way forward. In particular, mainstream medicos and alternative and/or natural therapy practitioners can suggest dramatically different treatments for the same problem.

Many of the fittest, healthiest individuals around us first started their fitness programs in response to an injury, a weight problem, a lack of energy, or chronic pain. Other people might be addressing more general issues such as weight, stress, or chronic tiredness. Often the reasons behind your motivation will be the key to your ability to stick at a new health program. So if you've been toying with the idea of introducing a more disciplined eating pattern and regular exercise into your life, what basic questions regarding your motivation should you be asking yourself?

Your health questions

- *What* – work out what you wish to change. How much do you know about this type of health change? Where can you get basic information on this?
- *Why* – what is the real reason for this change?
- *When* – what is your time frame?
- *How* – what is available to help you make these changes?
- *Results* – what are your expectations? Are they realistic?
- *Commitment* – what are you bringing to the program – have you tried and failed before? What will you do this time to make it different?

Adam Shostak: Refusing was easy

In my mid-forties I suffered from a prolapsed disc. I'd been a footballer until I was 30, which meant my body was constantly used as a battering ram. I also worked in the family grocery business, using the lifting and carrying as physical training. But eventually this aggravated my injured back severely.

One morning I couldn't get up. I had to be stretchered out of bed and was taken to see a specialist, who told me he would perform an operation to fuse my back the next morning. This would cost $5000.

Refusing this was easy. I went straight to my own doctor, and started on a series of acupuncture, for a year, three times a week. I was like a pincushion. This brought temporary relief, but it was really just a band-aid treatment. During the following year I also saw a chiropractor, an osteopath, and a physiotherapist.

Then I saw an advertisement in a health food shop for Stephen Barry promoting stretching for lower back problems. Stephen had learnt Iyengar yoga, and had the same back issue. He became concerned that the Iyengar was injuring him and so modified the yoga to fix his own back pain. I was his first disciple. He explained, 'This is what I did for myself – now let's see what it does for you.'

The first session brought dramatic improvement. There seemed to be an immediate cellular recognition. Because I knew this was something that could help me, I willingly set time aside for it every day. In two to three months I was 10 per cent better, and within four years I was 100 per cent better.

I also learnt to reverse my mind from the fast-fix mentality back to a slow process mindset, and then it became easier – once you see a tiny light at the end of the tunnel you become very encouraged. After five years I was fitter than when I was nineteen or twenty years of age.

About the same time as my back fell apart, my wife left me, and went to live in Mullumbimby on the north coast of New South Wales near Byron Bay. I missed my children, so went up there for long breaks and loved how green and wooded it was, with amazing creeks and mountain views. I tried growing vegetables, and started down the healthy organic path. I also tried the drug scene but it wasn't for me.

I had promised myself after four years that if yoga continued to work so well for me I would teach it to others. I call my next seven years my apprenticeship. I would do yoga for two hours, sometimes four, sometimes six because I just didn't want to stop. I also read as much as I could, grabbing books, videos, any material that was available on the history and practice of yoga. Then I came across an anatomy book. It's a funny thing about bodies, we are never given a manual, and so you don't know how you work. I could not believe what sort of machine our bodies are. I stopped reading yoga books and dived into anatomy and physiology texts, reading thousands of pages and discovering new things all the time. My yoga improved out of bounds – it became so much sweeter. I started teaching when I turned 51. I needed to go through all the pain in order to teach properly. Training as a footballer for twenty years had made me very disciplined. I carried that discipline into yoga. I had touched pain all the time so the barriers were familiar. Yoga has increased my awareness of self, breathing, and given me more flexibility and energy. I'm 64, but I'm 34.

I now live permanently in Mullumbimby, and have added a yoga studio to my house for my private students. I work hard at my yoga, and the older I get, it is not getting easier. I work the vital organs, the heart, the eyes, the prostate. Sometimes it's very hard; sometimes it's a joy. I experience the full gamut of life in my yoga. I might get lazy for a day or two, then I jump back into it.

Finding basic information

For the non-medically minded, it is often quite daunting to try to learn more about a specific area of health, when the terminology can be unfamiliar and there is often an assumption of prior knowledge. Start by reading a general women's health or men's health book or visiting such a website. Good books are *Everyman* and *Everywoman* by Dr Derek Llewellyn-Jones, useful websites are those of the Jean Hailes Foundation for women, and the Pfizer men's health website for men. Gain an overview of your particular area of interest, and then start to drill down through the layers of information until you reach the appropriate level for you to frame questions for your doctor. Yes, you do need to visit your family GP.

Your general practitioner

When you decide to change your health regime, although you are fully aware that your very first port of call should be your family doctor, this is often the very last person you consult. You will actively seek advice from friends, strangers you meet at dinner parties, fellow exercisers at the gym, the electrician, and the supermarket cashier. But rarely will you take the time out to make an appointment for a general health check-up and discussion of a program to fine-tune your physique.

Why?

Is cost a factor? Yes, the longer appointment will be up to double a normal consultation fee, which may be expensive unless your doctor bulk bills. But to put this into context, compare this to what you will spend on the new regime without blinking (new running shoes, shorts, food and so on).

Is it because they will tell you what you don't want to hear, or already know? That less fatty food and lower alcohol consumption should form part of your resolve?

Or is it because they are aware that you have 'tried' and 'failed' before? Surely this is all the more reason to discuss why it didn't work previously. What were the missing ingredients?

You might have a general aim, such as 'losing weight' or 'getting fit'. Your medical appointment is a good opportunity to discuss whether your exercise routine should be focused on aerobics, stretching or strength training. You can also evaluate your weight and body mass, and ask for an explanation of what this really means for someone your age and sex. Ditto for your blood pressure and cholesterol levels. The result of this visit should be a tailored health management plan. Expect nothing less.

Background reading on health change

There are a couple of excellent Australian resources for those serious about implementing a healthier way of living. The first, written by nutritionist Cyndi O'Meara, is *Changing Habits, Changing Lives*. This book looks at unhealthy lifestyles (big issue) and breaks them down into a series of unhealthy habits (much more manageable). The author then offers a system of small, achievable steps (34), which, if implemented one by one, a week or more apart, will gradually form a far healthier way of living. Primarily concerned with what you eat, and achieving a balanced, high-energy eating plan based on pure foods, O'Meara also explains, in layperson's terms, why certain foods, eaten in suitable portions, will maximise your wellbeing.

In a similar vein, but offering a more holistic approach to health, is *Re: Life* by Dr John Lang. Subtitled *Find your balance and master work, change, career, family, nutrition, exercise, sleep*, Dr Lang's book also takes the approach of explaining what lies behind successful long-term health changes. He looks at your reason for altering previously harmful patterns of eating or lack of exercise, and offers strategies to allow you to evaluate how you stay away from fads, but introduce positive long-term habits into your life. In particular the two chapters entitled 'Exercise and Fitness' (see his suggested ten-point plan) and 'Nutrition' are an excellent starting point.

IN THE MIND

Mental health is as important, if not more so, than physical. There are many resources to assist those who need some support with mental health concerns. A handful of these contacts can be found in the Resources section, but this list is by no means comprehensive. If you, or someone you know, is in need of assistance in this area, it is important to start with a general practitioner who can offer a primary diagnosis and refer you on to a qualified specialist suited to your needs. For those seeking background on depressive illnesses, the BeyondBlue website offers a 'why are you here?' button which leads to information, frequently asked questions, symptoms, and possible treatments for sufferers.

If you are interested in a government-sponsored fitness program, try visiting the Active for Life and Fitness Australia websites for more information. Another option for those who love walking is to consider the 10 000 Steps program, which started in Canada, but has recently been implemented by the City of Rockhampton in Queensland as a way or increasing all residents' health levels. This program suggests that 10 000 steps per day, when combined with the correct nutrition, will enable most adults to reach and maintain a healthy state. Your steps are measured by a relatively inexpensive pedometer which is worn on your hip. Be warned, once you start measuring your steps, the sense of achievement can become totally addictive as the kilos dissolve.

You don't have to go it alone

Sometimes the main reason for our lack of discipline in making changes to our routine lies in the lack of accountability. We reason that we are only letting ourselves down, and so when we falter on a rainy morning, and fail to rise to run or walk, we don't mind too much. If you are rising to meet a friend on the street corner, and the only reason they have got out of bed at 5.30 a.m. is because of their commitment to be there for you, the whole impetus shifts, and you are much more likely to get up. Consider asking a good friend to join you on your new routine, whether it is swimming, cycling, yoga or walking. Agree on the number of times per week you can both reasonably meet for mutual workouts, and agree to stick to it for four weeks. By this time hopefully the habit and pleasure will carry you forward.

You can also acquaint yourself with those who have successfully achieved what you are after. Try reading books by sporting identities who have worked hard to achieve their dreams. Try Lauren Burns' *Fighting Spirit*, or *It's Not About the Bike*, by Lance Armstrong. These books are not about aiming to win an Olympic medal or the Tour de France, but about how the authors trained their minds to help train their bodies.

Consider also joining a team sport where your fellow members will depend on you turning up to training as well as games. Such a commitment will almost guarantee regular exercise in your life.

THE MASTERS GAMES

The Masters Games provide an opportunity for older adults to keep playing competitively in one of forty or more sports. The first Masters were held in Alice Springs in 1981. Since then most states hold bi-annual Masters Games, whilst the Pan Pacific (formerly the Asia Pacific Masters) is held on the Gold Coast every two years. The games are distinguished by the fact that there are no qualifying standards or requirements to compete. To enter you only need to ensure that you reach the minimum participation age for your chosen sport. The World Masters Games, held in Melbourne in 2002, attracted more participants and spectators than the Sydney Olympics in 2000, with the majority of the attention focused on netball 'grannies' and Charlie, the ninety-something sprinter. The next Australian Masters Games are scheduled for Adelaide in 2005.

Christine Garth: Taking on the challenge

Despite the accumulating years I was convinced that I was as young as I felt and that I was successfully delaying the outward signs of ageing, although, for some time I had accepted the response of my inner self to time and gravity. For me 50 was the watershed age . . . The idea of 'ageing gracefully' kept echoing in my thoughts as I began a surreptitious study of over-50 females. Working in the health sector provided me with ample opportunity to observe the differing approaches to ageing from the resigned-to-be-old-before-my-time to the terrifying no-one-will-notice-the-plastic-surgery. Rather than identifying a group of inspirational woman with particular physical characteristics I began to appreciate an age independent 'attitude' encompassing a passion for life, love and taking risks. Age gracefully? No! It was time to be a woman with 'attitude' and age disgracefully with the codicil that the disgrace would be of my choosing.

During this period of reflection my life was becoming busier with work and running three children around. I found myself actively participating in my younger two children's sporting lives, particularly basketball. I had played basketball briefly in my teens and this provided the little bit of knowledge required to become involved with their club as a team manager, committee member, and eventually, coach, and player. *Did I say 'player'?*

Basketball introduced me to a wonderful set of dynamic mums from various backgrounds. Many of them had 'attitude' and I loved being in their company. I was already reasonably fit but nonetheless I was terrified of injury, trying to jump, running, everything. With strong encouragement from my partner and children and gasps of disbelief from many friends I ventured forth with my friends to take on the challenge. We looked like a team of tomatoes with our red uniforms but at least our embarrassment was well disguised. We laughed, cheered and cried our way through two seasons and have just begun our third. The team composition has changed due to injury and other life events; however, our commitment to play remains strong and our friendships grow stronger. We still get excited over each goal and yes, there aren't that many. We celebrate our improvement, our ability to work as a team, admire each other's efforts and contribution, and get together away from the games to discuss the meaning of our lives.

This old dog has learnt some new tricks and has found it exhilarating – especially sharing the experience with friends. My self-esteem has blossomed along with my physical and psychological fitness and as for 'attitude', I just love being an over-fifty basketball-playing mum.

Unexpected health change: The diagnosis

In a perfect world, if you must receive a diagnosis of a debilitating condition or terminal illness you will be accompanied by a sensitive, loving family member or friend, and the doctor concerned will give you all the information you need to negotiate your way through the initial shock, and subsequent issues. It's not a perfect world, and many people learn in a less than helpful way of the radical change that has just hit them. They are then left, largely on their own, to grapple with the medical information (or lack of), the degree of the illness or affliction, and the psychological challenge of this change. Time and again, those who have received such a diagnosis relate stories of leaving the surgery to go somewhere alone and sob their way through the trauma. Only weeks, months or years later do they learn about some of the support services they might have benefited from. If you, or a loved one, are encountering such a diagnosis, it is helpful to request five different types of information, from the very beginning:

1. A plain English facts sheet of your diagnosis, including the physiological and mental manifestations which may occur. If your doctor does not have such information, he or she should know where it can be obtained.
2. Contact details for a peer support association which will allow you, as soon as you wish, to meet and talk with others who have dealt with this condition previously. You are not alone, but right after diagnosis you may certainly feel that you are.
3. Information about government agencies which provide services for someone with your condition. These will be available at federal, state and local government level, some may overlap, but it is worthwhile knowing about the full range in order to widen your options as much as possible.
4. Other information about other people's management and experiences of the condition – books, films, tapes, and so forth.
5. Short-term management strategies – some kind of plan or structure to allow you to deal with the next few weeks, including exercise, nutrition, mental wellbeing, until the shock and sense of unreality fades and you are able to bring a more objective focus to your next stage.

STRONGER FOR LONGER

Older Australians are well supported by free or inexpensive health programs in every state. Many are offered by the federal government, often through programs delivered by other agencies. *Living Longer Living Stronger* is a program designed by COTA (Council on the Ageing) Victoria, and being rolled out nationally in early 2004. It aims to increase the range and quality of strength training opportunities for older people. The training sessions will be available from gyms, community health centres and neighbourhood houses for a maximum cost of $5 per session.

Seena Samuel: A real bonus

I was 24, and living at home with my parents and brother and sisters when I was diagnosed with multiple sclerosis in August 2001. I knew nothing about MS — I couldn't even spell sclerosis. I'd done the MS Readathon fundraiser as a child but had no concept of what was involved. I thought MS was a disease for old people. My symptoms started about a month before I was diagnosed. My left side was numb; it felt funny, kind of dragging. For about a week I thought it was because I slept on the wrong side. I couldn't use my left arm. My body was tired, I was just plugging on with my work in the finance department of a publishing company. My workmates could see how much I was struggling, and told me to go to the doctor.

He said it might be muscle problems. Later he confided he had suspected a tumour, but thankfully hadn't communicated this to me. The day I had my CAT scan I was planning to go back to work, but ended up in hospital for five days undergoing further tests. Those five days were so hard. When everyone around you is grieving, you end up having to be the strong one, not just for your parents, but also your siblings. I'm the eldest

> *it's all about suffering, and perservering, and hope*

and I've always been their support. It was really difficult to keep this going. My parents would go home, and my brother or sisters would come to me in tears, and ask if I was going to die. Having my best friend outside my family was an opportunity for me to open up, but being strong for him too meant I had no time alone to cry.

I went to the MS Society in Footscray one month after being diagnosed. I walked out of there and got in my car and cried. I just hated the thought of being labelled. I've spent the past year educating myself more about MS. At first I thought MS meant wheelchairs. I've now learnt you can continue on with life. Much of my knowledge has come from peer support groups, being around people with the same condition. I don't do research on the Internet — you can make yourself sick from that. Unless the MS Society endorses the information, I won't waste my time with it.

I've had to let go of many of my plans and goals. But I've replaced them with others. That's not a disadvantage. I do still have days when I ask 'Why?' I think if things in general aren't going well, if you have a condition like MS, you can begin to question it all. I truly believe the one thing that has got me through this is my relationship with God. About a year before I was diagnosed I went back to the church. I look back now and I know it was my time of being prepared. I did have an angry period in January 2002 when I went to Perth by myself. I just had to fight it out with God; I wanted to say out loud how angry I was. And I came to see that it is not God's fault, but it's all about suffering, and persevering, and hope.

For a long time I had thought about getting into social work and psychology. In July 2002 I resigned from my job and started a four-year social work degree at La Trobe University. The good news was that with recognition for prior units the degree would only take two years. I've met so many wonderful people through the course. I'm also working on placement in counselling for staff and students at Melbourne University. I just love it. I do get mentally and physically tired five days a week. During term I work part-time in a nursing home doing office work — I'm lucky living at home that I can afford to just do the part-time work. If I needed more money I doubt that I could do long hours of waitressing like I used to.

MS is definitely an uncertain disease. Things might get worse and they might not. But what I do know now is that nothing in life is certain. In this sense, I feel one jump ahead of others who expect life to be so. I still have days when I don't feel my best. When my leg hurts and my left side is weak. I wonder how I will manage if the MS gets worse, and then I think, 'Well, I've managed so far, if things get worse I'll just have to deal with that change.'

The one thing I know is that although at times I cannot control my body I can control my mind and my thoughts. If I based my life on my feelings I don't think I would be here today. I realise I have to manage what I can control.

The funny thing is, if I hadn't got MS I doubt that I would ever have stepped out of my comfort zone and given up work to pursue what I am passionate about. With MS, although I have lost a lot, I have gained a lot too and if anything it has allowed me to take risks I never imagined taking. I see this as a real bonus.

> *This year I was going to get regular exercise, lose weight, cut back drinking and get serious about my fitness. But, once again, it just didn't happen...*

WHAT'S STOPPING YOU?

It's highly likely you've commenced this radical life improvement program on January 3. You were at a friend's beach house and off you went for a quick jog (after years of gentle shuffling), and then you nibbled miserably on carrot and celery sticks, while you watched the rest of the gang quaffing champagne and eating tacos. Timing *is* everything, isn't it? Little wonder your resolution had dissolved by January 5. If you are serious about improving your health, fitness and nutrition, take yourself seriously enough to research what these changes might mean, and armed with this overview, work with your health practitioner to create a program which involves a long-term and achievable renegotiation of your health habits.

chapter eleven
ASKING THE BIG QUESTIONS

It might be reaching a certain stage in life or a certain age. It might involve a steady progression from a life started in faith to a deeper commitment or it might mean learning about a new faith and the gradual diversion to a different path. It could just as easily be the first time you have seriously considered living a more spiritual life.

You might be in your teens, twenties, sixties or never. You may have a faith in mind. Or just be full of thoughts about what faith really means. Your desire for more faith in your life could be triggered by a loss or trauma.

There are no good or bad reasons for a spiritual search — but there are also no quick fixes, or easy answers. And just as there is no 'right' way to change your life, there is no 'right' way to spiritual enlightenment.

What are the big questions?

Regardless of why and when you are starting to widen your questioning to seek an understanding of the essence of what lies beyond your day-to-day existence, the big questions often come back to a few core issues:

- What am I doing here?
- How can I lead a more meaningful life?
- What role does faith have to play in my life?
- How do I find a faith which allows me to be true to myself?

If these are the types of questions circling your mind and you suspect that until you – at least partially – resolve them, you will not be living the life which best suits you, you may be encouraged to set out on a spiritual journey to discover the best way forward. But as you take the first step, things have a way of becoming very confusing. The upside of increasing religious freedom in the western world also has a downside of virtual spiritual supermarkets with true enlightenment promised for all comers. There is much less certainty and more confusion. We have moved away from the days when our faith was inherited, when our community and family expected us to remain faithful adherents to mainstream churches for all our born days. We are now confronted with a bewildering array of religious choices, including very specific splinter movements of traditional faiths, causing schisms within these faiths.

This chapter does not offer an exploration of all of these different faiths. What it does do is discuss how those who believe there's got to be more to life can get started, including finding a faith, a way of entering that faith, making a commitment and, for those sufficiently motivated and able, sharing that faith with others.

Finding your faith or path

If you have absolutely no grounding in things spiritual, but just a vague sense that there might be a system of belief which will allow you to lead a fuller life, there are a myriad of questions you will wish to ask.

One of the first challenges will be defining the type of belief system or faith, and this will mean resolving your fundamental approach to religion. Do you see religion as a social construct, as part of a movement which, in time, will reform the world? Or is your purpose an inward journey, not requiring an external structure, but entirely dependent on your own ability to find your way? Some questions which may help are:

- Why are you searching?
- What type of answers are you hoping to find?
- Have you any religious experience which encourages you towards a particular faith?

- Are you seeking a god, or an absence of god? Do you believe in higher authorities?
- Do you see religion as a way of saving your soul?
- Are you seeking peace of mind?
- Do you believe in the concept of sin and sinfulness, or is this foreign to your way of thinking?

> The problem with the contemporary world is not that it has too little religion but that it has too much. With that, we have an abundance of texts that lay claim to some kind of sacred quality. For every text there are guides, although in many cases they are difficult to distinguish from salespeople. It has reached the point where most of us need a guide to the guides.
>
> — MICHAEL McGIRR

Philosophy as a way of life

It could be that your bigger questions are not inviting spiritual answers at all – instead you may be seeking a new way of thinking as a framework for the way you live. If your journey is more concerned with the philosophical than the religious, you will find a rich supply of material to start you on your path.

From the Greek *philosophia*, meaning love of wisdom, philosophy is a study of the truths and principles underlying knowledge and reality. A big subject indeed, and often more easily handled if you restrict your search to one particular area, such as Greek philosophy, Renaissance thinking, Marxism, Existentialism and so forth. But how do you pick your area of interest before you know what other thinkers were offering?

As with so many other disciplines, starting with an overview can often be the best way. Try a Council of Adult Education short course (often 5–8 weeks) for an introduction to the great thinkers. Many universities also run short courses in philosophy, although these will normally be more detailed and longer (about fifteen weeks) than those at CAEs. The beauty of starting your search in a class environment is the discussion which will form part of the class — an essential strand of the philosophical quest. If you have the time, try reading *A History of Western Philosophy* by Bertrand Russell. Or Professor Bryan Magee's book, *The Story of Philosophy*, for a fascinating and accessible overview of different ways of thinking.

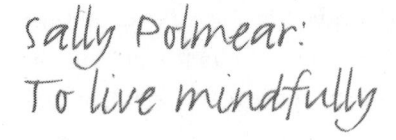

Sally Polmear: To live mindfully

As a child I struggled to understand the mysteries of life and death. When I was younger I was a committed member of the Uniting and Anglican churches as a way of exploring spirituality.

My husband Brian and I were married in the church but within a few years found it to be much less fulfilling than we'd hoped. On my spiritual quest, I found I needed to leave the structure of the church to find my own path.

I remembered back to when I was seventeen and spent a month at a monastery in Taize in France where visitors were able to experience a retreat. I wanted to recapture that sense of stillness in my life. About this time, when I was approaching 40, I visited the Ian Gawler Foundation for a three-day meditation retreat. I was introduced there to the writings of the American-born Tibetan Buddhist nun, Pema Chödrön, finding them accessible and practical, about how to live an ethical life, and what an ethical life might be. Her writings inspired me to accept myself. It was a huge relief. The Buddhist approach is not to reject parts of ourselves as 'sinful'; rather to see these very aspects as the fertile ground from which virtues can grow, as a lotus flower will arise from the mud.

I also responded to the central role of meditation emphasised in Buddhism. Now it has become the still wheel around which the rest of my day revolves. It allows me the opportunity to observe and understand myself and through this understanding take responsibility for my life and actions; to live mindfully.

The whole inspiring purpose of this is to learn and practise how to be of most benefit to others and myself.

Through reading *The Tibetan Book of Living and Dying* by Sogyal Rinpoche I recognised the need to have a spiritual guide. But where would I find one in Melbourne? After I went to hear Sogyal Rinpoche speak I was handed a flyer advertising Lama Choedak Rinpoche, a Tibetan Buddhist Meditation Master who was working out of Canberra but visiting Melbourne regularly. I felt compelled to go.

Looking back, it was a valuable lesson in paying heed to my own inner voice/wisdom to keep searching. That was five years ago.

My husband and children are very accepting of my faith, and give me the space I need to practise it. This has transformed my relationship with them, increased my patience and gratitude.

Where do you find out more?

There is a confusing array of resources which offer solutions of faith to most people's quests. The trick is to find the starting point which will best suit you. And this may well lie in a combination of reading, research and discussion with those already involved. In *The New Believers* Rachael Kohn offers a guide to contemporary expressions of age-old faiths. Kohn has been the presenter of *The Spirit of Things* on ABC radio since 1997, and in this book offers an excellent beginner's guide to current spiritual trends, and the faiths from which they have evolved. For those interested in specific faiths, she offers a reading list. Another useful book is *Spirituality Revolution*, written by David Tacey, which traces the protest against the more formal religions. For those wishing to learn the basics of faiths to which they have had no previous exposure, the 'Dummies' guides to Catholicism, Islam, Buddhism and other faiths are not, as the name suggests, a dumbing down of the subject matter but, on the contrary, useful guides that address basic questions which you might be asking. You can also search on the Internet, but this can prove more frustrating than it is worth, with a simple 'Google' search for Buddhism in Australia producing more than 30 000 results. Better, instead, to head for the source and make contact with a local church, synagogue, chapter or bible study group.

Too shy to do this? Then phone a regional, state or national body which can direct you to the best person within the faith to help with your questions. Remember, you are not asking for a favour, but expressing interest and curiosity about something very dear to their hearts. They will probably be eager to assist.

> *Cultivating spiritual wisdom and ardour begins with an open and inquiring mind*
> — **RACHAEL KOHN**

Consider also undertaking a course or attending classes, lectures, or talks. Your initial choice may not answer your questions but it is likely along the way that you will pick up leads and contacts to further your quest.

Radio and television documentaries are also a rich source of information for the spiritual novice. Look up *Compass* (TV show) and *The Spirit of Things* (radio program) on the ABC website for transcripts of previous episodes.

The retreat

As with so many of life's searches, there is no substitute for immersion. If you are serious about exploring a faith, rather than trying to understand what it represents while in the midst of your everyday existence, you might consider taking the time for an extended stay at a retreat run by the faith which interests you. For those seeking such an opportunity within Australia or New Zealand, *Sanctuaries*, written by Barbara Hasslacher, offers a list of spiritual and health retreats with details on the religious (or secular) order in charge, and whether spiritual direction, prayers, or mass are offered. Whether you seek a yoga and meditation centre for women and children in Queensland, or a Benedictine Monastery in Western Australia, *Sanctuaries* will list an alternative.

Entering the faith

If you determine that a particular faith will suit you, then another series of questions will arise:

- What time will I devote to this faith?
- What energy will I bring to it?
- What commitment am I capable of making?
- Do I know someone who has gone before me, with whom I can discuss these issues?
- Is there a local church, synagogue, temple I can join?
- Who will be my guide in this process?

Committing to your faith

At some stage you will need to decide on your level of commitment to your faith. This will involve asking the hard questions of yourself about how much time and effort you are prepared to give to the faith – what place it has, or potentially could have in your life. Essentially it is about abandoning

---

WHAT ARE WE WORSHIPPING?

For those seeking a new spiritual path, the good news is that, as an Australian, you can legally worship what you like without fear of losing your life or freedom. In the 2001 census conducted by the Australian Bureau of Statistics, the following major affiliations were recorded against a total population of nearly 19 million:

RELIGION	PERSONS
Buddhism	357 813
Christianity:	
Anglican	3 881 162
Baptist	309 205
Catholic	5 001 624
Jehovah's Witnesses	81 069
Lutheran	250 365
Orthodox	529 444
Presbyterian and Reformed	637 530
Salvation Army	71 423
Seventh-day Adventist	53 844
Uniting	1 248 674
Hinduism	95 473
Islam	281 578
Judaism	83 993
Other religions:	
Australian Aboriginal traditional religions	5 224
No religion	2 905 993

yourself to the faith, and not dwelling upon what the faith will bring to you. How will this fit with your family needs and other obligations? Which sacrifices might you need to make? Your desire to commit may be so strong that it may need to overtake some of these family needs. If your family is unaware of the strength of your commitment, it will be time to share your intentions. For many, their original commitment has grown into a fuller role as a guide in that faith – is this your ultimate hope?

Reverend Noyoun (Noah) Park: My journeys continue ...

I was born in South Korea, in the countryside, where I was educated at high school before attending university, studying to be a marine engineer. After achieving my degree I spent four years working on ships, in the engine room, including electrical and mechanical tasks. I was also involved in a lay ministry which encouraged worship and bible study onboard.

In 1999 I stayed in Melbourne for a year, touring and studying English. It was here I started to work for the Mission to Seafarers, looking after the pastoral concerns of visiting seamen. This was part of a natural progression towards the ministry, starting with my days at university where I was involved with the Presbyterian Church. In 1990 I joined the mission, and in 1994 I was appointed a lay chaplain. I worked for the mission full-time, and studied theology part-time at the Ridley College of the University of Melbourne. This was particularly demanding, not just juggling the work and study, but also because English is not my native language. But overall I enjoyed the course very much. I finished my study in 1999, and in 2000 I was ordained as a deacon and priest with the Diocese of Melbourne. All along I have worked with seafarers.

I was one myself, and I now see myself as a servant to seafarers. Part of my role is to work closely with other denominations – seafarers have affinity with many different religions including Muslim, Buddhist and Hindu faiths. Our goal is to provide every seafarer with a home away from home, with friendship and fellowship which shows Christianity to be a holistic ministry, meeting physical as well as spiritual needs.

The sea can raise the human spirits to the highest peaks of exaltation and it can strike terror into the innermost depths of our being. I experienced a world of adventures and many great inspirations during my time at sea. I still miss the feeling of achievement when you arrive at a safe port after a long journey full of rough weather and danger. I miss the camaraderie and teamwork between the sailors throughout the voyage, as well as the different people, cultures, and languages.

Yet my role as reverend is a journey which continues the excitement of seafaring. Jobs can represent life itself. I am serving the world, people and a community.

> *I know there has to be a higher meaning than just going through the motions on a daily basis. But the idea of seeking spiritual fulfilment sounds kind of embarrassing...*

WHAT'S STOPPING YOU?

Is a previous religious affiliation making you wonder if another way of worshipping can really be legitimate? In fact what, you might ask, is legitimate?

Are you carrying a legacy of guilt from previous affiliations, or are you concerned about the disapproval of your family? Do you have a deep-seated fear of commitment? Are you afraid attending a church or temple or synagogue will signal commitment above and beyond that which you are prepared to give?

Are you worried that your ignorance will be revealed, and that you will ask stupid questions in your quest for meaningful answers?

These are common concerns, but surely not sufficient to get between you and a serious resolve to find out more about your place in the scheme of things. How will you find out anything about anything unless you're prepared to ask a few dumb questions? Try talking to a representative of the faith of your choice about how other members of the congregation or community overcame their reservations. You may find this both surprising and comforting.

What Rebecca experienced

Remember Rebecca from page 75? How did she get back on track?

Stages of change:

1. A sudden change involving loss of health, independence and control.
2. A rude awakening in a ward full of people 50 or more years older.
3. A rapid learning curve about health services and how the system works.
4. A realisation that testing the boundaries was the only way to make progress.
5. A necessity to relinquish day-to-day responsibility for her daughter.
6. A determination to work towards greater mobility.
7. A two-armed hug at Christmas.
8. A rejection of pity.
9. An appreciation of the support from fellow volunteers.
10. An understanding of what your family can really do when you need them.

ON PRIORITIES:
Things that were important no longer seem so. I don't take people for granted now. Being able to walk the dog with my daughter is such a gift. So are all the things that, by rights, I shouldn't be able to do.

ON FRIENDS:
The good ones never treated me any differently.

ON HER LIFE CHANGE:
My life is not worse. It is different. It is not bad, I just have a different way of living.

ON INDEPENDENCE:
Needing people to help with your personal care takes your control away – it was only a few months ago that I took that control back.

some questions worth asking

- Do I like myself? Am I comfortable in my own skin?
- Am I acting out a life to please others?
- Do I want to work on different aspects of my personality, but feel negative about my chances of sticking at it?
- If I am negative, how did I get to be like this? Was I always this way?
- Do I enjoy time spent in my own company?
- How would I rate the relationships in my life? Does the thought of doing this frighten me?
- If my relationships aren't very satisfying, do I have any ideas about how I can change this?
- Am I pleased with my health and fitness levels or am I in total denial?
- Do I have a spiritual element in my life, or a curiosity to seek one?
- How much control do I think I have over my own existence?

Part Three:

CHANGING YOUR WORKING LIFE

Work is the primary site in which people find and create meaning in their lives; [this is] one reason why people so badly want to do it

— MARTIN HEIDEGGER

The greater part of most of our lives is taken up with our day jobs. For many people their work is their life and their life is their work. You might try to make a distinction between your work life and the rest, but it's usually like trying to remove the flour from the cake once it's been baked. Part Three looks at the different elements of your working life and how, at different stages of your life, you might choose to change them.

The opening profile of Brandon will give heart to everyone who has spent time out of work, and believed they would never find meaningful employment again. But in Brandon's case, he didn't just find a job for himself – he created work for many others in the same situation.

Leaving your job by choice can be sometimes as demanding a task as finding another job when you are retrenched. You might be wanting to make the leap, but feeling powerless to get started. Often this lack of resolve can stem from confusion over why you are leaving, as well as a lack of clarity over where you might go. Chapter 12, 'Your Choice', looks at this confusion, and the four different ways of creating a meaningful career change.

Often a high proportion of your self-esteem is formed by the type of work you do, and how well you feel you do it. Yet if that work is removed without notice, you can be left feeling intensely vulnerable.

Chapter 13, 'Their Decision', examines what can be one of the most soul-destroying events in your working life – the Don't Come Monday note with your pay advice. Yet whilst this may initially feel like a total assault on your dignity and self-esteem, for many people a forced departure has also led to new opportunities and career highs. Redundancies or retrenchments can be managed. Part of this management comes from a clear understanding of the different vocational options you have. These are covered in Chapter 14, 'Your Work Options', including achieving life/work balance, portfolio work and starting or buying a small business. For those at the more leisurely end of the work cycle, Chapter 15, 'Not the Retiring Type', is a celebration of how not to retire, but how to pursue meaningful activities for as long as possible. And Chapter 16, 'Looking Outward', encourages those who are able to look outward and give back their time and efforts to those who need assistance.

Brandon Charlesworth: It's not about the money

It's important to accomplish something in your life — to have done something of benefit to others.

I was born in Melbourne and attended agricultural college there until my parents decided to move to the Gold Coast. They bought some land, sight unseen, and so were surprised to find it going underwater when the Tallebudgera creek flooded.

My first job was working in their restaurant, but then I worked in the mining industry in Mount Isa. By this stage I was married, and an enforced stay in Sydney when my first wife had appendicitis led to a job in the rag trade. I started as a storeman, and ended up as manager at Marco, the proud manufacturers of crimplene safari suits. By now we had three children, and two of them travelled with me to Malaysia, where I was to run a factory for my company, and set up a house so my wife and our eight-week old baby could follow. The day they were due to arrive, the call came. She was leaving me for my best friend. Within a few weeks my 24-year-old brother brought the baby — plus two nappies. I met my second wife in Malaysia, and converted to Islam for her. We had two children together. After we returned to Australia I sold life insurance, and made quite a lot of money from it. I was caught out in the late 1980s — I had invested in property, was too highly geared, and I lost everything. I can still remember the police escorting the bailiff and locksmith to the house as my wife, children, the Chihuahua and I stood on the nature strip.

Unfortunately the reversal in our fortunes had a similar impact on my marriage, and I ended up, a year or so later, travelling in a 4WD and caravan with five kids and a bird in a cage across to Perth. The youngest was two years old. It was a great bonding trip, but being on the sole parent's pension meant living in housing commission accommodation when we arrived.

I tried to get a job. I tried so hard. I was 50, and I applied for 200, maybe 300 jobs. I thought I had a lot to offer, so I set my sights high, and expected replies to my applications. When they didn't I lowered my sights, and tried again. I got to the stage of 'lying' — omitting my date of birth. I was occasionally told I was overqualified, but mainly there was no reply. I would get up to make the kids' lunches and send them to school, and then I'd sit around, and other unemployed friends would drop in, and we'd drink too much. I was convinced my life was over, in fact I thought I had cancer. I didn't. Then a miracle happened — I saw an advertisement to win a trip around the world on the *QE2*, and I entered. A few weeks later I was listening to the radio and heard my name read out. I'd won the $14 000 trip. Everything was supplied — so my sixteen-year-old son and I went. We lived like millionaires — there was just one hitch. The sea voyage finished in Hong Kong, and we were to fly back but we didn't have the $100 per head airport tax on us. Happily the Australian consul bailed us out.

When I got back to Perth I realised I had become a bum, and I had to do something to change my situation. I decided to take the family back to Brisbane, hoping for more job opportunities there. I was wrong — I kept getting knock-backs. So when I saw an advertisement for someone to erect real estate signs — the receptionist said they really wanted a university student — I offered to work for nothing for a month, so they could see how hard I would work. The receptionist went away to check with the director, he came to check me out, and then said I could start the next day, and they would pay me from the very first day. I cried.

I was now earning $180 a week, and with the pension, the kids and I actually had enough to live off. At the weekend we would ride our bicycles to Broadbeach and barbeque sausages — it felt like luxury.

I was still trying to get a 'real' job, but had very little self-esteem. I would go through stages of hating everyone, thinking the world was very unfair. I had about $25 in the bank and decided to run a newspaper advertisement in the local paper:

ARE YOU OVER 45 AND TIRED OF BEING UNEMPLOYED?

Four hundred people responded. We would meet to discuss the issues — how we could change employers' attitudes. It was the first time some of these people had shared their story, and I realised I wasn't so badly off — I'd never contemplated suicide but about 25 per cent of my respondents had. We spread the word around, and many employers said what a great idea it was to employ older people. Words are cheap — they may have thought it was a good idea, but nothing happened. So we decided to do some work for widows — many of us had handyman skills, and a newspaper ran a story on us. The response was very strong, because we were offering security, particular to older women, we'd turn up on time, get the job done, and often the younger people thought having us there was like having dad call in to do the repairs. The critical issue was that our work had to be good — people would hire us for the 'feel good' factor only if our service was comparable to that in the marketplace.

This was 1997, and most of the workers would arrive at my place and wait for the phone to ring in response to small ads we were running. It didn't take long, and I would chart the work, workers, and their skills on a white board. At the end of each day we'd pool the money, and I would keep 5 per cent for administrative costs, and the rest would be divvied up. When we got to five whiteboards, we knew we had a business. We had to apply for permission from the Department of Defence to call it the Grey Army. Happily, they decided we were not a threat to national security. After a while I became aware of the possibility of franchising the Grey Army, and ran an ad in the paper. Within a week I had sold the first one. Now there are many franchises in all states. The original purpose remains — the Grey Army exists to help anyone over 45, and this includes the customers as well as the staff, and we do quality work for a reasonable price.

I've learnt a lot from the Grey Army experience. For me, having a job has always meant your sense of self-worth, that you are of some value. It's not about the money, but it is about the job. Affluence can ruin your life more than going broke does.

> When we got to five whiteboards, we knew we had a business

chapter twelve
YOUR DECISION: YOU JUST CAN'T DO THIS ANY MORE

You're fed up. You're sure that there has to be more to life than this. But you're less sure what that 'more' might be. In fact, generally speaking, you're very good on the negatives, the things you really don't like about your working life, but there's a huge blank white space when it comes to finding an alternative.

These feelings are common. Some people act on them. Some partially act on them. Some just buckle down for the long haul. Some become resigned, vaguely unhappy. Others work through the problem. Others become bitter, and frustrated by a sense that they had much more potential than they have been able to realise.

Where you fit into these different reactions – or where you ultimately plan to fit, is a very personal decision. An exploration of the different feelings you might have about what a 'day job' constitutes, and how you can maximise your sense of work satisfaction is a good starting point.

Consider the following statements and try to measure the strength of your reactions to them.

1. I am working merely to pay my bills.
2. I would really like to do more meaningful work.
3. I would like more control over my working existence.
4. My definition of success has changed.
5. I do not feel rewarded by my work.
6. The hours I am working just to cover my financial obligations are ridiculous. People tell me to get a life. They are right – I just do not have one. Workers during the industrial revolution had more life/work balance than I do.
7. I did not choose this vocation – I am here, not for reasons of interest or passion, but merely by default.
8. I am desperately in need of a break – and I am not talking about a three-week holiday.
9. I am seriously bored, and just drag myself through my working day. I feel as though 90 per cent of the tasks I perform are repetitive.
10. My best friend died of cancer recently, and I am wondering what it's all about, and I just know it's not all about the job I do 60 hours a week.

There is no rigid score system to determine whether you are sufficiently disenchanted to require a change of career, rather than momentarily fed up. But before heading off to the Internet or newspaper classifieds to select another job, it might be a good strategy to understand the different types of career changes available to you, and how one of these types of changes might be far more suitable than just finding another job in the same line of work.

These types of career changes are more fully explained by author Richard Bolles in *What Color Is Your Parachute?* in Chapter 1, 'What are you looking for?'

Let's consider the example of accountant. You are currently working as an accountant in aged care, in Hobart. You have been doing this for five years, without a promotion or variation in your job description, and you are bored witless. If someone opens the window, you feel like you will jump.

POSSIBILITIES?

There are four broad avenues of escape here:

1. Remain an accountant but change your work environment (work as an accountant but for a travel company specialising in water sports).
2. Remain an accountant but retrain over a period of time to something you really care about – perhaps a writer or a nurse?
3. Undertake some CPD (continuing professional development) as a positioning strategy for a promotion within the same workplace.
4. Take a total leap, and apply immediately for a different type of job in a different field (waiter in a café?).

So the four options to move from any one job can be summarised as:

1. same job, different environment
2. retrain to different job
3. same career, different responsibilities (not always a promotion, could be to take lower responsibilities but supplement fewer hours with other highly valued activity)
4. different job, different environment

By considering these differing magnitudes of job change, it is possible to start to order your thinking about the aspects of your current job that you wish to change. You may find that you actually do enjoy your role as veterinarian, but do not like the large animal work, long-distance driving and all-hour call-outs which are part of this role in a remote rural area. By seeking a role in an inner city practice, you might be able to achieve more controlled working hours, less driving and more enjoyable work with family pets. No career change, but job change instead.

Timing

The phone rings, and it's a friend who has just been appointed casting director for a new reality TV show. No, she doesn't want you, but your house would be the perfect location for the show. The producer is willing to pay $100 000 per annum to secure the location for twelve months. Are you interested?

YES! You fling down the pen, trowel, thermometer, or tea towel and march on in to tell the boss exactly where to ...

But no, you are dreaming. It just won't happen this way. Sudden financial windfalls are dreamed about on a daily basis – in an exactly inverse proportion to how often they occur. Dream on, but don't wait for this way to get out of a bad work scene.

The art of timing your move from a job can be extremely difficult – often because your ability to objectively measure your level of discontent, and to assess other possibilities is affected greatly by the fact that most people are spending 40-plus hours in the environment they are seeking to measure. Getting away from the workplace for a few days in a row aids objectivity immensely. Touching base with a valued, but honest, friend increases your likelihood of good decision-making. But perhaps your best gift to yourself will be the gift of patience and good planning. Understanding there is rarely a 'happy ever after' (no matter what the advertisements say), but just new challenges, and new opportunities, may encourage you to spend some time looking at the possibilities for a longer term transition to something you really want, rather than a quick fix (new job, same responsibilities, same industry, same boredom factor).

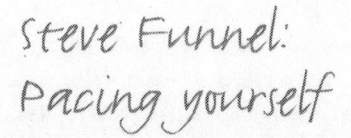

Steve Funnel: Pacing yourself

My first job was as an assistant geologist for the mining company CRA. I worked there for several years and held many different roles, in human resources, business analysis, exploration; you name it. During my time there I also completed a business degree and an MBA. I left in 1997. I was overwhelmingly tired of working for the same company. My wife, Vici, was also holding down a 'big' job and we needed one spouse to be more flexible, to be there when the kids needed us. Up until this time we'd had live-in nannies, but we wanted this to change.

I'd always had a passion for wine, and Vici was the same. I'd developed this interest during my travels with CRA, and when Vici and I discussed possible career changes, we set the goal of growing our own grapes on our own land, and building a small winery. This was very much a joint decision, Vici was really supportive, enthusiastic and keen to see me do what made me happy.

What resources was I bringing to the project? Probably my attitude was the key factor. I am passionate about this opportunity and feel if you start with passion, most else can follow. But this enthusiasm needs to be tempered by constant reality checks. Many people go into viticulture with bucketloads of passion, but less idea about running a business. Yet if you want a good small-business investment, there are about 1001 different options which make more sense than viticulture. You also need to know beforehand that both spouses are fully committed, and what your plans will do to the rest of the family. I didn't want to rush it, then wonder why I choked. It was always going to be a huge project to finance, and my experience in finance, understanding business plans and monitoring cash flow has been invaluable. It's all about how you pace yourself.

This change was for us a very, very long term retirement planning project. It takes about seven years in a vineyard before you break even, and in this time our family had to be capable of living off one income. I needed to do a degree in viticulture. This degree wasn't just about technical knowledge, it was also about credibility and confidence, and delivered a huge bonus of networking with some fantastic wine professionals.

We also spent a long, long time choosing our land, looking for a magical combination of soil, climate and rainfall. We were also seeking a location within an hour or two of our home. We drove all over Victoria for six years before finding a lovely small acreage on the Bellarine Peninsula. Apart from buying the land, the set-up costs are about $40 000 per acre. I'm very averse to taking risks, so I don't like borrowing money, but sooner or later you do need to secure a loan to plug holes in the cash flow.

Apart from the myriad of tasks I do at the vineyard, I spend an awful lot of time in the car commuting back to the family home in the city. I have also immersed myself in the local wine association, as this provides a wonderful life-long learning opportunity as well as the excellent networking.

We celebrated our first vintage of pinot noir in 2003. I am striving to make a top-end, savoury handmade wine, using traditional winemaking methods. Our vineyard is named Hat Rock after an outcrop named by Matthew Flinders, portrayed in a first-edition atlas I have. This map is now on the label.

My next personal challenge is to work on the marketing of our produce, and I will research this as thoroughly as I have all other aspects of our venture. My feeling on such life change is that you can't just run on emotion, you need to know yourself thoroughly and what your limits are. I would say 80 per cent of the population don't. You also need to be aware, up front, of what you will need to do without. If I'd stayed in a mainstream occupation, we would have probably lived a much more 'comfortable' life. What we have started has been very capital intensive, so Vici and I have gone without a lot, and what extra we do have goes to the kids. But what we have achieved is really, really pleasing. We believe we've held back in the present, to build for our future.

TEN STEPS TO ESCAPING JOB BOREDOM AND CREATING THE LIFE YOU WANT

1. Get the Point
2. Get the Picture
3. Get Clued into Your Calling
4. Get a Grip
5. Get Real
6. Get Informed
7. Get Ready
8. Get Support
9. Get Going
10. Get Present

(from the website <www.changingcourse.com>)

Letting go

Do yourself a favour and let go of linear thinking.

Imagine a whiteboard.

Imagine a line drawn on it passing through dots representing your time at school, any further education, your early jobs, your current work. Imagine this line to be straight, starting lower on the left-hand side, and gently curving up to the right, ending on current work.

This is how many of us have been conditioned to expect our life trajectories to go. But life events have a habit of intervening.

Now force yourself to imagine this straight line being pulled in all directions — dipping down, up, down again. Another line moving vertically off the first one — a third moving down. This is the kind of thinking you may need to incorporate in your search for a new way of working — it's also going to help you stop thinking of a career as a straight line, a steady progression, and start thinking of it as a dynamic launching point for opportunities you may never have heard of.

☞ But I've always been a teacher...

WHAT'S STOPPING YOU?

You've looked at changing career a few times, but always pull back. It's not that there's a shortage of new directions you'd like to take. Every year you go on holidays you vow the first thing you'll do on your return to work is to resign. But you never do.

Maybe what's stopping you is your commonsense. You may have a risk-averse personality and resigning without a clear alternative is just not a smart way to go. Instead try exploring some of the other directions which are of interest while you are still teaching. Look at the crossover points between your teaching skills and those needed for a new venture. Maybe you have an interest in starting a bed & breakfast. Can this be done where you live? Wouldn't many of your teaching skills, particularly the people skills, be well suited to this choice? So what else is involved, apart from the obvious location requirements? Try a B&B course at a TAFE. Does it still interest you after learning about the capital investment, and long hours? See if your next holiday can be spent working in one. Start drawing up plans for your transition. Can the teaching become the part-time job while your B&B becomes established? Get the picture?

chapter thirteen
THEIR DECISION: DON'T COME MONDAY

Redundancy, like divorce, is hard not to take personally.

As we have seen in Part One, work change can come from within, often as the result of a long and clearly discernible build-up of frustration, boredom or dissatisfaction with your occupation. It can also come from without – when your employer decides you are no longer needed. There may have also been a long-term build-up to this decision, but often the subject of the work 'divorce' is totally shocked when the boss invites them in to say a permanent goodbye.

For some workers, this will lead to immediate euphoria. 'Hi, darling, they've finally let me go and, great news, the package is large enough to buy the goat farm' is an actual quote from one such retrenchee. For many others, however, it can be the beginning of a period of huge turmoil and emotional trauma, sometimes likened to the grief process of losing a loved one. But why? As you walk out of your boss's office, you probably still have two arms, two legs and a beating heart. What is it about job loss that we can take it even more seriously than relationship issues?

The job

Why are we identifying ourselves by our job? Why is 'What do you do?' the first thing we ask a new acquaintance?

The answer goes back to the long-term conditioning to which most of us have been subjected. From the cradle, we were asked, 'And what will you be when you grow up?' 'Just myself' was rarely viewed as an appropriate answer. Similarly, 'A clown', 'A friend' or 'A cowboy' all met with little approval. Instead, something vocationally focused: 'A lawyer', 'A pilot', 'An architect' would win smiles. Parents also led by example, showing approval for those with 'important' jobs with high salaries. If family values didn't influence a mainstream vocational choice, then the education system would certainly kick in at the end of secondary school with an overwhelming focus on results, and specifically those results which would lead to tertiary education and a qualification to do a particular job. If you didn't achieve the results for a chosen course of study, you were a failure.

This conditioning is usually much more deeply ingrained with men than women. They continue to see themselves as breadwinners, primary providers who bring back sustenance for others – their self-esteem is often

RETRENCHMENT AND REDUNDANCY FACTS

- In the three years leading up to 2001, 596 400 Australians were retrenched.
- Of these, 65% were men, 35% women.
- This represented 8% of the workforce.
- Relative to the number of employees, the three 'worst' sectors were mining (25%), communication and services (19%) and construction (16%).
- Main reasons given were 'not enough work' or 'job cuts' (42%) and closure of business (18%).
- Less than five weeks' notice was given to 77% of the retrenches – with less than one day's notice for 25% of employees.

dependent on this. Until recently, women have been less likely to define themselves by their jobs. But with more women in the workforce ascending to higher positions, many have changed to a radically different lifestyle than their mothers and made a conscious decision to have a career, and not children. One of the results of retrenchment can be a questioning of their whole value system. Many have experienced their job as a relationship and now ask painful questions. *I gave up having a family for you – and now you've dumped me*, is a not uncommon response.

How are you likely to feel if you are made redundant?

You may have many fears on the day you are made redundant. These can continue for weeks, perhaps months. Some of these are rational, some are irrational; all feel bad. If you are not receiving professional career transition services, it is helpful to find an objective friend or mentor with whom to share your thoughts.

Some common reactions are:

- The mortgage – how will it get paid?
- I'm of no value.
- I'll never get another worthwhile job.
- Oscillating from 'Great, I'm free to do what I want', to 'I'm devastated'.
- Relief – I suspected this was coming and it's better to know than to dread it.
- Anger – how dare they do this to me?
- I've given up my manhood.
- I'm no longer superwoman.
- I've been cut off from the most important thing in the world.
- It's because of that report I wrote, that remark I made, that meeting I missed for Jane's ballet concert.
- Revenge – I'll show them.
- Total shock – my world is spinning out of control.

- Embarrassment – how will I tell my family, friends, and acquaintances?
- Sense of betrayal, futility – the investment I made going in this direction has not paid off.

All these feelings are legitimate, and worth discussing with an objective counsellor, mentor or friend.

How long are these feelings likely to last?

This roller-coaster can remain until you can consistently direct your efforts towards your future. As you move into a position where you can again take the reins, some of these feelings may still occur, but with less violent oscillations. Most people move from a position of 'I have just been told I have lost control of my life' to taking that control back because they are thinking about objectives, planning, being assisted with job search skills, and support in the market. The amplitude of emotions decreases, and the general direction is up. This turnaround could be as brief as a few weeks, or take many months.

In the meantime, try *not* to:

- phone and abuse your ex-employer
- hang around ex-colleagues, desperate for news of how they are managing without you
- think of being retrenched as an ending, rather than a turning point
- feel negative towards friends who are obviously enjoying their careers

What can you do?

First, take a reality check. It is rare to enjoy being fired. But, also, it is unlikely that you have been retrenched because you are incompetent.

Second, face the dollars as soon as possible – it may not be as bad as you think. Dread of financial ruin can be a totally debilitating emotion. Facing your financial reality is the first step back. Hopefully it is unlikely you are about to lose your house and your entire life savings. It probably just feels that way.

Consider how you view your package — buying time to do a thorough and methodical job search or time and money to take a much-needed holiday — the money is not sacrosanct, or a nest egg that can't be touched.

Do your sums

Attending a redundancy seminar is an excellent way of gaining an overview of your employment termination, and what it means financially as well as emotionally. You might also wish to locate a financial adviser who specialises in redundancy and, with their help:

- Understand your payout.
- Understand your payout options, including social security and superannuation rollovers.
- Understand your debt, and whether your payout should be used to reduce it.

These financial issues are complex at the best of times. When you have just lost your job, although your most recent income stream has been dramatically removed, it may be prudent to invest a few hundred dollars in the best redundancy/tax advice you can afford. Not long-term financial planning advice — you may not be able to plan the long-term right now — but there are immediate questions such as:

- How will I handle my payout?
- How will I cover my mortgage and any other loans for the next few weeks?
- What are the tax and superannuation implications?

These questions need to be addressed by an expert. A good start is your accountant, or a specialist financial adviser.

MORTGAGE WOES

TALK TO YOUR BANK

Just about the first thing most people think about when they lose their job is their ability to cover the rent or mortgate repayments. It is common advice for those who think they may renege on a loan or mortgate payment to talk to their bank. No one minds talking to their bank — but will they listen?' Before you contact your bank, do a budget of day-to-day expenses, and estimate funds you will require for any special expenditures. Then make an appointment to see your lender, to work through your needs and options.

Some strategies you may be offered are:

TAKE A REPAYMENT HOLIDAY

- Recheck your mortgage repayments on the contract. If there is a short-term need to lower repayments, take a repayment holiday (using built-up specials), pay interest only or extend the term. Some people may find taking a basic loan at a lower rate of interest may be worthwhile — sacrificing some flexibility.

SECURE A LINE OF CREDIT

- Provides cost-effective finance when required (much cheaper than cards, personal loans etc.) — this might help manage cash flow, rather than forcing you to sell or break investment terms if you need access to quick funds.

CONSOLIDATE YOUR DEBT

- Particularly useful if you have a mortgage and can take advantage of borrowing at home-loan rates. This can be done by redrawing against overpayments or by approaching the bank for a top-up loan. This can save on personal loans or store cards etc.

There are a variety of ways a bank might assist — the point is to talk through the options as soon as possible so that the best individualised solution can be provided.

Start with the short term.
Then medium term, then long term

If you can possibly afford it, take some time out by yourself. It may be that in addressing your immediate finances, you can factor in some money for a short break, somewhere you've been longing to go, but couldn't afford the time. Well, now you've got it. This break doesn't need to be far away, or luxurious. On the contrary, it may be revisiting a childhood holiday destination you haven't seen in years, allowing yourself the opportunity to look at mountains, farmland, bush, or to embrace the coast. Take a book you've always wanted to read, and a journal to record your thoughts. Challenge yourself, taking time alone to be reflective, remember your simpler self, and to enjoy being spontaneous.

Receiving outplacement

How does an outplacement professional counsel you?

If you're one of the fortunate minority who receive outplacement or career transition services as part of your retrenchment, this is how your initial meeting might go. The counsellor will normally address your feelings first, getting you to talk about the full range of emotions and how you might go about handling them. They will also try to pinpoint your greatest concerns and true causes of loss – what really hurts the most, the loss of ego, income, structure, security? They will also draw you out about your family situation, how this will affect those closest to you, as well as your financial capabilities. Counselling with a chartered accountant may be provided. This is not for financial advice, but to perform an analysis, evaluating the length of time for which you are able to fund yourself. Many who are retrenched have a financial buffer for at least a few months, to allow them to do a methodical job search and not just take the first (inappropriate) thing that's offered. The counsellor will also ask what your best guess, at this stage, is that you will do occupationally. They will usually try to alert you to the fact that the next 48–72 hours can be a very tough roller-coaster of emotions. You may wish to call your ex-employer and argue. You will probably be advised to write down your thoughts in a letter, reread it in a few days, and then, hopefully, shred it. Most counsellors will try to get a commitment for the next meeting, or give you some homework. If you are switched on and functioning, they may supply some self-assessment work. Alternatively, they may suggest that you need more time to work on your emotions.

Janene Murdoch: An amazing ride

My first career was as a flight attendant before taking twelve years out to raise our daughter and son. During this time I helped run my husband Jeff's electrical contracting business. In 1997 I returned to the paid workforce, working in customer service in the Australian Stock Exchange bookshop in Melbourne. Less than a year later, my husband was not well enough to work full-time, and I was told my services were no longer required.

I had no idea I would be sacked until we were all asked to stay back for a video conference. It was April Fool's Day. About eight staff went to the boardroom and were told that, as of the end of June, the ASX would be shutting all investor bookshops. I wasn't bitter at the time. Some young ones shed a few tears. I was just cross, because I thought they had known. They just didn't see us as part of their core business any more. Others worried about finding a job or getting a résumé done. I didn't worry much until I got home and I sat down in a chair, poured a glass of wine, and burst into tears. Not just tears, but absolute, heartfelt sobbing. Then the kids and Jeff came home and said, 'What's *wrong*??'

My first real thoughts were, 'I'll never find anything. I'm never going to get another job like this.' I just loved it. I can see now how illogical this was, with twelve months of workforce experience in a rising stock market behind me.

Straight after that we made an offer to buy the investor bookshop from the ASX. It was Jeff's idea. We could buy it, and I could run it. He has great confidence in me, Jeff. I was very excited at the prospect – I had an idea of the running costs, and although the rent was huge ($120 000 per annum), I knew I could negotiate this down, and achieve the necessary turnover.

But the ASX wouldn't sell. And to this day, five years later, there is an empty space. I'm still not sure why.

I was very unhappy when they said no. So I worked through to the end of June, and checked the newspapers and went for, and was offered, three different jobs. I was basically prepared to do anything, and I settled for an administration position at a school.

Meanwhile, we had decided to set up our own bookshop almost next door to the ASX. Jeff negotiated leases, and organised the trades, phone and fax, but I knew I would be running it. He still wasn't well – this wasn't just a token job, I was becoming the primary breadwinner. When I signed the lease, all I could think was that we could lose the house.

We opened Educated Investor on the first of November, with just $15 000 worth of stock – a bare minimum compared to the $80 000 we hold today. It was a good day's trading. And what an amazing ride we've had since then. Jeff has started a coffee shop out the back, and is really enjoying it – last week you couldn't get a table. Now the markets are down again, but I'm a positive thinker, and believe it's starting to turn. And whether it's a bull or bear market, you still have to trade.

The most important lesson I have learnt is about networking. I was helping people because they were nice. This desire to give people good service probably stems back to when I was a flight attendant. I wasn't looking for anything in return, but invariably a few months later, they would be helping me. And I think that's been one of the keys to the bookshop being successful.

> *When I signed the lease, all I could think was that we could lose the house*

After the first shock

Take time to work out your best possible career options slowly, carefully, and with full cognisance of your values. Establish your core values, and how they can assist your next vocational decision, whether more paid employment, purchasing an existing business or starting up your own, a portfolio career, or something else.

Ask yourself:

- What are my abilities – what have I become good at?
- What things have I accomplished using those abilities?
- Which things do I think are fun?
- Which things do I like, whether I'm good at them or not?

Try to find a crossover between things you're good at and those you like to do – this is where the fun should be found, whether work, activities or hobbies. If you can get at this, you will have a strong foundation on which to seek your next area of work.

Using a book such as *What Color Is Your Parachute?* is a good start, as it addresses the role a job plays in the whole of your life, rather than viewing a job as a total representation of who you are.

BENEFITS OF REDUNDANCY

- Time out for a thorough self-examination.
- Opportunity to take a different direction, which fear of the unknown has previously prevented.
- Outplacement – assistance with skills audit, CV preparation.
- Nest egg – some packages are generous, and can provide a down payment on a new business, career, lifestyle.
- More time with family and friends.
- Regaining of perspective generally lost to someone working more than 60 hours a week.

You may also wish to work with a career transition professional. A good starting point is the Australian Association of Career Counsellors. Alternatively, you may already know someone you can trust, who will be objective, and who can get you motivated to do the painful thinking. It may be someone you went to school with, or a former colleague, who will maintain your confidence and provide an objective sounding-board. Talking to your spouse can be very good or bad, depending upon their outlook. At this stage, you may not wish to alarm them with your secret dream to sell up and move to a third-world country. Family and friends can also have limiting beliefs about your abilities, or a vested interest in telling you that being in any job is better than none. You don't want someone to be sorry for you, or to share your problems. Better to talk to someone who won't cry with you, but will honour your ideas, not offering a solution, but letting you work towards your own best solution.

Above all, remember there are many myths about job searching. In particular, the commonly held view that it is best to look for a job when you are in one. Since the late 1980s when very competent people came on to the market because of a spate of global 'downsizing' decisions, the stigma of unemployment has lessened. Looking for a job when you are working twelve hours a day is very difficult. It is usually far more productive to use good methodical networking which is a full-time task.

Relationships and redundancy

Bob experienced the least inspiring example of familial support when he was retrenched as managing director of a large company. He went home to tell his wife he had lost his job, and the perks that went with it. She stopped talking to him. This made Bob's job search program rather difficult, his career counsellor noted drily. However he persevered and, a few months later, he secured a new position on a slightly higher salary. He went home and shared the news with his wife, and she started talking to him again.

Few families are as unsupportive as Bob's wife. Some relationships will be strengthened by the adversity of one partner's experience, and with unexpected time to re-evaluate life priorities many workers choose a new job with fewer work hours so they can maintain the increased time with loved ones. If you are out of work for a long period of time, and money pressures are mounting, it may be wise to seek some objective relationship counselling to help you over the rough patch.

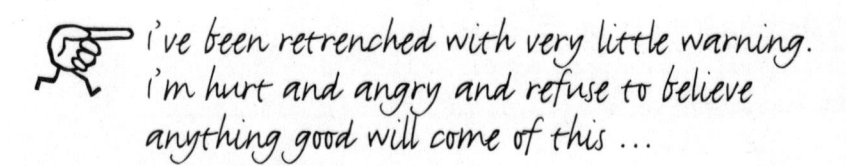

> *I've been retrenched with very little warning. I'm hurt and angry and refuse to believe anything good will come of this ...*

WHAT'S STOPPING YOU?
Go back to other situations in the past that involved an abrupt change, seemingly for the worse. Maybe it was also unfair? How negative were your perceptions? Can you say now that these U-turns were 100 per cent bad? Or can you see some value in those experiences? What was that value? Did you learn something about yourself? Did you rise to the challenge? You may feel so deflated at the moment that you suspect you will never rise to anything again, but do yourself a favour and talk to someone, anyone who has been through this situation, and come out the other side. Grab a copy of *What Color Is Your Parachute?* and start dwelling on the things you've always wanted to do, rather than those in the past you've had to do.

chapter fourteen
YOUR WORK OPTIONS

Work is where we develop ourselves, intellectually as well as personally

— RICHARD REEVES

We all have many more options than we think – it's just difficult to recognise them at times. This chapter looks at the broader picture of work life balance, portfolio work, starting your own business, buying a business, never retiring, and possibilities for those with the time to volunteer.

Life/work balance: Getting it right

In recent times work has received very bad press. It is blamed for a variety of ills, including stress, heart disease, a poor sex life, and dysfunctional families. This is not dissimilar to the way in which it has been fashionable to blame television for declining literacy rates amongst children. Along with the perception of work as being bad and taking over our lives in a negative way, has come a growth industry in achieving life/work balance. And if work is 'bad' and life is 'good', then the usual reaction is to reduce the level of bad (working hours), and increase the 'good' (time with family, leisure) to achieve the optimal life balance.

But is it correct that work is bad? And do all those who are working long hours really want fewer? Not necessarily.

Research from Duke University in North Carolina, USA, reveals that the top predictor of a long life in the United States – even more important than good health habits or good genes – is work satisfaction. So before jumping to conclusions that simply adjusting the ratio of work to leisure time in your life will solve most of your problems, take the time to consider what work adds to your existence. If you are feeling dissatisfied and frustrated, are there other ways of manipulating the life/work structure to achieve the best mix for you?

Satisfying work can provide:

- companionship
- structure
- a sense of achievement
- self-expression
- challenges
- the opportunity to learn
- a sense of belonging
- a sense of identity

Some people's work provides all of the above. How does your day job stack up with this list? If it's not providing more than half of these benefits, can you think back to a time, or another role, which has previously given you this?

Does it have to be a competition?

In 1991 Faith Popcorn, the future trends guru, predicted a change in emphasis for baby boomers wishing to 'cash out' of the corporate world. She declared, 'In the seventies, we worked to live. In the eighties, we lived to work. Now we simply want to live – long and well'. And the concept of whether you work to live or live to work caught on and became a dichotomy implying you can't have it both ways.

Why not? Some would claim they don't have a division between their life and their work – their work is their life because they love it so much. Others would read this statement and view it as sad evidence of workaholism. Either point of view is valid. The object is to achieve what's right for you.

If you are of the former persuasion, and are feeling very fulfilled in your work, and have no trouble working long hours, then there seems to be very little reason to change – *except* if you are travelling in a bubble and have no idea of the impact of this work commitment on the people around you.

Greig Whittaker: I'm not sure who you are ...

Greig Whittaker was a busy marketing manager ten years ago. He also owned a string of video hire franchises. He describes himself as a success junkie, always chasing the next deal. His working week would stretch to 80 hours as he kept close control of the detail of his businesses. Then came the wake-up call. A Father's Day card from his young daughter with a picture of Daddy in the daytime (working) and Daddy at night ('coming home after I've gone to bed'). This was followed by a comment from his wife that she couldn't get him a birthday gift, as 'I'm not sure who you are or whether I like you'. He realised it was time to redefine his thoughts on wealth, and in doing so, assess his relationship with God. The time he took to work out this redefinition opened his eyes to the needs of other people.

'I started to get involved in other people's lives; first my family, and then more widely. We took someone just out of drug rehabilitation into our home.'

Greig then returned to university to study theology, and became involved with the Salvation Army in Ryde, New South Wales. Wanting to spend more time on spiritual pursuits, he relinquished his marketing role, and determined to change his business priorities from working for the profit motive to one of helping and enriching other people's lives. Consequently, the family income has decreased, but he rates his family as wealthier than ever. He has no office, but oversees a scaled-back business, saving his real energies for helping others, and his relationship with God.

If you view long hours and total commitment to your work as a sign of becoming a workaholic, the following dialogue might assist:

1. Do I feel like this because I think work is essentially bad, just something you 'have' to do for the money?
2. If I do, is this because I have drifted into the wrong career? Are there things I am passionate about which might lead to a more satisfying career where work hours would fly rather than drag?
3. If this is the case, is it too difficult for me to change to such a new role? What would be the steps involved?
4. Or do I just not like change, and if this is the case, can I happily accept the idea of staying in a job which doesn't thrill me and just do the hours, one day at a time?
5. If so, can I introduce into my leisure time some activities which *really* thrill me? Can I pack those out-of-work hours with fun times, exhilarating activities and satisfying family moments so my week contains a lot I can look forward to?
6. How will I go about doing this?

The good news about life/work planning is that the remarkable changes in the workplace over the past two decades have seen some real benefits as well as negatives. It is certainly the case that 'downsizing' has seen many workers lose jobs, and spend too long trying to re-enter the workplace. Older workers have often borne the brunt of this, and 'older' refers to 40-year-olds, not 70-year-olds. Some types of jobs have disappeared forever, replaced by new technology. Some would claim there has been a de-humanising of the workplace.

But the upside of these changes surely lies in the physical and psychological flexibility which now exists in many work opportunities. Part-time, contract work, working from home, job portability, increased ability to combine jobs, and opportunities for home small businesses now exist. The scenario of a young mother at home in her pyjamas, looking after a sick child yet participating in a conference call with suited locals in a high-rise hotel in Dubai, achieving professional outcomes, is not at all unusual.

No-one can evaluate the most suitable life/work balance for you, except yourself. And your ability to achieve a harmonious mix will more likely be achieved by a full assessment of all the available options. The following chapters address some of these possibilities.

> *I have absolutely no balance in my life. I just live to work ...*

WHAT'S STOPPING YOU?

Are you lacking any sense of separation between your work life and your home life? Maybe you are dragging yourself through very long work days, and then lacking energy when you get home to do anything more than slump in front of the TV, eating reheated leftovers. Weekends might be continually reduced by take-home work, or extra trips to the office or workplace. No wonder you don't feel as though you have a life. It sounds as though you need a total revamp, not just of the way you think about work, but also the way you think about your own wellbeing. Instead of tinkering at the edges of your working life and achieving very little real change, start with the non-work component. Map out a reasonable fitness routine which includes exercise and some regular walking (Chapter 10 may help). Now add a hobby or fun activity or two. Put these activities (health and interest) into your diary for the next two weeks. Next look at your workload for the coming fortnight, and work out how, with more efficient prioritisation, better delegation, and dumping on the least important, you can fit the 'life' back into your life. Also schedule a two-hour review of how this has worked for the end of the trial period. If your working hours have been truly horrendous, it won't be easy to stick with this plan, and your work colleagues might be unforgiving, but it could prove the better alternative to crashing and burning at some future date.

Portfolio work: Becoming a business of one

Having reached a denouement in your current employment (either because you have chosen to go, or been pushed), it may be that a simple career change is not going to be the most satisfactory solution for your needs. A traditional job may no longer provide the income or stimulation you need, or you may just be finding it difficult to achieve the required amount of work this way.

A new way of thinking about your options is to consider the merits of a 'portfolio' or 'modular' work model. In *Making Your Future Work*, Marcus

Letcher describes modular work as a composition of connected activities, centred on your core priorities, with 'gap fillers' (short-term tasks undertaken to keep your momentum going and your bank balance in the black), for when time and income needs fluctuate.

Portfolio work is a structured combination of paid work assignments, performed concurrently, by one individual. This creates 'the business of one'. There are many reasons why you might adopt a portfolio work lifestyle. You may be seeking the variety of activities which three main work tasks will provide as opposed to one traditional job. It may be the variety of workplaces or diversity of colleagues that you are seeking. It could be a defensive strategy against losing a job and losing all income from that job in the one hit. You may not have sought out this situation – your portfolio work may have grown like Topsy when you could not get a full-time position. Older workers might be using a portfolio work life to create a transition into retirement – a way of lessening their dependence on one main job.

Ideally, the combination of income-earning activities will complement each other. It is good if you can use skills you have accumulated during your previous career, and if at least some of the tasks are highly enjoyable.

Grace Johnston: My soul was dying

My portfolio work consists of consulting, teaching, counselling workshops, writing and running workingconnections, the job matching service of the Over 50s association which helps mature-aged workers get a foot back in the door.

For me it's been a way of getting back into the workforce productively, using my skills and knowledge to work in the area I love. It is not a secure way of working, but it is satisfying. It's still hard to juggle the bits. It's definitely not the best way to fund your retirement. Portfolio work is not the same as consulting – it's often the only way mature people can stitch together various activities to generate enough income to survive – after they've reached the conclusion they will never again get a full-time job.

I have had a fairly chequered work history. I am a journalist who worked on country newspapers and in regional TV, but at 35 I found myself a single mum with three children to raise. For some years I worked full-time for the public service in a really demanding job. It was secure, but my soul was dying.

At 50 when my children had left home, I re-assessed my options. Leaving the public service gave me a life with a bit of work here, and a contract or two there, but none of it was ongoing. I really wanted to return to journalism, but my technical skills were out of date. Then I got a lucky break – a publisher picked up a brochure of mine about a work and purpose workshop, and offered me a book contract. But more importantly, I was asked to do some regular editing work on a three-days-per-week basis. I could survive on this income, it also gave me the time to write my book, and I connected with the Over 50s association, where I run *workingconnections*. I often get exhausted – I deal continually with people who are scared, people who have had their egos stripped. Along the way I've gained qualifications in counselling and pastoral work which have helped the work I do with the unemployed.

Running my portfolio business is a real challenge – I have to think like I'm a business, define the skills I lack, and how I can access them. I'm now trying to move to the next level of my portfolio career where instead of doing it all by myself, I will become a micro business and will do various contracts with people who do core work, whilst I do the creative and developmental side.

The best things about my portfolio career are that it uses and develops many skills and enables me to really tap into my creativity. It has forced me to address business skills such as time management and financial management. I also know how to go out and get what I want. At times it has forced me to do what many would consider menial jobs to secure regular income, and underpin my portfolio. You certainly learn about being at the bottom of the pecking order. One such job was working at nights in the dementia unit of a retirement hostel. I'd always said the only bottoms I'd ever clean would be mine, or those of my children, but I learnt to see the beauty of these older women – there was so much beauty in their 'lived-in' bodies, and I ended up loving this job.

How do you get started?

1. You are becoming a business of one. Acquaint yourself with as many aspects of business as possible, whether for sole traders or large corporations. This includes time management, marketing, bookkeeping, and break-even points.

2. Decide upon your *required* income, as well as your *desired* income. Work out where, between the two different incomes, you will be happy for your business to sit.

3. Define the activities which will combine into a portfolio lifestyle.

4. Decide upon the geographical area you will cover.

5. Ensure that you have included a fun factor (for example, a task you love, as well as others you like, a location you like, and people with whom you will enjoy working).

6. Seek out those who are also conducting a portfolio work lifestyle. Pick their brains about what works and what doesn't.

7 Understand how gap-filler activities can work for you. Make sure you have such an activity in your proposed schedule.

8. Plan your ideal week incorporating these activities – is it achievable? Is the balance right for you? Are the activities compatible? Are you spending too much time in transit from one activity to the other? Will you be physically exhausted?

9. Have a long hard think whether this really sounds like a good way to work or if it is just a response to panic over not finding the right full-time job as quickly or easily as you would have wished. If this is the case, reconsider full-time work possibilities.

10. Ask yourself whether you will miss the companionship of working in a team. If being a team player is one of your core skills, this may not be the path for you.

11. Look at the balance of activities – is one more prominent than another? If so, why? There may be a good reason for the mix, but you should enter the arrangement with that knowledge.

12. Is your remuneration commensurate with the effort?

NEED-SPOTTING

Those who are good at 'need-spotting' will often seek out or create work opportunities in emerging industries. Do you know what skills the new age economy needs? Are you good at following societal and demographic trends to see opportunities for small businesses? And before writing yourself off as 'technologically inept' and therefore not suited to the new age, consider that the need for genuine old-fashioned customer service exists in just about every sector of the economy, particularly with more than two million Australian consumers now aged over 65.

REALITY CHECK:

Are you good at:

- picking up on popular culture?
- spotting trends?
- finding needs?
- working out ways to satisfy these needs?

Are you:

- Excited by new ideas?
- Lateral in your thought?

If not, train your brain, and keep it alive by:

- reading a new non-fiction book every fortnight
- listening to ABC Radio National on any subject
- watching SBS television documentaries
- surfing the net for new products, new ideas, new thoughts
- talking to everyone you know about what they do, why they do it, if it works for them, and what gaps in their industry are unfilled

Modular work is an excellent risk-managed option for starting a small business. Rather than using the 'all or nothing' approach of changing from employee to self-employed status overnight, the model helps you to develop an enterprising outlook incrementally.

— MARCUS LETCHER

Modifying your situation

Recognise that through circumstance or choice, you may be unlikely to ever hold a full-time job again. Test your feelings about this. For some people the only true sense of security comes from having a full-time position. If this is the case for you, put your energies into getting one.

Maybe you like your current full-time job, but are a bit bored. Could you create a better situation by reducing your working hours by one or two days a week and supplementing this core position with something you adore?

Think the boss won't wear it? How do you know until you've asked? Give him/her a chance to see it your way by finding a suitably skilled potential job-share partner *before* you ask. Make it very hard for him/her to refuse . . .

Call in the consultants

It's quite a common reaction when retrenched, or just plain fed up with your day job, to consider reinventing yourself as a consultant. But what does a consultant do, and will this suit your personality?

A consultant is someone who is hired to solve a specific problem, by specifying the nature of the problem, and offering advice and skills to ultimately solve it. Different consultants may perform different parts of these tasks. A consultant differs from a contractor in that the consultant will set the parameters of the task, whilst a contractor will work within them.

Becoming a consultant as a rebound response to a bad work experience is not the best motivation. Good consultants need a variety of skills, including:

- flexibility (with different 'bosses' and workplaces)
- strong networking skills to maintain workflow

- good people skills
- self-motivation
- self-discipline
- technical knowledge of the area in which they will work

If you do not possess these skills, and are not a genuine self-starter, you may find the role of consultant stressful, isolating and lacking in structure.

The best guide to help you evaluate your own potential as a consultant can be found in *Consulting, Contracting and Freelancing: Be your own boss* by Ian Benjamin.

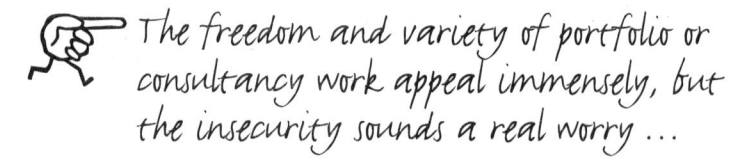

> *The freedom and variety of portfolio or consultancy work appeal immensely, but the insecurity sounds a real worry ...*

WHAT'S STOPPING YOU?

Undertaking a portfolio work life is a deliberate decision that you will work two or three different work assignments concurrently. It can offer variety and a chance to work in different workplaces, on a variety of tasks. It can also, ironically, sometimes offer greater job security than a full-time job. Should you get a DCM in your full-time job, your income will cease. Should you lose one of your portfolio tasks, you may still retain about two-thirds of your income. So much for security. When you are considering using your talents for a portfolio work life, think long and hard about the gap filler aspect. Many people are surprised to find that their painters also hold down a job as an ambulance driver or a fireman. The skills associated with driving and fire-fighting are very different from house painting, yet the combination suits many. Write a definitive list of all the skills you have. Note those which fit with a general career direction (design, administration, medical). Now note those which could be used, if necessary at short notice, to earn a wage (coffee making, waitressing, handyman). Now consider growth areas of the economy (hospitality, aged care, horticulture). Is there a fit between these areas and your gap filler skills? You may decide you need more such skills – a short stint in a voluntary capacity could help with this.

Small business startup: Doing it for yourself

The ultimate in enterprise is starting your own business. So many yearn to do it, so many *do* do it, and if you glance at business closure statistics, so many can fail at it. What's the big attraction? Why would you want to? This section looks at why you might wish to start your own business, how you can get started, the resources you will need and what assistance is available for startups. This is only a very brief overview of this subject, but will hopefully provide enough starting points for you to get going with your own research.

SELFISH WORK

In a business of one, the buck definitely stops with you. Your skills will need to be totally self-ish:

- self-reliant
- self-motivated
- self-organised
- self-confident

What's the big attraction?

There are many reasons why people start up their own businesses – some better than others as predictors of how they will go. Why do you want to start up a business – it could be for one or more of the following reasons:

1. AS A WAY OF EXPRESSING YOURSELF. You may have a skill, talent, vision or dream which just refuses to let you rest until you've had a go at turning this concept into commercial reality.

Not sufficient reason on its own but a great starting point.

2. TO MAKE MONEY. It might be as simple as this. You have an idea or have spotted an opportunity where you just know there is money to be made. It may be an emerging market, or an existing one which is poorly serviced.

A good reason, but hopefully you have some passion for the project as well.

3. BECAUSE YOU WANT TO BE YOUR OWN MASTER, AND CONTROL YOUR OWN DESTINY.

Valid and very common. Just remember this includes putting out the rubbish and replacing the toilet paper.

4. BECAUSE YOU HAVE JUST RECEIVED A SIGNIFICANT SUM OF MONEY (INHERITANCE, PACKAGE, SUPERANNUATION LUMP SUM) AND THINK THIS WILL BE A GOOD FORM OF INVESTMENT.

A small business startup has proven to be an excellent form of investment in many cases – it has also been the wipe-out factor in others. Do your homework and do not invest the entire inheritance, package, or lump sum – leave yourself with an escape route if things go belly-up.

5. BECAUSE IT LOOKS MUCH EASIER THAN THE WORK YOU ARE CURRENTLY DOING. Many people have started successful businesses by transferring their skills from someone else's company to creating wealth in their own.

It is completely valid to wish to reap the benefits of your own hard work. Are you convinced your skills will translate into owning and running the business as well as doing the work?

6. BECAUSE YOU HATE YOUR DAY JOB.

This is simply not enough.

7. BECAUSE YOU'VE BEEN RETRENCHED AND CAN'T GET ANOTHER JOB.

Not a great reason. If it is the only reason you are doing this, it is very much 'rebound' driven. If it is combined with reasons 1 and 5, it may be a good starting point.

8. BECAUSE YOU ARE AN ENTREPRENEURIAL CREATURE BY NATURE. You can't imagine not doing it for yourself.

Useful, but not sufficient in itself. Be careful, also, that your self-belief and enthusiasm don't lead you to miss key resources that you may need to bring on board. You can only do so much.

9. BECAUSE YOUR OWN BUSINESS WILL ALLOW YOU TO WORK HOURS WHICH SUIT YOU BETTER.

Many business startups have had this as a major factor. Don't forget to consider how this will work if the business takes off and you need to employ staff, and work longer hours.

10. BECAUSE YOU WISH TO WORK WITH A PARTNER, SPOUSE, FRIEND OR FAMILY MEMBER.

Be careful, be very careful. In fact see if you can trial this situation first. Some marriages thrive because of the shared experiences in their own workplace. Others falter. Parent–child relationships are particularly fraught with difficulties in the workplace, especially when more than one child is in the company.

11. BECAUSE YOU HAVE RELOCATED TO A PLACE WHERE YOU CANNOT GET ANY OTHER WORK.

Again a common reason, particularly for those moving from the city to the country. It is usually combined with the instigator seeing a new opportunity, or a gap in the market, where their previous skills can be successfully applied. Just make sure your local market research matches the level of those previous skills.

12. BECAUSE IT IS A LIFESTYLE CHOICE.

Beware. The lure of the caravan park in Port Douglas knows no bounds. If the new business offers a fabulous exotic location, and few working hours, check it out thoroughly. It might deliver – then again, it might not.

13. BECAUSE IT IS A LOGICAL EXTENSION OF ALL THE SKILLS, TALENTS, EXPERIENCES AND IDEAS YOU HAVE EVER HAD.

Convincing!

SMALL BUSINESS IN AUSTRALIA

Small businesses employ fewer than twenty people. Micro businesses employ fewer than five. There are 1 233 200 small businesses operating in Australia, and this represents 97% of private sector businesses. Small business employs some 3.6 million people – approximately half of private sector employment.

Over 50 per cent of small business startups fail within three years – but as the years pass, the likelihood of success increases, with only nine per cent of those in business for five–ten years heading into trouble.

Summary

Only you know which reasons might apply to your situation, and whether the combination of these reasons is both logical and will lead to a fair chance of your business not just surviving, but hopefully thriving. If you don't know, you need to do more research, and talk to someone who is honest, objective and has a degree of knowledge about running a small business. Your tax accountant may well be the best starting point.

MAKING THE GOVERNMENT YOUR ALLY

It's usual to moan about government when you are running a small business. Too many taxes, too much paperwork, too many requirements. But utilising the information available from government when you are contemplating a business startup can be the fastest way to understand your obligations and submit required information. Two websites in particular provide a comprehensive walk-through of the issues you will need to address. The Australian Securities and Investments Commission (ASIC) site takes you through starting, running and closing a business. The Business Entry Point (BEP) site also steps you through setting up, managing, expanding, and financing a business.

Getting started

There are many steps involved in starting up a business. Using some of the listed resource books, as well as the directions on the Business Entry Point and ASIC websites, will give you a fuller picture. The following summary is cursory, but should help you start with an overview of the work involved. You will need to:

- Decide on the nature and structure of your business (sole trader, partnership, trust, etc.).
- Decide upon the location (home-based, rental, purchase premises).
- Decide on your staffing requirements (employees, outsourced services).

- Obtain legal advice on all of the above.
- Obtain financial advice including funding a business startup, as well as taxation (including GST) implications.
- Learn how to manage cash flow, or find someone who will do it for you. Even if you delegate this task, you still need to understand how cash flow works.
- Check out government resources and requirements.
- Register the name and/or website.
- Define insurance requirements.
- Research risk management.
- Appraise your own management skills.
- Know about marketing or how you can let people know about your business.

DOMAIN NAMES

Most new businesses, as a matter of course, will have an Internet presence. When you have decided upon your trading name or product name, check this out on the Melbourne IT website <www.melbourneit.com.au> which is a quick way of ascertaining availability of all com.au, .com, .net, .net.au, .biz names. It may save heartache later, if you choose a name already owned in cyberspace by someone else.

Invaluable advice

The best advice of all will be free – as long as you have the ears to listen. Ask friends and colleagues about their small business startup experiences. Who did they go to for a loan, how did they choose their location, why did they start up when they did? Then ask them the five key points they wish they'd known *before* they started. Write them down. And make sure these are points you've got covered. Reading about business startups is often as inspirational as it is informative. Gloria Meltzer has written two excellent books on Australian business startups (*Minding Their Own Business*, and *Minding Her*

Own Business). They consist of case studies of individuals who have taken an idea, and made it happen. They share the highs and lows of their achievements, and summarise this business experience with tips and traps.

> *I've got a great idea for a new product, but it seems like too huge a leap from this idea to a functioning business ...*

WHAT'S STOPPING YOU?

The gap between an idea and a business is substantial, but not insurmountable. The best framework for exploring how one can lead to another is in substantial research into how other, similar, concepts got off the ground. Write out your core product/service idea. Write a hypothetical proposal to a corporate entity for venture capital to develop this concept. Make it as detailed as it would need to be if you were seeking $3 million capital. Outline all set-up costs, and ongoing operating expenses. These will form part of two documents you need to author – proposed profit and loss statement, and a cash flow projection for five years. Understand what the break-even point for your business will be. If this isn't clear, refer to Noel Whittaker and Des Knight's *Driving Small Business* to learn more about this. Write another document which addresses the unique selling point of your product or service. If it doesn't have one, what will you be doing better in order to gain customers? Now look at the obvious gaps in your knowledge, and think about how they can be filled. You don't have to know everything about small business, but you do need to know where the answers you require may be found. Draw your small business idea as a tree. The roots are the great idea, the trunk is you, and the branches the various components you will need to get started. Put ticks on those that you think you have covered. Think of the unticked branches in terms of a numbers game – a certain number to be covered, then you can really get going.

Buying a business

Much of the information about starting a business will apply to buying one. The critical difference when buying an established business is that the market has, to a certain degree, already been tested. The major point you will be trying to assess when purchasing is how well the business you want is currently servicing its market sector and therefore how much growth you can expect to achieve. This is not dissimilar to the 'best house in the street' real estate analogy. What are you looking for? A property (investment) which has already 'peaked' with no room for value to be added? This might be seen in a restaurant business, where the business has grown into a highly successful outlet, but now sits in a strip centre with another 25 thriving restaurants. Is the growth potential now flattening, and could this be a reason the owner is selling?

A good starting point for understanding some of the key issues involved in purchasing an existing business (as well as starting your own) can be found in Noel Whittaker and Des Knight's book, *Driving Small Business*. See Chapter 4 of their book, where the authors outline the dos and don'ts of making a decision to purchase.

DON'T
- be rushed into a purchase
- fall in love with a business you intend to buy to the point that your judgment is clouded
- purchase if you lack the necessary technical expertise or ability to gain it

DO
- your research
- seek expert advice
- pay off the vendor in installments
- beware of enthusiastic vendors

Mandy Chalmers*: Business with a friend

I trained as a teacher but left Australia when I was 21 to live in Florence and London. In the 1970s I married, and my husband and I started supplying clothes to boutiques in the youth market. It was a crazy time, crochet dresses were big news, and we just couldn't make enough of them. We started a cut-and-sew business, and opened a shop, but were overextended and went broke. We had one baby daughter at the time and nearly lost our house, but fortunately my mother stepped in and helped us out. My husband then started a wholesale fabric business which did really well, but it didn't really satisfy him, he had dreams of being a lawyer. We bought a magnificent Victorian house in Prahran, Victoria, and we spent six years living in virtual squalor while we totally restored it. I enjoyed my time mothering our two daughters, but I still wanted to work as well. In 1989 our marriage broke up – we'd been together for 23 years. I would have left much earlier, but I was scared of being alone. I was so wrong – I'm just so happy on my own and I'm never lonely.

I worked in hospitality for years after that – mainly in a friend's hotel. The clientele used to call it 'Mandy's place'. During this time I became friendly with the DJ and his wife. We decided to go into business together and bought a reception centre. From the beginning it was a disaster. The DJ wanted to run it as a nightclub – I thought we'd bought it as a wedding venue. Within three months we'd hit the wall. I'd put up two-thirds of the money, but when the business went down, they declared themselves bankrupt and I was left to pay off the creditors. I didn't want to become a bankrupt – I really wanted everyone to be paid back, so I increased my mortgage and went back to work, and after three years, I'm nearly there. If I had my druthers, there are a few lessons I'd observe. I'd consult someone about using home equity for a business investment, I'd try not to be so impulsive and gullible, I would check all the detail more thoroughly, and I wouldn't move so quickly. I would never go into business with a friend again. But everything has an upside, even losing a business, and I am still amazed at how quickly my friends supported me and gave me courage. I'm still a great optimist – no matter how bad things are, something good always happens.

✳ Name has been changed

Franchises

A very particular type of business purchase is the franchise.

Analysing the business failure statistics can be quite heartening for those wishing to purchase a franchise. Whilst more than 69 per cent of business startups fail within five years, the success rate of franchises over the same period is a staggering 80 per cent. It is clear that purchasing into an existing network of business has its advantages. But is a franchise the answer for you?

WHAT IS A FRANCHISE?

A franchise is a business which has network support. It is someone else's idea, developed into a successful business, and this concept has been sold, as well as trading rights, to another party in an agreed area or business zone. McDonald's is a high-profile global franchise, but many others only have two or three shops or outlets in the network. The success rate of franchised businesses is high compared to independently run small businesses. They are also more likely to return a profit more quickly.

WHAT ATTRIBUTES DO YOU NEED?

- sufficient capital to not just purchase the franchise, but also to cover running costs for at least twelve months
- energy to run the business
- team skills – this is not a business of one, you will need to work with your staff as well as fellow franchisees, and the head franchisor
- promotional knowledge
- willingness to get your hands dirty doing menial tasks
- specific understanding of the retail sector if this is the nature of your franchise

HOW MUCH WILL A FRANCHISE COST?

The answer to this question entirely depends, of course, on the product and current trading performance of the business – the price could be anything from millions for a prominent fast food outlet, to a few thousand for a mobile dog-washing service. The price also varies, depending on whether the franchise is retail, service sector and/or fixed site. Recent estimates suggest the

CODE OF CONDUCT

Franchises in Australia are bound by the Franchising Code of Conduct which requires franchisors to disclose specific information and to follow certain rules. Familiarise yourself with this code of conduct and check if the franchise you are considering adheres to it. Assistance for small business operators who are buying, extending or renewing a franchise, or who need help with resolving disputes, may also be available from state and territory governments.

---

median price (ex GST) for mobile or home-based franchises is around $45 000, whilst retail outlets have a median price of $208 000. What you get for this money can vary from one franchise to the next. Some include premises, delivery vans, and zoned territories whilst others are little more than a great idea, a name and some goodwill. Of course, this upfront payment does not take into account the running costs, advertising, and legal expenses.

HOW CAN YOU FIND OUT MORE?

Start with the Franchise Council of Australia. This is the peak body for the vast majority of franchise businesses in this country. Visit the website, and under 'Businesses for sale' go to the franchise finder, and enter the category of franchise you wish to purchase. This is not the only listing of franchises for sale in Australia, but by shopping around, you will start to get a feel for the type of industry opportunities which exist. The site also lists business specialists such as brokers, financers and lawyers. For those who prefer printed matter, the council has a bi-monthly magazine called *Franchising & Own Your Own Business* with a wealth of information about how to start, buy or sell a franchised business. The government also provides useful information for prospective franchisees via the Australian Tax Office (visit the website and click on Franchising and Tax), as well as via the Australian Competition and Consumer Commission (ACCC) Franchisee's Guide for those buying, extending or renewing a franchise.

Good books and magazines to read are *The Franchisee's Guide: Everything you need to know as a franchisee*, from the Franchise Council of Australia, *Franchising & Own Your Own Business – 2004 Yearbook Directory*, edited by Pamela Oddy and Ros O'Sullivan, and *Own Your Own Franchise* by Garry Williamson. These books, as well as some useful websites, can be found in the resource section.

> *I'm not the type to start up a business, so buying one sounds like a better idea, but why do they all have to be so expensive?*

WHAT'S STOPPING YOU?

Think about why you're not prepared to start up your own business. It's probably something to do with the time, effort, risk, and income forgone necessary to create a profitable venture. One or more of these factors will be making it seem all too hard. And yet you are hoping to purchase someone else's creation at a rock-bottom price? If you consider this transaction from the vendor's point of view, it's not unreasonable to expect a return for all the hard work and capital they have put into their business, as well as the goodwill they have created along the way. Measuring this is no easy task. Educate yourself about the prices of businesses in the field which interests you. Look in the classified ads, talk to business brokers, and gauge the real selling prices of these companies as opposed to the original asking price. Try to break down this cost into elements including original capital input, owner hours to develop, goodwill and so on. Then do a comparison of starting up such a business, and running it for a similar period of time. Consider also the shabby house theory, and look at businesses with potential that are currently trading poorly. If you are confident you can add value and turn them into profit, then hard negotiation with reference to the profit and loss statements may reduce the price to a more affordable level.

chapter fifteen
NOT THE RETIRING TYPE

It was much easier in the good old days. Almost like the bumper sticker, *You're born, you live, you die,* life was a predictable and clearly segmented existence; childhood, education, work life, retirement. And for many males the retirement segment could be as short as five years. Over the past twenty years, workplace changes in technology, gender roles and working hours have forced a societal rethink about the place of work in our lives. The old notion of retirement could not be quarantined from this rethink.

With greatly increased life expectancies for most men and women in the Western world, few are contemplating 30 years of just fireside chats and improving the golf swing. Former concepts of retirement are now being rejected, replaced by a new understanding of later-life options. This understanding involves a transition from the notion of full-time work (wherein a balance of life/work is the goal) to a more clearly articulated desire for life/work balance – the 'new' retirement being not a retirement (withdrawal or cessation) but a life adjustment. In many cases it represents a new beginning, whereby the transitioning worker plans a structure which firstly addresses their goals, dreams and ambitions, and secondly seeks to incorporate some elements of work into this structure, as part of the glue of self-worth, as well as an income stream.

> *Employment is nature's physician, and is essential to human happiness*
> — GALEN

How does it all work?

Until now the impetus for someone to retire has largely come from the workplace – research from the Australian Institute of Family Studies shows the majority of 'early' retirements to be, in fact, forced redundancies. Industry and government have tended to collude on this point – some companies deciding older workers have a use-by date, and the government encouraging this attitude with tax concessions for those who leave their work place at the age of 55. Belatedly the realisation that forcing retirement on those in the demographic bulge caused by the post–World War II baby boom, and migration, will have two negative impacts. First, a greatly reduced tax nest egg, and second, a severe dilution of business knowledge, experience and history. If all baby boomers charge out of the workforce at the same time, the country will not be able to support itself. Now the message from governments and large corporations is changing – come back, older workers, you are a valuable resource. Yes, we understand you might wish to cut back your hours, so let's see how flexible we can be to retain you.

Cynicism aside, this can be good news for everyone. A much more flexible workplace is gradually emerging, creating job-share, part-time and off-site work opportunities for young and old alike. So how do you best tackle the idea of your own later years? Is there any research which assists in the best strategies for you? In a word, yes.

Research on ageing well: Those who've gone before

The most comprehensive research on ageing, which has followed teenagers from high school into their early eighties, has been conducted by Harvard University in America. Called the Study of Adult Development, it broke new ground when it commenced in 1932 by concentrating on adults who were well as opposed to sick. The study draws from three cohorts – male Harvard graduates born around 1920, socially disadvantaged inner city males born about 1930, and 90 intellectually advantaged women born about 1910. The findings of the research have been drawn together by Professor George Vaillant, in his book, *Ageing Well*. The conclusions are:

1. Happiness is not determined by negative life events, but the good people in your life.
2. Relationships are important. Healing relationships will enrich, and are brought about by a capacity for gratitude, forgiveness and the ability to love.
3. Good marriages at age 50 are a better predictor of positive ageing at age 80 than low cholesterol levels.
4. Alcohol abuse is a negative predictor, particularly because of the social consequences.
5. Learning to play and create as well as to continue to add younger friends is of vital importance.
6. Subjective good health is more important than objective – that is, it's not how you are, it's how you feel you are.

In particular, generativity was singled out by Vaillant as a critical factor in happy ageing. This quality he defines as the giving of oneself, and the taking care of the next (younger) generation in a way that outlives the self. This, he maintains, we can only do after our true selves are formed.

More recent Australian research, conducted by psychologist Michael Longhurst as part of a postgraduate degree, has also found its way into a book, *The Beginner's Guide to Retirement*. Longhurst's research, *Retire 200*, comprised a national sample of 100 men and 100 women, all retired, and living in both urban and rural areas. The aim of the research was to evaluate the behaviour and activities of those who were happy with life in retirement and of those who were not. The findings tend to corroborate those of the Harvard Survey. Respondents with a degree of control (that is, those who had retired of their own free will, at their own time, with financial security) were more likely to be content, as were those who were proactive in all aspects of their lives – relationships, health, education, life planning and purposeful (as opposed to leisure) activities. *Retire 200* also notes the critical role of emotional support.

> *I am more myself than ever before*
> — MAY SARTON (AGED 70)

RELATIONSHIPS: TOO MUCH SPOUSE ON TOO LITTLE INCOME?

Like so many clichés, the old joke about twice the husband on half the salary is based on the very real experiences of a multitude of retirees over the years. Suddenly the spouse who seemed to have energy and purpose in the workforce is everywhere – telling you how to drive, which tin of beans to buy, how to compost the potato peelings. Serious thoughts of divorce enter your mind. And then the guilt kicks in, because you think you still love him or her – just not 24 hours a day.

Happily, you will not be the first person to feel this way. Try to see this as a blimp on the marital radar screen, and use the opportunity to improve communication and define key life areas as yours, theirs and mutual.

The findings of both the Harvard survey and *Retire 200* research are corroborated by the readership surveys conducted in *Your Life, Your Retirement* magazine. Surveyed in every issue over the past five years, readers are asked, 'What are the key ingredients for a happy second life?' and requested to rate, from one to six: health, purpose, financial security, variety of activities, good relationships, and work. Results of the survey, and years of reader feedback emphasise the following points:

1. Growing older is not perceived as a negative. Some functions may decline, but there are many compensating factors.
2. Staying connected with the wider world is vital.
3. The ability to 'give back' – to grandchildren, family, the community, the workplace, the environment – is of paramount importance to your own sense of wellbeing.
4. Physical and mental wellbeing are inextricably intertwined. One leads to the other.
5. Financial security is important, but within the scope of the type of lifestyle you have already afforded, not in terms of being wealthier than you have been.

6. Continuing to grow and learn is also of high importance.
7. Travelling to different cultures and regions at a more leisurely pace is one of the true bonuses of leaving full-time work.

What is the message here? How do you apply this information to your own situation? There are a handful of useful strategies when thinking of your post full-time work years:

1. Make your own list of priorities from the research you've seen.
2. Beware retirement danger zones of shutting down your existence.
3. Recognise new opportunities.
4. Get the money in perspective.
5. Grab the discounts.
6. Consider joining a club.

Ageing seems to be the only available way to live a long time
— DANIEL FRANCOIS ESPRIT AUBER

Listing your priorities

Not all of the findings above will have relevance to your situation. If you've been happily divorced for years, and very much enjoying your own space, and your ability to make decisions as a onesome, it is highly unlikely the findings on happy marriages as a predictor for happy eighty-somethings will move you deeply. Other findings, however, will have a degree of resonance. Make a list of those concepts which appeal (generativity? active physical health? lifelong learning?) and try to evaluate how successfully you can incorporate these ingredients into your day-to-day existence. *Note that this is not retirement planning – this is planning how you choose to live.* It will also assist you to maintain some structure in your week. Recognise these recurring themes:

- the importance of structure
- the importance of relationships

- the need for a work component
- the value of ongoing mental stimulation
- the need for regular physical activity

Beware the danger zones

There are many, and most have a similar theme. Question why, if you find yourself saying:

- I always wanted to, but ...
- I'm too old.
- It's all very well for him, he's much .... (insert younger, richer, stronger, braver, luckier, etc.)
- I've run my race.
- I'd like to but I just can't seem to find the time.
- I just can't be bothered.
- I don't have the energy.
- Younger people are ... (insert ruder, more hopeless, more aggressive etc.) than in my day.
- I would have liked to make a difference, but I just never got around to it.
- The slipper syndrome – it's just so comfortable at home, why would you need to go out?

Recognise the opportunities

One of the best poems to be written in the past few years is called 'Warning' by Jenny Joseph. It starts with the line, *When I am old I shall wear purple with a red hat that doesn't go* and goes on to describe a wish list of convention-breaking activities one woman dreams of doing when she is old enough to get away with it. Surely the mature years should offer everyone this possibility? If you've raised and educated children, or built a business, or paid off a mortgage, been a diligent son or daughter, whatever your contribution has been, hopefully now it is your turn to do what you want:

- start a business
- stop a business
- grow tulips
- trek over mountains
- learn Swahili
- eat garlic every day
- travel on a cargo ship
- wear purple, pink, lime or black

This list can be inexhaustible, or limited – but only by your imagination.

Ged Lawrence: I felt I needed a change

I have had three major shifts of direction in my life.

My first career was in the army, but when I was 41, after 25 years, I decided I wanted to do something different. Call it male menopause if you like, no big crisis, I just felt I needed a change. For the next twelve years I held the position of executive director of the Real Estate Institute of Australia. And then, again, I thought I'd done as much as I could for that organisation, and it was time to move on. During the last couple of years, we'd been living in Canberra, but had a holiday house in Batemans Bay. We had previously set up a small record shop in Batemans, and it was going well. My son was interested in working in the business, and had had experience in the music industry, and I wanted to be independent for the first time in my life, so we went for it. In 1995 we moved into online music sales, selling CDs. We were using cutting edge technology, and sold more online than in the shop. We deliberately aimed the online component to sell Australian artists overseas – there was particularly strong interest coming out of the United States, and the exchange rate was working in our favour.

About this time my son had an accident, preventing him from working in the shop. I was in my mid-sixties and didn't quite like the fit of an older man in a record shop, so when I heard Festival/Mushroom records were thinking of setting up a website, I got in touch with them, and sold our business.

At this stage I was wondering what to do with myself, so I got on the Internet and researched retirement. There were so many gaps in the information provided, I saw a niche I could fill. So, again with the assistance of my wife and son, we launched a website called *About Seniors* in September 2000. It's not exactly a fourth career, as I only do about six hours a day, and make sure I have time to walk on the beach every morning. My son is the chief technical consultant, and I provide the content. There are about 150 pages of information on the site, and it's all about helping seniors find out what they need to know about housing, finance, care associations, what the government is offering. Websites such as Centrelink are strangely complex, so we get many emails every week asking us to help our members navigate their way around to find the answers they are seeking. After just three years, we have more than 8000 subscribers who receive a free newsletter, and some 1400 unique site visitors every day.

It's a very good business to run, and we still manage to get away for short breaks about six to eight times a year.

RETIRING BUSILY

A few years ago, Jill and Owen Weeks took time out from work to travel Australia and list their 24 recommended retirement living destinations in *Where to Retire in Australia*. In the process of gathering information for this book, they kept meeting up with people who had taken an idea and created a small or large business from it. Some of the income-earning ideas were résumé writing, oven cleaning, minding pets, dancing lessons and tutoring mature age students. More than one hundred accounts of these businesses are listed in the resultant book, *RetireBizzi: How to Start a Business without Risking Your Retirement Income*.

Getting money in perspective

Ensuring a retirement income stream is an integral part of your 'second life' planning. There are usually one of two main responses to the idea of retirement income planning – those who have spent a long time planning their retirement income, and those who have not addressed the issue at all. Just about every financial services company in the country has you in their sights – and many will promise if you leave it up to them, you can forget about the stress and strain of managing your money. Don't believe them. No-one except you is capable of making your own financial decisions. However, the best result will usually come from a partnership – an informed you, and a qualified and principled financial planner.

Becoming informed about retirement income streams can be confusing, but there are a couple of excellent resources to give you a clear and objective overview of what you need to know. The first is a book called *Retirement Income Streams*. Written by Dr Ed Koken and Barbara Smith from the Taxpayers Association of Australia, it is a clear and easy-to-follow summary of the ways you can get paid in retirement, whether on a full pension, a part-pension, an annuity, or other forms of income. The federal government has also set up an organisation specifically to inform Australians about their retirement income options. This organisation is called the National Information Centre on Retirement Investments (NICRI). NICRI is a treasure chest of information for those planning retirement income, and seeking to understand it thoroughly before leaping in. It also addresses issues such as redundancy, first mortgages, and many other potential pitfalls in the planning process. It is a free, confidential and objective service. Phone, email, fax or visit the website for a wealth of information about specific planning issues.

Grab the discounts

An advantage of extra birthdays in your life is hitting an age when you are rewarded exactly for that – your age. One of the main examples of this is the seniors card program. This card is available to Australians aged 60 and over, who are no longer working full time, and are now entitled to a range of benefits. The card is free and is issued by state and territory governments. Eligibility and benefits vary, but most programs annually mail to all members a booklet listing discounts on travel, recreation, food, consumer goods, entertainment products and services. Participating businesses often have a seniors' card sticker on the premises, but if they don't, it is often worthwhile asking if such a discount applies. Taking advantage of these discounts can also encourage you to try new activities, and stretch your horizons.

Consider a club

The world consists of two types of people – those who are joiners, and those who can't think of anything worse. If you belong to the latter category, skip this next section and go and water the garden, or read the paper. If you're one of the former, then there is a virtual smorgasbord of clubs awaiting the pre- and post-retiree. Some have a focus on your finances in retirement – Australian Association of Independent Retirees, The Older Persons Action Centre and the Australian Pensioners and Superannuants Federation. In the past twelve months the two largest seniors organisations in the country, the National Seniors Association and the Council of the Ageing have joined forces to form NSA–COTA, representing some 270 000 50-plus Australian men and women. Members benefit from advocacy, information, political lobbying, discounts and a bi-monthly magazine.

TRAVELLING SLOWLY

For those with extra time to travel and the flexibility of late booking, a trip on a cargo ship makes a lot of sense. Facilities can be basic, you will dine with the crew, and you may have long stretches of time in which you will need to entertain yourself. Great news for readers, writers and deep thinkers. This mode of travel can also be inexpensive, and allow you to see a very different aspect of other countries and cultures. Companies which take passengers on their cargo ships include P&O Containers, the Columbus Line, and Star Blue Lines. A visit to the Freighter Travel website will provide a good overview of different passages and prices.

I couldn't wait to leave work and pursue all my interests, but now I've retired the days stretch ahead with boring monotony. It's really starting to get me down ...

WHAT'S STOPPING YOU?

Many people make the transition into retirement by cutting back working hours and increasing leisure hours gradually. This gives them a chance to develop other interests and friendship groups so the change isn't too sudden if they leave work permanently. It may be that what you really wanted was an extended holiday and not a full-time departure? Is it possible to organise some part-time work to reintroduce some structure back to life? Because, love it or hate it, work certainly gives a sense of structure to our existence. If paid work is difficult, can you offer your services as a volunteer? This will have a few benefits. It will get some meaningful activity back into your life, create some definite appointments in your diary, force you to interact with those in need of assistance, and stop you thinking about the negative aspects of life for at least a few hours a week. At the same time, choose one subject about which you would like to learn more. It doesn't matter what it is. Then go to your local library and, using community listings, the Internet, and reference books work out how you will pursue this interest. Via a class, self-directed learning, and Internet-based search? Plan to devote six weeks to this course of action. And before your leave the library, borrow two novels by authors you've never read. Challenge yourself to finish them over the next two weeks. Remember, you're the one with all that time ...

chapter sixteen
LOOKING OUTWARD

In times past, the system of tithing, or pledging one-tenth of your earnings to the church, enabled communities to take care of the needy. With the development of state intervention, and a robust taxation system, many social welfare functions have been subsumed by the state. But there are still many organisations not in receipt of government funding, and heavily dependent on donations of money and time to continue to exist. For some people, giving money is the most involvement they wish to have. Others, however, prefer a social contract which allows them to give their energy and skills and receive back an immense sense of satisfaction and achievement. This can be particularly true for older workers who are moving out of the full-time workforce, but keen to stay involved. Two such areas of involvement are volunteering and mentoring.

Volunteering

Volunteering is an activity usually undertaken through a not-for-profit organisation, which is of community benefit, of the volunteer's own free will, and for no financial reward. It is also a vehicle for individuals or groups to address human, environmental and social needs. Currently 4.4 million, or more than one in five Australians, are involved in volunteering.

Why do people volunteer?

People will volunteer for a broad variety of reasons. It may be to add something to their own lives (companionship, work, adventure, structure, or travel) or with the express intent of adding to the lives of others (education, skills, caring, practical support). Many older Australians move to volunteering as a way of seeking satisfaction beyond the normal material gains they have received from long years in the workforce. These volunteers are often looking for activities which will have an impact on their soul, offering new and stimulating experiences, different types of relationships, and allowing them, in some cases, to make friends for life.

When shouldn't you volunteer?

When you are wishing to work over other people, to 'get them better organised' or because you think you have all the answers. No-one does, and most volunteers claim to learn more than they teach.

How do you get started?

Fill in the volunteer checklist in the Resources section. Start by thinking about the sectors which really grab your interest, and see if you can come up with three or four strong options. Then list your skills, allowing for basic, often unrecognised talents such as 'dancing with children', 'soothing babies' or 'don't mind repetitive and menial tasks'. Try to objectively assess your personality for those traits which can add real value to the volunteering brief – commitment, compassion, sensitivity, enthusiasm, persistence, or tenacity. Think laterally on this one. Then assess your reasons for wishing to volunteer and don't be afraid to include those reasons which may, on the surface, sound selfish: getting out of the house more, meeting new friends, adding some structure to your day, achieving a sense of self-worth. No one is 100 per cent altruistic, and these reasons are just as valid as the more philanthropic ones.

Lastly, get practical and list the maximum number of hours per day, week, month or year to which you are prepared to commit – remembering that once the commitment is made, even though this is not paid work, you will have asked an organisation to trust in you. You will need to deliver on this promise.

ATTRIBUTES OF A GOOD VOLUNTEER

- flexible
- adaptable
- good at group dynamics
- team workers
- proactive
- sensitive to cross-cultural issues
- resilient, particularly if there is conflict or times of difficulty
- prepared to make a commitment
- willing to learn and share, and don't assume they have all the answers
- possessing a sense of humour
- know yourself well enough to select the correct task for your energies and one that matches your values
- respectful of the rights, dignity and culture of others

GOOD VOLUNTEERS DO NOT

- need to direct others
- use work as an ego or power trip
- feel overtly 'sorry' for those they are assisting
- treat volunteer tasks as a social outing. It's not an excuse for a chat – there's work to be done!

Having listed your thoughts, now look for connections – is there a recurring theme here? Perhaps your passion is animals, and you are fit and love the outdoors, so animal welfare work is sounding like a possibility. Maybe you are a patient person with strong driving skills, and would consider work driving the disabled or elderly to be a worthwhile task, or perhaps communication skills are your forte, and assisting in public relations work for a startup community organisation will suit you better.

Once you have a fair idea of the type of volunteering you might like, go to the 'Go volunteer' website and punch in your postcode – look at the types of opportunities which exist. This website is a recruitment site for Volunteering Australia, which is the peak body in Australia for organising and promoting volunteering. At <www.govolunteer.com.au> you will normally find at least several hundred opportunities in the cities, and proportionately less in regional areas, to get you moving. However, do be aware that although you keep hearing organisations are crying out for volunteers, some actually have too many on their books. Don't be offended or discouraged if you are not snapped up immediately. It may be that they are top of the list of favoured volunteer organisations, or that your skills simply don't suit their requirements. Move on and try somewhere else.

Brad Mander: The passionate volunteer

I did not choose to be a volunteer. My working life has been a mix of nursing and IT. I'm 41 and still don't know what I really want to do work-wise – I've never been passionate about a career, but I am about Camp Connect. That really inspires me.

I formed the Australian Camp Connect Association earlier this year, three years after my marriage broke down. My son was three and my daughter five, and I had no idea of the process of a breakdown, nor the effect it would have. It was a total eye-opener.

At this time I started helping a friend with his website. It was for the Australian Information & Support Services For Men (now known as the Australian Family Support Services Association). This organisation gives practical initial support and information to non-custodial parents going through a family breakdown. I really enjoyed helping out – it was exactly the distraction I needed from my own situation. It also inspired the formation of Camp Connect, which I started as a project to help non-custodial dads who generally have limited contact time with their children. We got together for Father's Day last year. We were strongly supported by the YMCA Parent Link program, which helped with expertise, contacts, networking with other organisations, all manner of things.

Our first camp ran on the Father's Day weekend in 2003 when sixteen dads and 24 kids spent from the Friday evening to the Sunday afternoon with us, while another six dads and ten kids joined us for the Sunday only. It was wonderful. Our motto is 'Ensuring contact time is quality time'. From the feedback we received from the participating dads we succeeded. We certainly also put fathers back into Father's Day.

But it wasn't just about being with the kids. I did some research about what was beneficial for children long term when parents split up. After separation, contact time drops right off — in 34 per cent of cases there is no contact, in 17 per cent it is daytime only. So 51 per cent of dads do not have sleepover contact. This greatly reduces the dads' feelings of parenting competence and confidence. I wanted to look at ways of raising the confidence and have now set up workshops, including Dad Talk. It is amazing how many fathers will open up and share their issues — in many cases this will be the first time they've felt secure enough to do so. Finding out they are not alone has been so important for them. Camp Connect is now supported by some of these first dads, with technological and other skills. For me, I now know I can do powerful things. This has certainly had a positive effect on my children as well as the other dads and kids. I know I can never get back the time I'm not with my children, but running Camp Connect keeps me inspired as well as focused.

Australian Camp Connect Association Inc. website: <www.campconnect.org.au>

Mentoring

Mentoring involves a mutually beneficial relationship where a more experienced person will help a less experienced person achieve their goals. It normally happens on a one-to-one basis. It can exist in the paid workforce, often with older–younger worker partnerships, where research reveals the benefits flow through to the partners and the companies involved, as well as the co-workers.

In the general community, mentoring is an increasingly popular way for older workers to choose to 'give back'. Often they will have spent years honing their skills in a business discipline and, having moved away from paid employment, still maintain a desire to keep active in their field. The Plan-It Youth (PIY) program is one such example. This mentoring scheme is run by community groups and sponsors on the central coast of NSW. It is a response to research which shows that that young people who leave school early are twice as likely to be unemployed at the age of 24 than those who have completed Year 12. Young people are offered the opportunity to plan a career, and find a positive pathway into employment, in partnership with a mentor. The program consists of four stages conducted over a twelve-month period, and linked to a TAFE course.

How do you become a mentor?

A good starting point is the National Mentoring Association of Australia, and its website, Mentoring Australia, which is sponsored by the not-for-profit Dusseldorp Skills Forum. The aims of the National Mentoring Association are to create a communication network for mentoring programs, educators and researchers, sharing ideas and resources. A visit to the website and a click on the 'Get Involved' button will reveal mentoring initiatives around the country, often involving mature-age mentors matched to younger people.

THEY'RE SATISFIED

Volunteers stand out from other workers for having the highest levels of wellbeing, according to research conducted by the Australian Unity Wellbeing Index. The survey found that the majority of Australians in unpaid voluntary work were aged over 55, more likely to be female, and worked for 20 hours or less per week. These volunteers outscored other cohorts in personal wellbeing (77 per cent), satisfaction with work (85 per cent), work hours (83 per cent), leisure time (80 per cent) and how they spent it (79 per cent).

☞ *I'd really like to volunteer, but I'm afraid of getting stuck with a bunch of do-gooders and not being able to extricate myself...*

WHAT'S STOPPING YOU?

It all comes back to your basic motivation, and your core values, doesn't it? Maybe you had a bad experience the time you volunteered at the school canteen, and got bossed around, and went home distressed, and thinking your services had been totally undervalued. They might have been, or you might have been a tad sensitive in a strange environment. Try to work out what the real issues are here. If you *would* really like to volunteer, ask yourself why. Is it because you feel society expects it of you now you have some spare time? Lousy reason. Is it because you do think, in the right environment, you can make a difference? Then think harder about what that environment might be. And what type of difference you are really hoping to make. Rather than shopping around for a volunteer organisation which needs help, check out the mission statements and core objectives of these groups. Or better still, talk to the volunteers organiser about the attributes they are seeking, and how their volunteers have made a difference to the community or the environment. But watch out – before you know it, you may become a do-gooder!

How Brandon survived

Remember Brandon from page 143? How did he create meaningful work?

Stages of change

ENDINGS
- '... the call came. She was leaving me.'
- Property investments and high gearing don't mix when a credit squeeze comes.

NEUTRAL ZONES
- Travelling across the Nullarbor, bonding with five children and a bird.
- Trying to get a job and getting no response.
- Sitting around the house with unemployed friends, drinking.
- Going through stages of hating everyone, thinking the world was very unfair.

BEGINNINGS
- Winning the trip and experiencing a different side of life.
- Realising 'I had become a bum and I had to do something to change my situation'.
- Being told I could start the next day. With pay.
- Using my last $25 to run an ad.

ON THE GOOD LIFE:
... the kids and I actually had enough to live off. At the weekend we would ride our bicycles to Broadbeach and barbeque sausages – it felt like luxury.

ON CREATING OPPORTUNITIES:
I offered to work for nothing for a month, so they could see how hard I would work.

ON THE IMPORTANCE OF WORK:
For me, having a job has always meant your sense of self-worth, that you are of some value. It's not about the money, but it is about the job.

some questions you may wish to explore

- How closely is my self-identity tied up with my work?
- Have I ever had a job which was so engrossing, I wasn't aware of the time?
- Do I want to feel like that again?
- Does thinking about my vocational options bring on a headache? Would more clarity of thought be achieved by using a vocational counsellor?
- Am I spending too much time being fed up with my job and not enough researching options?
- Do I still hanker after the job I had, but lost? Do I need some help to move on?
- Is my job dissatisfaction part of a deeper longing for a simpler life?
- Do I believe all 'successful' work must be well paid?
- Is it possible to contemplate a salary cut to do something which I will find more meaningful?
- If I am working more than 60 hours a week, is this out of fear of losing my job, disorganisation, or because I'd rather be at work than at home?
- Does my work ultimately benefit mankind? Will I feel proud to have devoted a large part of my life to this?

Part Four:

MAKING YOUR SEA-CHANGE

> For my part, I travel not to go anywhere, but to go. I travel for travel's sake. The great affair is to move.
>
> — ROBERT LOUIS STEVENSON

Does place matter?

Do you define yourself by your location? Are you living where you want? This question is not about the merits of owning or renting, or the relative luxury of your house, or the 'desirability' of your suburb or region. Instead, it is all about whether your place, be it inner city, country, seaside, or suburban, is a confirmation of the type of life you desire. If it is not, and you are ready to spread your wings, this chapter is designed to help you define the type of geographical change which will best suit your purposes, as well as to remove all the excuses for dreaming rather than doing it.

Changes in location can vary from the permanent, to the trial run, to a brief sojourn. Biographies about 'happily ever after' sea-changes abound. *A Year in Provence* by Peter Mayle, *Under the Tuscan Sun* by Frances Mayes, and, more recently, *Almost French* by Sarah Turnbull, have struck a responsive chord with those who dream of selling up, ditching their cares and woes, and moving to a quintessentially European location where they will be initially amused by local eccentricities, but ultimately seduced by a much more exotic culture. If only everyone had such a positive experience, with book royalties as well! Such a dramatic leap from a mundane suburban life is not always guaranteed to be so successful.

Why do some people's sea-changes work and others' don't? Part Four concentrates on understanding your reasons for a change in location, measuring the degree of change which will suit you, and encouraging as much research as possible before you commit. Happily there are many ways of testing your resolve, including house swaps, and renting, and these usually offer the best research of all. Christine and Marius Webb moved their family to a small village in Italy – but achieved this rewarding life change only after years of planning, preparation, and a few diversions along the way.

The chapters are divided into the main ways you can change your sense of place, firstly by relocating where you live, in Chapter 17, 'Home'; secondly, by allowing travel to be a trigger for personal change, in Chapter 18, 'The Journey'; and lastly, by trading nations in Chapter 19, 'The Expatriate Experience'.

Christine and Marius Webb: Think of anything in the world you would really like to do

In 1999, when my husband Marius was 57 and I was 45, we moved to Citerna, a small village in the province of Umbria in Italy. We had both had very successful careers in media when Marius took a redundancy from the ABC after 23 years. We had our second son soon after and the high-pressure life of Sydney was leaving a lot to be desired. I was attending many management training seminars for my job at News Limited and one in particular was about using Edward De Bono's 'six hats' for creative thinking. One evening I was explaining it to Marius and asked him, 'Just think of anything in the world you would really like to do and we'll work on a way to make it happen'. Unexpectedly, he said that he'd always wanted to live in Italy. His mother was half-Italian and he certainly was an Italophile, so we set about making it happen.

We wrote down a series of objectives that we wished to achieve. These included:

- more family time together
- personal expansion
- learning the language,
- a return to painting (for me)

We also addressed some of the difficulties we might encounter such as:

- language problems
- visas and house ownership
- schooling and various options such as correspondence school
- banking
- health

Initially we thought we would plan an eighteen-month holiday, renting our Balmain house to finance the weekly expenses. Then a succession of tragic events (the death of my mother and also Marius's father) turned our ideas around and we found ourselves taking a four-year sea-change in Sorrento, Victoria, looking after Marius's aged mother in her final years. Marius spent the better part of his early retirement organising his father's estate, then his aunt's and finally his mother's. He also developed a property nearby as holiday cabins. I started painting and held three exhibitions as well as teaching once a week, and freelance writing. Despite being based in regional Australia, through the Internet we were able to do a considerable amount of research that made our subsequent adventure more successful. Once we got to Italy we did not experience any serious setbacks. Which is not to say that we have not had periods of doubt, challenge or worry – but nothing so serious as to make us change our course.

By moving to Sorrento we managed to achieve many of the objectives we were aiming for in Italy, including more family time and my return to painting. Our lives also slowed down to a much more comfortable pace but we were still drawn to the idea and challenge of Italy. After the death of Marius's mother we inherited part of a property in London which was sold, allowing us to buy a small house in Italy.

Our boys were very young (six and ten), and Julius, the older one, was very reluctant to leave Sorrento, particularly the beach and the bay which are a ten-year-old's idea of heaven. We had done a lot of research about the impact on children of moving countries and found that on children younger than ten it can have a tremendous character-building effect, but for children in their teens it can be quite damaging. We were very apprehensive about the boys' capacity to cope. Luckily we found the ideal house in the middle of a vibrant but ancient town and there were plenty of kids to play with.

We searched the web and found an estate agency that had consistently cheaper prices than the others. Most of those properties offered by EPN (Euro Property Network, a real estate company on the Internet) were in the Upper Tiber Valley and worth investigating. Some prices in Italy seemed to be incredibly cheap by Australian standards. On a trip to England I stopped in Italy for five nights, made an appointment, spent a day driving around looking at properties and took the last one seen that day even though the agent didn't have the keys to get in. I returned and saw the interior, took home photos and Marius was brave enough to say yes.

We were very well prepared. We planned the move for five years, deciding on such details as what time of year we would arrive and if there would be anything to sit on when we got there. Marius could already speak good holiday Italian and he attended weekly classes for several years. Our fallback was to structure in a review timetable of six months, two years and five years so that we could return to Australia if things were too difficult. Other defining factors were that if the kids failed at school or one of us became seriously ill we would return. I think our review periods were a good idea. It gave us sensible time frames to put problems in perspective and also to reassess what we were achieving. Our nearest town, Arezzo, has proved a valuable boon in the transport sense. It is a major rail stop between Rome and Florence and means we can get to and from those towns quite easily. When we realised we were not seeing enough of places like Florence and Rome, we would organise a day for one of us to just spend some time there cruising galleries and the like.

We didn't bring any furniture so we had the cost of setting up house again, airfares as well as a new car and renovations to the house after we got here. The house cost roughly A$165 000 and we spent about another A$80 000 on the rest. With the exception of wine and coffee at the bar, everything is much more expensive than in Australia. Heating and petrol are double, food is about one-third more and you can really only buy Italian products so it took more than a year to find jasmine rice and ingredients to cook the Thai food we love.

> *We told them if they could do this, they could do anything in their lives*

I miss libraries. What I wouldn't give to be able to have the Rosebud or Balmain library down the road. We miss the ABC, of course and I hope that we can get the latest series of *Kath and Kim* on video. I read *The Age* and the *Sydney Morning Herald* every day and feel very proudly Australian but at the same time have the privilege of learning the heritage of being European. It has been harder on the boys as Aussie kids make friends easily and there is a lovely naturalism that they miss. Another difficulty is the massive distance and expense to get home.

One of the things we anticipated positively was that by simply spending time here the children would become bilingual. Whilst this has been achieved, don't believe all the clichés about kids learning the language in next to no time. They certainly learn quickly. That's true. But school has been incredibly hard. Their first day was excruciating, as they could barely understand a thing. We told them that if they could do this, they could do anything in their lives. The younger one, Fabian, has risen to the academic challenge and topped his class in the first year. He speaks perfect Italian, like a newsreader – it bowls the locals over. Julius, on the other hand, has always found school much more difficult. Julius has always been the litmus test as to whether we'll be able to stay. Whenever we have come up to one of our review periods we have had some agonising moments as to whether the experience is working for him. But now he is in a class of eleven, he is getting incredible attention from very capable teachers and we are confident he will benefit from completing his education in Italy. Now, he loves it here.

We have a very unstructured life. For two months in 2003, Marius was in Melbourne presenting an Italian Theatrical Performance for the International Festival of the Arts while I remained in Italy, looking after the boys and researching a book I am hoping to write. I am also the de facto town photographer and so am continually called on when there is a communion or some such. I am developing a very large photographic archive of all aspects of the town and its life. We also offer a personal accommodation referral service in our area, the Alto Tevere Region or Upper Tiber Valley between Arezzo and Sansepolcro.

We feel incredibly privileged to be here. It is wonderful. The landscape, the heritage (we found we have a 2500-year-old Etruscan Tomb under the house), but most of all the people of our village, who have welcomed us like extended family.

Chapter seventeen
HOME

It's meant to be where the heart is — but what if your heart is determined to wander? Is the former house of your dreams now something which you blame for keeping you shackled? Is it time to move on? And if so, how far? What are the intelligent questions to ask before deciding it's time to call the removalists?

Moving home is something some people do twenty or more times during their life. Others refuse to budge. A much-loved neighbour of mine died, aged in his early sixties, in the house in which he was born and grew up. In between he spent a few years posted overseas with the army, but when allowed his own choice, he returned to the neighbourhood of his childhood.

For others, this is anathema. Not only would they be bored beyond belief staying in the same familiar neighbourhood all their lives, but work commitments and other responsibilities often force more frequent moves. Many Australians have also taken advantage of a long-term property boom in nearly all the capital cities to renovate and sell, renovate and sell, as a wealth creation strategy with the asset unlikely to attract capital gains tax — the family home.

The reasons you might choose to move home are many. Some are valid, others perhaps less so; all should be evaluated carefully before taking the leap. Whether you are renting or own your home may also have a huge bearing on your decision-making processes. To simplify the issues, this chapter will discuss moving home as though you are an owner-occupier. If you are not, some of the detail on costings and tax implications can be skipped.

A look at the pros and cons of moving may help you progress from vague desires to a plan of action.

Reasons for moving

- You need a change.
- Your locality no longer reflects the real you.
- You hope that a change in location will be the beginning of a whole new life.
- Your work prospects are better in another area.
- Your house is costing too much in maintenance and rates.
- Your family situation has changed and you need a smaller/larger abode.
- You are leaving someone.
- You are moving in with someone.
- This is part of a financial strategy to release some equity for other purposes.

Concerns you may have about moving

- Your current home holds many dear memories.
- You feel very comfortable in this neighbourhood.
- You are close to amenities which suit your lifestyle.
- Your family is not in agreement about this move.
- You are not overly familiar with the area to which you are moving.
- You are frightened at the thought of making this change.
- You are not clear about the financial implications of the move.
- You are concerned you may want to reverse this decision when it is too late to do so.

These lists are by no means exhaustive, but they do help to crystallise some of the major issues involved in moving home. The good news is that there is a wealth of information available to help you evaluate the strength of your reasons for a move, and to arrive at a sound decision.

Your move can be best understood within the following categories:

1. research
2. the trial run
3. the holiday house
4. decision-making time
5. staying put

Doing your research

Let's assume you are living in a suburban setting in one of Australia's cities, and you are thinking of moving to a more bucolic location.

How do you know if your dream destination will stand the test of time? It may be that you are living in Perth, and have spent summer holidays and long weekends in the Margaret River region, and now feel this is where you would like to call home. The first step is to organise some time which is not a holiday break, but a research trip, to check out the detail of the location in a way holiday visitors never do. This may be an expensive exercise in terms of time away from work and dollars spent flying or driving to a different area. However, if you are investing thousands or hundreds of thousands of dollars in relocating, it may be the best investment you ever make. Consider the magnitude of the potential relocation, and commit to this exercise. In their book, *Where to Retire in Australia*, authors Jill and Owen Weeks nominate 24 key areas around the country which have features conducive to 'the good life'. Whilst the title of their book refers to retirement, the information contained within is applicable to a move at any age, and the location checklists are an excellent way of evaluating facilities.

So once you believe you have found an ideal location for your next home, try considering the following aspects of the potential move:

About you

- What are your work requirements? Does this location satisfy them?
- If not, is there another type of work you can easily obtain to allow you to still consider this move?
- Is there a local employment service where you can gather this information?
- How do you currently use your free time? Are these activities available where you are thinking of moving?
- Is there a new project or activity you hope to incorporate in the move? If so, is this achievable in this location? If you are moving to Darwin as part of a newly leisured existence, and hope to do more bird-watching, a visit to the Northern Territory website will soon reveal the myriad of opportunities close to Darwin for those who enjoy bird-watching. If you are moving to the Shire of Wyalkatchem in Western Australia and intend to start a bookshop, you may find the resident to area ratio of one of the sparsest shires in Australia is unable to provide the critical mass for your new business.
- Are your spiritual needs likely to be met in this new setting?
- Is your social life going to be satisfying? Will the locals be welcoming?
- If volunteering is part of your life, will there be an organisation which can utilise your talents and skills?
- Can your pets go with you?

Your new location

- Discover as much as you can about the local history from the town library.
- Go to the council chambers and ask for a new resident's kit. This will usually provide the best overview you can get, with a listing of all key services you may require, as well as many

residents' associations, clubs and amenities. If the council does not have such a document, try the local Rotary Club or Lions Club. See also if you can meet with locals through such organisations to ask questions about day-to-day life in the area.

- Is this region experiencing growth, or decline? It may be that you are prepared to accept a region which is in decline, but it is important to have realistic expectations on capital growth of property prices if this is the case.
- Regardless of whether you are a young parent, grandparent, likely to need aged care facilities, or are currently fit and healthy, medical facilities are important. Living in cities often means taking for granted health care services (including 24-hour access to emergency facilities). If you are going to a regional area, these facilities should form part of a checklist when it comes to decision-making time.
- What about the weather? Contact the Bureau of Meteorology for average local temperatures during the year. Mango fever in Darwin's wet season was so named because locals grew so discontented they felt they would burst. Try living through such a season to see if it is compensated for by the endless sunshine at other times during the year.
- You know what your current cost of living is, but if you are going to a remote location, you may find grocery shopping, fuel, transport and basic services are much more expensive, or, if you are lucky, more affordable. Find out before you move. Is shopping going to be easy? Are basic goods and services readily available? Will the luxury of nipping out late at night for a coffee or carton of milk become a forgotten dream?
- And what of the converse – if you are heading to the inner city it may be just as difficult to locate basic goods and services out of hours. Can you stay in a nearby hotel to assess what this part of the city is like on weekends, how the parking is affected, what type of people are around?

IT'S TIME TO GET FRIENDLY WITH LOCAL GOVERNMENT

Local governments (councils or shires) are one of the richest sources of information for potential residents in a new area. They are also one of the least utilised resources. Take the time to visit your new town or shire via their web page, as well as making a personal visit when you are gathering information. Ask about recycling policies, local clubs, zoning regulations, recreational facilities, historical societies, volunteering opportunities, shopping areas as well as the size and population of your area. Check where the library is located, and its opening times, and then make this your second port of call. Be relentless in your questioning, and learn from the answers.

Visit the Australian Local Government Association website for a hotlink to all councils. <www.alga.com.au>

The trial run

Having researched the main features of your dream destination, you may still feel concerned or, at best, ambivalent about the wisdom of a move. This makes you a prime candidate for the trial run. Moving home does not have to be forever. In fact, some of the most successful life changes are trialled by renting, home-swaps, and short-term contracts which enable you to get a feel for the new without totally losing the known – a transitional time to ease you into a very different life.

Glenn & Andy: Breaking the rules – the no-plan method

Glenn and Andy broke all the rules for a smooth transition from one location to another. Rather than careful planning, a trial period of time in the new state, or remaining within close proximity to family and friends, they moved from suburban Melbourne to Darwin after a snap decision made on holiday.

The only reason they were in Darwin on holiday was that that was the destination of the plane tickets given to them by Glenn's children to celebrate his fiftieth birthday. At the end of their short holiday, they were so impressed by the energy and ambience of the Top End, they returned to Melbourne, sold their house, packed their pets and possessions, and returned to board with Glenn's nephew at the RAAF airbase while they sought rented accommodation. After years in Melbourne commuting to a job in an advertising agency, Glenn had felt he had moved away from his creative skills, and was stuck in a management role he didn't enjoy. Moving to Darwin allowed him to return to his craft. Andy worked as a veterinarian nurse, but then took time out to retrain as a chef. They get around Darwin quickly by bicycle and Mini Moke. Both consider the move has given them energy, excitement, and true life balance. Melbourne in winter now seems far away.

Many Australians are now availing themselves of home-swapping or house-sitting services as a cost effective way of testing different locations and lifestyles, both domestically and abroad. These swaps can be for as short as two weeks, or as long as a year or more. The advent of the Internet has meant it is much quicker and easier to view properties and book without delay. The potential savings can be significant, particularly for those wishing to try out the new location for an extended period of time. There are also traditional catalogue homeswap companies contactable by phone and mail, although if the properties are simultaneously listed on the Internet, it may be a frustrating process if availability keeps changing by the time you have tried to secure them.

A recent search using the term 'home-swap' with the Google Internet search engine produced more than 60 000 listings. This makes it very difficult for a prospective swapper to define which service will best suit them. Within the category of 'homeswap', subcategories such as 'single home exchange', 'golf course homes' and 'boat and yacht swap' can also be located. The only way to research the bona fides of the site hosting the swap you want is by checking references so that you can reassure yourself there will be a bed at the end of the journey. Do the hard work of requesting referees, and be assured that many travellers are using this method of testing other locations and finding it is highly enjoyable. It also saves thousands of dollars of hotel bills, and you get to meet some very interesting pets and neighbours along the way.

Dianne and Mike Cecil: I can't think of a downside

Mike and I spent ten and a half months in Europe after I retired from teaching last year. Living in Queensland on a hobby farm, in drought conditions, we were more than ready for the cooler green landscapes in Europe. One of the difficulties in booking such a long trip was that airlines will not allow you to commit to a ticket for more than six months in advance, and similarly, with the houses, we found the earlier swaps easy to organise, but few owners really wanted to commit more than six months in advance.

We were really pleased with the accommodation we secured. We used HomeLink, which is an organisation that started in Brussels 50 years ago, but now goes all over the world. We left Australia at the end of October and stayed throughout Scotland, Wales, England and Europe. In between homestays we visited capital cities where we stayed in hotels. Most of our swaps were non-simultaneous, which means our home has forward bookings for 2004 and 2005. We met none of the other homeowners as they were travelling out as we travelled in, although we did meet some of their pets. The homes are often outside major cities, so that is worth checking, but the family car can be part of the deal. In Amsterdam we were in an apartment in the centre of the city – up five flights of stairs. I was glad I was fit. That owner left us a car and two bicycles – and we certainly used the bikes. One of the tiniest homes was a bedsit on the main esplanade in Brighton, England. It had a picture window with a view of the ocean, and our visit coincided with the Festival of Brighton – we couldn't have planned a better stay.

I can't think of a downside to the home-swap arrangement – I was pleased to have someone in our own house for reasons of security. I locked valuables, such as family photos, in a spare room, but in hindsight this wasn't particularly necessary. And the whole system felt quite secure as both parties are required to sign a contract for the swap, and forward a copy to the HomeLink head office.

How much does a home-swap cost?

This will obviously vary from company to company, but some sample costings are as follows:

HOMELINK

There are three forms of membership available: Domestic membership – exchange only within Australia (A$160 p.a.); International – exchange only overseas (A$240 p.a.); and Combined (A$330 p.a.), exchange everywhere – overseas and Australia. The one-off annual fee includes listing your property on the website and in the hard-copy directory.

AUSTRALIAN HOUSE SITTERS
The longest-established Australian based company, available via the website, or telephone. Registration of A$185 per year will give you access to domestic and international residences for periods of between one week and one year.

INTERNATIONAL HOME EXCHANGE NETWORK
Some other companies encourage members, but also make their listings available free of charge for non-members. The rationale behind this is that the bookings for members who list will reach a far wider audience, thus enhancing the value delivered to paying members. The International Home Exchange Network, based in Florida, USA, charges US$29.95 per year membership for those wishing to list as well as locate a property to rent or swap.

How does it work?

Once you have paid your membership, you can arrange as many exchanges as you please. You contact the members directly. A lot of members offer non-synchronised swaps. Some have second homes so they will stay in those or they might have arranged an exchange elsewhere for the time that you want to come.

Most home exchanges are organised so you actually exchange – they vacate their house, either to stay at yours or elsewhere and you stay in theirs.

Before the exchange most members will have been in regular email/written contact and will have spoken over the phone. They are not only getting to know each other but sharing tips for their holidays – recommending restaurants, places in the region that might be of interest, and so on. Often they will meet their exchanger at the airport and have a meal with them before they depart for their destination.

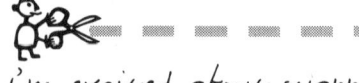

I'm excited about swapping houses, but ...

Q. What is my guarantee that the property I get resembles the Internet image of the property I book?
A. Do your research thoroughly. When you have located a company with a property that you like, choose another property they have somewhere nearby to you. Look at the description on the website, and then go and check it out. Does the description match the real thing? If there are no available 'test' properties nearby, ring the company concerned and quiz them on the property as thoroughly as you can.

Q. What if we swap house and car, and then have an accident in someone else's car?
A. For both home exchange and car exchange, make sure there is a current certificate of insurance – request a copy.

Q. What if my house gets trashed by the swappers? Do I have any comeback?
A. Same as above – check insurance before you go.

Q. How secure is the Internet booking arrangement?
A. You can contact by letter, email, telephone, or fax – whichever you prefer. The booking arrangement between members is as secure as you want to make it, from the most informal to the most formal, having a solicitor draw up a contract.

Q. What if I want to shorten or extend my stay?
A. This often happens and often suits both parties, particularly extending. Shortening may be a problem depending upon your original agreement/contract. Think about this before you commit.

Q. How clean/new/well-maintained does my house need to be?
A. It must be very clean, and you need to be totally honest in your descriptions of your own home.

Decision-making time

Now it's crunch time.

The research is over and you're ready to make a decision. You're convinced of the emotional need to move, but want to evaluate whether the house you have in mind is the right purchase for you. Let's break your decision-making down into manageable steps:

1. understanding your motivation
2. working out your priorities
3. costing all aspects
4. deciding whether to buy or sell first

Understanding your motivation

When it comes to real estate, there are three broad reasons why you are investing a large sum of money in this house:

1. You are purchasing an asset for capital growth (i.e. financial investment).
2. You are purchasing a centre of family life (i.e. lifestyle investment).
3. You are purchasing a destination for possible retirement (i.e. lifestyle investment).

You may feel your reasons are a mix of two or three of the above. But one of these reasons will be your primary motivator, and it is imperative you understand which one it is. Only then can you evaluate the property you have in mind against your main purpose for buying. For instance, if you are purchasing an asset with capital growth in mind, rather than investing this money in the share market or other forms of investment, say this out loud, and then compromise on the lifestyle elements associated with the purchase (for example, other friends have purchased in Byron Bay, but you see better growth potential in Yamba). If your motivation is lifestyle, and you are seeking a sea-change to a coastal area, with sea views and the ability to walk along the beach every day, proximity to the beach will be a primary factor, and you may choose to purchase at above-market prices to satisfy this need. You will need to make a conscious trade-off against capital appreciation if this is the case. You may be choosing a property or location which is where you hope to live for the rest of your life; in other words, a possible retirement destination. If you are choosing a location which already has a large population of seniors, consider your own feelings about this. Will the town still have a vibrant economy and social aspect? Do you want to mix primarily with older people? Will you feel as though you are in a quasi retirement village? Consider also the move to a location which has always been magical as a retreat. When you are living there 24/7 will the magic remain? Or is it better to recognise the magic lies in the occasional visit, and that your day-to-day life is better lived elsewhere?

Working out your priorities

Having clarified why you are buying, try to sort the priorities for the purchase under three different headings; your priorities, your family's, and the ten non-negotiable features of a new home. Fill in the Is This the Right Home for Me? checklist in the Resources section to help work your way through these.

Tony Dyer: sea-change — let's see what happens

In 1996 a few things came together in our life to convince me the time was ripe for a sea-change. My daughter loved horse-riding, and we were agisting horses out of town, but dreaming of a little more space where we could do this ourselves. We were living in Moonee Ponds, and thought we'd like a country home with a few acres. A note was dropped in our letterbox from a prospective buyer who was interested in our house. We named a price beyond reasonable expectation, and to our surprise, it was accepted. This really put us on the spot — I wondered if this was just a crazy whim, but we had a family meeting and decided to go for it. It wasn't quite so easy finding the country home. We'd looked and looked, then one day we were driving down a lane in Gisborne, and upon retracing our steps, a sign had miraculously appeared on a house that looked just right. The funny thing was, the owners suddenly arrived and said the sign was for the land next door, the house was not yet on the market, but would be after some road work was completed. After some discussion our offer on the house was accepted, but it took two and a half years before we owned the house outright.

It was the driving that did us in. At first it was fine for the kids to go to school – using a bus. But as they got older and went to university, and had part-time jobs, we managed to clock up 300 000 kilometres in record time. We didn't mind hopping down to the city for restaurants and entertainment, but our city friends just saw it as a long drive, and didn't reciprocate. We weren't able to make many friends locally – many were commuting to Melbourne, and the weekend was the only time they were really in residence. And since our kids' activities increased, and my wife worked in the city every day, they spent waking hours downtown and only returned home in the dark. The maintenance on 12 acres was huge – I would need to mow the lawn twice a week in season, and this took a full day out of my schedule. I had planned to work on my textile hangings in the studio there, but fencing and the garden kept me busier than I'd intended.

When I needed surgery my wife and I both questioned if she would be able to maintain the property if I couldn't, and the short answer was no. We were still driving up and down to the city for our work, and so we decided to move back to town at the end of 1999. Prices in the city in our area had nearly doubled – not so in the country. So I guess, financially, it was a bit of a disaster. I don't think the move itself was a failure – I'm glad we had a go. I like the fact we made a decision and acted upon it. But even though we were born in the country, I think my wife and I are both city dwellers at heart.

Costing all aspects

A Costing Your Property checklist is also included in the Resources section to help you factor in all possible costs associated with your change in location. Before filling it in, take a guess at the highest amount you believe you can afford to spend, then fill in the worksheet, and see if the add-on costs of buying or buying and selling *plus* the purchase price will still enable you to proceed.

Deciding whether to buy or sell first

There are no easy answers on this one, but here are a few basic guidelines:

- If you are selling in an area of high demand, buy first, secure in the knowledge that you will be able to confirm a purchase price, as well as have a strong chance of moving your own property afterwards. Buy at 120-day settlement if possible, and sell at 60–90 to decrease the chances of needing (expensive) bridging finance.

- Assess your own personality, and if you are selling first, make sure you can confidently handle the wait, and not panic-buy. Factor in a twelve-month rental period to avoid making a hasty decision.
- Talk to an objective real estate professional (that is, one who is not handling your sale or purchase) and ask their assessment of the merits of either course of action.

Staying put

Chapter 6 highlighted ways of finding more meaning in the familiar places of our lives. This can apply to your home as much as it does to your marriage or your career.

You may be extremely keen to introduce change into your life, but feel so connected to your current home or neighbourhood that you just don't want to leave. Maybe it's time, instead, to consider revamping your home environment in a way that expresses your personality and better fits the 'real you'. This does not have to mean a renovation you can't afford – but it can mean a very satisfying program of room-by-room 'makeovers' which make your home an exciting place to be.

A wonderful starting point for such a revamp is the book *Clear Your Clutter with Feng Shui* by Karen Kingston. You don't have to be a Feng Shui devotee to get the author's point. Her concise suggestions encourage you to review the possessions you've built up over a lifetime and crammed into drawers, on shelves, under beds, and to try to streamline this miscellaneous matter to create a simple, functioning home. It's amazing how much clarity of thought can be achieved by a wholesale attack on the junk room – a task you may have dreaded and put off for years. It's also amazing how much we accept the familiar arrangement of furniture and effects in our rooms – and how going to the trouble of removing all furniture, and knick-knacks from a room, then putting back only the items you love, can force you to rethink what is optimal. This reworking of your possessions is similar to the 'green-bagging' process for your wardrobe. If it is something you have worn within the past twelve months, it can stay. If it's not, into the garbage bag it goes, and off to someone who needs it more via an appropriate charity.

And while the spring-cleaning bug is buzzing, consider a serious reorganisation of your personal files. In *From Thought to Action*, Antony Kidman offers a very simple method for reorganising home files and information, proving that you don't need an MBA to maximise your efficiency with bill paying, filing and general household management. For those who maintain this more disciplined approach, the bonus is a minimisation of frustration looking for lost files, unpaid bills, library fines and missed deadlines.

THE REVAMP

Are you a fan of lifestyle 'reality' shows where the TV team arrive and create order out of mess, style out of disaster? Why not turn your own clutter-clearing project into a revamp? Schedule your makeover date, invite family and friends (with compatible taste) to put aside a weekend, with you shouting the pizzas and wine, and get started. Just remember before the 'team' arrives to have cleared all extraneous clutter yourself, and to have a clear idea of the final effect you are hoping to achieve.

☞ *I think I want to move, but am worried about losing money if I sell up and then decide to move back ...*

WHAT'S STOPPING YOU?

Everything! It's all very well to be dissatisfied with where you are, but unless you have a clear idea of where you want to be, it's best to put the decision-making on hold until you have gathered a little more information. Consider the main aspects of moving — your family's attitude, work considerations, costs, your knowledge of real estate, including purchasing and renting options. How well-informed are you about these aspects of a sea-change? Finding out your family's attitude might be as simple as sitting down and chatting with them, but exploring work options and costs involved might take a major commitment of time and energy. That's probably a good thing, as the financial risks can be high, and a little research up-front will more than likely save heartache further down the track. Consider a 'real estate for beginners' course at a local CAE. Try the sea-change checklist in the Resources section. If you still have absolutely no idea of where you might wish to move, convert the search into family activity days, or go with a good friend to check out desirable locations *just for fun*. The worst that will happen is an enjoyable day in a different location. The best could be a whole new world waiting for you to arrive and claim it.

chapter eighteen
THE JOURNEY: USING TRAVEL AS A TRIGGER

*If we don't change our direction,
we are likely to end up where we are going*

— CHINESE PROVERB

One of the most satisfying ways of rejuvenating yourself is by travelling somewhere new. This chapter is about using experiential travel as a way of exploring your future directions. It is not about the more passive travel offered in coaching or cruising holidays where you might be ferried from start to finish, or sit in a deckchair reading in the sunshine for the bulk of your trip. It is about using travel as a trigger to place yourself in an entirely different set of experiences and activities from those you've experienced before.

The goal is to challenge yourself by placing yourself outside your comfort zone. This can be done in a variety of ways, and this chapter offers three different approaches. First it looks at the opportunities to transport yourself from the familiar and into the unknown, perhaps as a catalyst for deeper life changes. Too much travel information assumes you will always have a companion, and because we often learn more and experience more deeply when we travel alone, the second section addresses the strategies and opportunities for those who need and/or want to go it alone. Lastly, there are those for whom a few weeks' vacation a year is never going to suffice. For such personalities this chapter addresses opportunities to combine work with travel – both for full-time careers or short work opportunities in a new location.

Life-changing travel

How *can* travel change your life? Think back to Part Two and the ways you might want to change yourself, and how this might be achieved through travel. Maybe it's all about changing your relationship with yourself. Maybe you feel that up to now you've been too safe, too fearful, lacking attitude. Maybe there is an aspect of your personality you are keen to work on. Or you might intend to enhance your wellbeing, your spirituality, your relationship with the wider world, your learning experiences. The type of travel experience you select should be directly driven by this end aim. This is not about holidays, but about experiences which will add to your understanding of yourself. Because there is such a bewildering array of travel options, and most destinations will offer the full gamut of opportunities for adventure, learning, volunteering, ecological pursuits, and so on, it might help you to narrow your search by first picking a location which:

- you've never before visited, or haven't been to for a long time
- is exotic in the true sense of the word, and which will give you sufficient fracture from your day-to-day environment to enable some profound thinking

Let's say you are hoping to explore some of the more spiritual paths in life. Consider a destination which will be conducive to this search. If, for instance, it is Catholicism which beckons, for those who can afford a trip to Europe, a retreat in a monastery in Ireland or France or Italy may provide an experience which helps your search in the following ways:

1. It will take you far away from your daily routine and responsibilities.
2. It will take you into the heart of Catholicism, the towns and villages where it was first practised as an organised religion.

3. Undertaking a retreat within a monastery will provide a total immersion in the religious experience.
4. You will be surrounded by like-minded people who can further your understanding.

Another example of changing your life through travel might be planning a trip to help you work on your fear of risk and the unknown. Perhaps you are hoping to leave your job and start up your own small business but keep coming up with excuses which, so far, have kept you desk-bound in an environment you loathe. Because of the new business plans, your travel budget is small. What low-priced 'attitude changing' travel adventures are available?

Many Australians undertake challenge programs for a week or longer at locations such as Camp Eden in the hinterland of the Gold Coast, where they expose themselves to physical and mental challenges. Not everyone can afford this type of resort, so other ways of achieving a similar outcome might be to join a walking tour or cycling tour across terrain which is unfamiliar. If you undertake such a trip on your own, for example cycling in the outback, you will probably encounter at least three major challenges:

1. The dynamics involved in such small group adventures (overcoming shyness, getting on with different personalities).
2. The physical challenge of the walk or the bike ride.
3. The mental challenge of the landscape and different environment.

By the end of your trip you may know enough about yourself to be able to make sound decisions regarding your business plans.

Travelling in order to make a difference in your life can often prove expensive. Being prepared to lower your expectations regarding accommodation can help, but often it will come down to making a decision about how much this trip might mean to you, and therefore how important it will seem in retrospect to those meals out, new clothes and other expenditure you will need to forgo.

For those unsure of how to make useful connections between the types of change they wish to implement, and the places they might go, a great starting book is *The Art of Travel* by Alain de Botton, a whimsical and enjoyable look at the way we are created by our journeys.

Katie Richards: Getting a new life in London

I was 21 when I set sail for England on the old Chandris liner, *Australis*. I'd reached a plateau in my job; after three years it no longer excited me. What did excite me were visions of foreign cities, and names like Piccadilly, Florence, the Sorbonne, and St Petersburg. I had to go. I had to know these places as more than names in an atlas. I had to go now. Within three months I'd bought the one-way ticket, given notice and told my parents. Most of my friends and work colleagues told me I was mad, and that I would never get a job on my return. This only made me more determined to go. I contacted my friend Sally with whom I planned to stay in London, to let her know I was finally on my way. 'Great,' she said, 'but I'll be in Edinburgh.' In for a penny, in for a pound I thought, and went anyway.

Saying goodbye to my family and friends was the toughest thing I'd done in my life. I suddenly realised that all my support structures, and all the love I'd ever known, was there, lined up on the dock, waving and throwing streamers, and I was on the vessel slowly moving away. I went down to my cabin, and the three strangers on the other bunks, and howled my heart out. The passage from Melbourne to Sydney took two days and was so rough most passengers stayed in their cabins, too sick to even make meal times. Sydney meant solid shore, and dinner with an old friend, who offered wine and a shoulder to cry on before pouring me back onto the ship. By Auckland I had made many new friends, including one with whom I would share a flat, boyfriends, clothes, cigarettes and many travel adventures. Very quickly I learnt that up until now life had been safe, predictable, and usually lived with other people's expectations in mind. Now was my chance to be the type of person I wanted, and to seize or create pportunities and challenges as I wished. I was away for eighteen months, and that trip not only began a lifelong love of travel and adventure, it opened my eyes to the wonderful possibilities the world has to offer for those willing to take a risk. Thirty years later I am still enjoying the benefits of my first big travel adventure.

What types of experiential travel are available?

Experiential travel, special interest travel, travel with a purpose – call it what you will, this form of travel is probably the fastest growing category across the world. Why? Because so many people genuinely want to experience another region or country in a more intimate way than sitting on a coach

CHECKING IT OUT WITH THOSE WHO'VE GONE BEFORE...

The best thing about travel contacts is that one leads to another, and the Internet, in particular, offers a rich source of travel possibilities. How do you test if the travel company you source via the web or from a book or brochure is financially sound? Simply telephone them and ask for contact details from clients who have previously enjoyed their tours. They will probably have a list of clients who agree to this. They may need to check the client's availability, but if they refuse outright, or say no such information is available, it will be easy to draw your own conclusions.

and looking through the window as the vehicle moves quickly past the great sights of the world. They want to smell, taste, touch and absorb the different environments.

Experiential travel is a wonderful way of challenging yourself. It will vary enormously according to the period of time you have available, your budget, your interests and your courage. There are no right answers, or one-size-fits-all solutions to your search of the ultimate experience, but starting with your dreams and passions makes a lot of sense.

The resources for this chapter can only offer a starting point. They fall into seven categories of travel:

- learning
- volunteering
- adventure
- activity
- cultural
- wellbeing
- spiritual

many of which will overlap, but should provide a useful framework with which to start your research. Because there is so much material on offer for these forms of travel, this chapter concentrates on two or three easily accessible resources in each category, with more listed in the Resources section. Most of these resources will lead to others, and you will quickly be able to refine your search to those which are most useful.

Learning journeys

Educational tourism can provide a fabulous opportunity for you to test a new skill, career or area of academic interest without a full commitment to a diploma, degree or change of profession. It can also allow you to learn at a more intense pace, if the normal day-to-day distractions are removed. If the environment is a match to the subject matter (archaeology in Eritrea, for example), then you will probably experience the ultimate learning journey. Many companies specialise in learning opportunities for the young, the older and those in between. Language courses, in particular, abound and often it is best to start with the particular language association. For instance the Goethe Institute, Alliance Français, and the Centre for Italian Studies all offer courses in language 'on site'. Archaeological experiences are offered by the magazine *Archaeological Diggings*, as well as Archaeology Australia, a not-for-profit organisation. Another useful starting point is Alumni Travel which commenced at the University of Sydney in 1987, and now handles inbound as well as outbound tour groups.

FAMILY HISTORY

A very special form of travel learning sits in a category of its own — genealogy. This form of travel requires a lot of homework *before* you leave. Do not be like David who rocked up to the records office in Dublin seeking his family history — only to be told that unless he had information on his grandparents' departure from Ireland (available from records easily located in Australia), there was little that could be done. Don't let this happen to you — contact the Society of Australian Genealogy which holds national and international records, and start your journey here.

Through the eyes of a volunteer

Travelling as a volunteer worker can prove to be one of the most satisfying experiences of all, not only because of the value you have added to another community, but also because of the unique perspective you can gain on a different destination, and the fellow volunteers you may meet. Usually you will be required to pay your own transport costs to and from the project, and in some cases, you may be required to pay towards your board and food. Deciding whether you wish to volunteer within your own country or abroad is usually a good starting point for your research. Australian Volunteers International is Australia's largest international volunteer organisation, sending people to 68 countries throughout Asia, Africa, the Pacific, Latin America, the Middle East, as well as in Indigenous communities in Australia. Projects vary from sending accountants to Afghanistan to sending mechanics to South Africa. For those with a strong interest in environmental activities, Earthwatch Institute, Conservation Volunteers Australia and AESOP offer well-run programs, many of which include international volunteering projects. For something a little closer to home, contact WWOOF (Willing Workers on Organic Farms) for their handbook of farm-stay options in Australia.

Asking for adventure

How do you define adventure? For some it might be as simple as a walking holiday in the foothills, instead of driving, for others it may be a full-on bungee jump from New Zealand's highest peak. Adventure travel does not necessarily mean having a life-changing experience. But it might provide a way of removing yourself from your daily distractions and experiencing a sport, activity or environment for the first time in a way that refreshes you for your regular life, or offers new insights into other possibilities.

Walking is one of the most popular forms of active travel – probably because it is cheap, most people can do it, and you actually see and experience more from street level than any other form of transport. The flexibility is also appealing. You can walk alone, in small groups, which are self-organised, or book a tour where your luggage is ferried to the next destination by minibus, while you amble across the fields with a small backpack and map. Walking tours are readily accessible in just about every country on the face of the earth. Inspire yourself with some of those listed in the Resources section – but don't forget International Park Tours who offer some excellent tours in Australia and New Zealand as well. You might also whet your appetite checking out adventure magazines in newsagents.

Renee Shapero: Achieving the dream

I was 74 when I climbed to the top of the Great Wall of China. This was the fulfilment of a lifelong dream, starting from the day, as a nine-year-old in London's East End, that I learnt about a wall in China which was so massive, it could be seen from the moon. Soon after I went on my first big journey, when I was sent to Ely in Cambridgeshire, to escape the bombs of the Second World War. After the war my new husband and I took a bigger journey still when we migrated to Australia.

After raising and educating three sons, we travelled back to see family in the UK many times, and included side trips to places like Germany, Italy, Israel, America, Hawaii, and Hong Kong. But my husband wouldn't agree to go to China. So when my 40-year-old son David was planning a break, and knew my 'Great Wall' dream was very much alive, he volunteered to travel with me.

Our first stop was Hanoi, in Vietnam, where we stayed in a two-star hotel. My white hair earned me great respect, and I enjoyed that enormously. An overnight boat trip to Halong Bay was very basic – at best it would rate half a star – but so much fun, with younger travellers and delicious food. Clambering from one boat to the next for a dim sum luncheon was challenging, but I yelled at everyone not to worry, I'd manage it, and I did. This was also thanks to the years of adult netball which kept me fit. I just loved the atmosphere of Hanoi, particularly the different shopping streets – the street of shoes, the street of haberdashery, and the street of saucepans. While in Vietnam we walked, dined at street stalls, travelled in cyclos, and even navigated mountain roads on a motorbike. From Hanoi we flew to Beijing and stayed in the Hutongs – these are comfortable motel-style accommodation, with gardens and waterfalls, hidden behind huge gates. Finally the day came when we journeyed by taxi to the Wall. We slowly climbed the steps to achieve my dream. At the top, we hugged each other, and shed a few tears. It was worth waiting for, I'd wanted it so badly, and we stayed up there for hours, just soaking it all up.

I felt as though I'd really made it. With David, I'd experienced a real adventure and not just a holiday.

The activity-based break

Activity-based travel has a huge crossover with cultural tourism, but can best be defined by the fact that you are travelling to a destination in order to do something rather than just look and see. How will this change your life? It may not, but by exploring your passions and hobbies in a different setting with like-minded people, you may be able to see possibilities for turning this interest into something more significant in your life. It is impossible to list all the different types of activities that might be included in this category, but just about anything you enjoy as a hobby or career can be enhanced by deepening your skills and understanding of this pursuit in a different location. Perhaps it's wine appreciation, cooking, singing, creating mosaics, tango dancing, embroidery, or stamp collecting. Searching for a course or program on the Internet or in the *Yellow Pages* is a good start, but so are local guilds and associations such as the Mosaic Associations of Australia, or the Embroiderers Guild. Another excellent starting point is the small group tour companies such as Peregrine, Headwaters, Explore Worldwide, and Sherpa Expeditions. If your activity is sporting based (either as a spectator or a participant), again there is a wealth of tennis ranches, golfing clinics, or horse-riding trips which may fit the bill. Start with the sporting resources listed in *Traveling Solo* by Eleanor Berman, or contact a local sporting association for a national body. If you are keen to gain a greater understanding of the natural world, visit the World Wild Life Fund for Nature at <www.panda.org> and click on the 'how you can help' button. The United States branch also offers a free travel newsletter at <www.worldwildlife.org>.

Culturally inclined

Cultural travel enables greater insights into a country's history and the way the local people have lived, or currently live. This is a huge category, and may be academically or historically focused (studying Minoan society at Knossos, for example) or more generally linked to the current culture – gastronomic tours in Thailand or opera appreciation in Vienna. As with activity-based travel, a good starting point for cultural tourism is with local associations and societies (wine appreciation, cooking). You may also consider contacting specialist travel agencies (Travel Associates, Mary Rossi Travel, The Travel Store) or visiting specialist travel bookstores as a starting point. The index at the back of *Gourmet Traveller* magazine also offers some interesting alternatives.

Biddy Naylor: My time to have fun

Last month in Tuscany one of the guests on my walking tour was a 40-year-old woman who had given herself the holiday as a birthday present. On the night of her birthday, we gathered for dinner, had a great meal, lots of wine, and wore masks to celebrate her day. It was so much fun, and great to be with women who felt so free. I love doing my tours with Australian women – they have so much humour, and are so flexible.

I began my Valentine Tours in 1998 when I was 49. I had been on a walking tour in Europe with friends and I was sure there was a market for the type of trip we did – not as tourists, but some serious walking in Italy or France. I had been a social worker for 25 years, and was definitely ready for a more light-hearted occupation. My husband was really supportive – he loves travel as much as I do. I speak French and Italian – they had been my favourite subjects at school. So I spent some time registering the business, seeking legal and marketing advice, working out brochures, promotion, publicity and what the bottom line would be. I don't think I was courageous – I was just seeking a fun thing to do.

The trips are working really well. I have a minimum of six guests, and enjoy my time with them so much. We don't stagger from town to town, but are based in one small village and walk out from there each day for a few hours. They are for females only, and we tend to attract women who are seeking travel on their own terms – not those of a partner or children. Most have been to Europe at least a few times already, and are now seeking an experience different from the mass tourism one. They are also interested in the essence of the journey, and the company of the other women, rather than the more goal-oriented style of male travel.

I don't see my change of career from social worker to the travel industry as a particularly courageous move. I get to spend four months a year in Europe, and indulge my love of language. Maybe I could have known more about marketing before I started, but nothing replaces your own steep learning curve. And if I'd known how much fun this would be, I'd just have done it a lot earlier.

Wellbeing

Travelling to enhance one's physical and mental wellbeing is becoming more and more popular. Initially associated with the more affluent visitor to exclusive spas and retreats, there are now many programs on offer which cater to all budgets as well as to those seeking not only physical but mental wellbeing. Whether your ambition is to lose weight, improve your fitness, clear your head, challenge your fears, or give up an addiction, there is a program available. Again, knowing what you want is of most assistance in finding information, but if it is a domestic adventure, starting with the state (or regional) tourism office is probably the quickest way to assess what's on offer. If you are seeking a wellbeing experience offshore, try an Internet search with 'wellbeing retreat' as the subject. Maybe a yoga or pilates retreat is for you? Try reading *Sanctuaries* by Barbara Hasslacher, for a listing of some alternatives.

Seeking spirituality

Retreats, immersion, monasteries, time out to ponder … and to learn about different religious orders. Perhaps the most significant form of journey you might take — but how do you know about what's on offer? Again, coming back to your area of interest is your best starting point. For instance, Buddhism is such a vast area of spirituality encompassing many different orders. Try starting with a local Buddhist organisation, find out a little more about that group, and then use the information you gain to move toward the most appropriate retreat, experience for you and your connection with this religion. Don't just focus on the faith — consider the areas where this faith might be strongest, and contact organisations, temples, individuals who might know more (for example, the Australian-Tibetan society). If you have no particular faith in mind, but would like to explore mind-enhancing opportunities such as meditation, or to test yourself in a silent order, obtain a copy of *Sanctuaries* by Barbara Hasslacher, which lists retreats in Australia, New Zealand and the South Pacific. The Ian Gawler Foundation in regional Victoria offers retreats, as well as being an excellent resource for contacts and books on this subject. If this all sounds too local, try searching on Google for 'spiritual retreats', adding in the country you prefer. This will bring up thousands of listings, but somewhere in there may be the one for you.

SEEKING INSPIRATION?

The great thing about serious travellers is that they are often adept at sharing their experiences via the written word. Exacerbate your travel bug by reading accounts by other travellers who stopped dreaming, and started doing it.

Try *Full Tilt* by Dervla Murphy who rode from Dunkirk to New Delhi on her bicycle, or *Long Distance Information* by Julie Welch who used marathon running in France as a way of solving family issues. Lynette Chiang who searched for, and found, *The Handsomest Man In Cuba*, and Ben Kozel who spent *Five Months in a Leaky Boat* in Mongolia and Siberia. None of these travellers had a huge budget – but all created a new space in their lives by venturing out into the world. Prefer anthologies? Don't go past *A House Somewhere*. Edited by Don George and Anthony Sattin, this is an evocative compilation of writings from those who have chosen to move their hearts and homes.

Going solo

Too often the world of travel advertisements and tour brochures seems based on the concept of twin share. But the reality is that the single households in Australia and the Western world are the fastest growing category. Many travel specialists are starting to recognise this and to offer opportunities for single travellers. But solo travel is not just for singles – it's also for those in relationships who wish to have a separate adventure from their partner. As with so many aspects of our lives, with travel the grass can be greener. Often those who have to travel alone would kill to have a companion. But the converse can also be true. Many times one half of a couple will desperately want the space and freedom and sheer selfishness of solo travel.

Regardless of the reason why you are a solo traveller, take the time to understand expectations and concerns you may have about your trip.

CHECKLIST – GOING SOLO

- Why am I going?
- What do I hope to achieve?
- How will I guard against isolation?
- What associations or groups can I utilise?
- Does this trip coincide with my interests or passions?
- Have I researched the destination thoroughly?

This is how the Going Solo checklist was used by a widower forced to travel for the first time by himself:

Robert is 48 and recently widowed. His wife had loved the countryside and they spent most of their holiday time together driving in the outback. He has always had a strong desire to visit New York, and is planning a two-week trip in the northern autumn.

Why am I going? Because I've never had the opportunity before, and I'm extremely keen.

What do I hope to achieve? I want to break out of my personal rut, see new sights, feel the energy, and have a drink at the Algonquin Hotel.

How will I guard against isolation? I will take a three-day photography course which I have located and booked on the Internet. Hopefully this will enable me to meet some like-minded souls.

I am being met at the airport by the Big Apple Greeters, and will be taken to my hotel by a friendly New Yorker.

What associations or groups can I utilise? Apart from the Big Apple Greeters, I will meet some members of the Long Island Rotary club.

Does this trip coincide with my interests or passions? I am so ready for a city holiday – art galleries, shops, restaurants, culture – this will be the fulfilment of a dream.

Have I researched the destination thoroughly? Not yet, but I am ready to get on the Internet, and I have the *Lonely Planet Guide*, so I am feeling pretty confident.

Robert's perspective won't suit everyone, but he has shown an ability to think through potential lonely spots in his trip, and structure it so he will have a degree of companionship, which he can build upon if he wishes.

Expectations

Your expectations of travel may vary from trip to trip, but if you are clearly aware of what you hope to gain from a travel adventure, you are more likely to achieve it. If, for instance, you are newly widowed, feeling isolated and depressed, and think a break from home will help, it is vital that you ensure where you are going will provide some support structure so you don't end up lost and lonely in a hotel room on the other side of the world. A comprehensive guide to travelling by yourself is *Traveling Solo* by Eleanor Berman. If you plan to go away a lot by yourself, this is an excellent resource book. Or try the Going Solo checklist in this chapter.

Don't forget that there are degrees of solo travel — try to work out if part of the thrill of your journey will be the opportunity to travel totally alone, whether you wish to be alone for just part of the time, and would like to hook up with a group or a tour for the remainder, or whether being part of a small group adventure the whole time will suit you best. If the latter is the case, check the Resources section for Sherpa Expeditions, Headwater, Peregrine, Intrepid, and Explore Worldwide tours.

FEARS OF SINGLE TRAVELLERS

Security — *I am afraid I will be vulnerable in strange locations on my own, particularly at night.*

You may well be — but you may be equally vulnerable in your own neighbourhood. Check out the list of strategies in *Traveling Solo* to help allay your fears.

Loneliness — *I am just scared of going alone and being by myself and depending on myself. I may just end up really lonely.*

This is a possibility — but it's one that can be minimised by careful planning as in the Robert example above. You may also return home more independent, and totally triumphant at not just surviving, but actually thriving, in a foreign location.

ADVANTAGES OF SOLO TRAVEL

- You get to go where you want and do what you want.
- You get to read as much as you want.
- You will probably notice more when you are on your own.
- People are more likely to strike up a conversation with a single traveller than with a couple.
- The sheer independence of getting around by yourself is a very heady (and addictive) drug.

Maximising your enjoyment of solo travel

You may have chosen to be a single traveller, or this could just be a situation you are in. Either way, you can maximise your enjoyment of the experience by thinking through the following tips.

- Follow your interests and passions – even if you are lonely you will still be doing something you love.
- Don't go looking for romance – a great bonus if it happens, but terribly disappointing if it doesn't.
- Force yourself to talk to as many people as possible – practise before you go, in your own language, or that of your destination. Expect some knock-backs, and determine to be philosophical if you receive them.
- Check the state or national tourist offices for your destination to see if they have a greeters' program. These are in place in locations as diverse as Melbourne and New York. They will not guarantee a new best friend, but they will organise for you to be met as you arrive, and transported to your accommodation by a friendly local.
- Consider backpacker or hostel accommodation at least part of the time. Not quite the Ritz but far more likely to bring you into contact with fellow travellers of all ages and persuasions.

- Eat your main meal at lunchtime. This will help keep food bills down, allow you to return to your accommodation in daylight if security is an issue, and prevent you from feeling like the only single in a candlelit restaurant full of couples holding hands.
- Try to negotiate regarding the dreaded single supplement usually forced upon those who book single accommodation – it's always worth asking, and some companies do not apply it.
- Keep a journal. It's not just a great record of new sights and sensations – but also a trusted, discreet friend to whom you can pour out your heart if you have an attack of the blues.

A career in travel

Working in the travel sector sounds like a dream job for those who are passionate about travel. Others will point out the antisocial hours, long periods of time spent away from the family, and low salaries. But for the true travel aficionado these are mere inconveniences on the way to their idea of nirvana – a suitcase, a ticket and a map.

If this describes how you feel about the possibility of working in travel, take heart from the following statistics gathered by the Australian Tourism Commission in 2001–2:

- The Australian tourism sector provided employment for more than half a million people during this period, some 6 per cent of total employment.
- International visitors spent 17.1 billion dollars on goods and services.

The tourism sectors of most countries are also showing similar gains, and so opportunities for employment are very positive. These opportunities are not just restricted to the young and athletic. They exist at all levels, and for all age groups.

So how do you get started? Apart from the general career change strategies outlined in Part Three, you can research specific tourism prospects by firstly defining the type of tourism which interests you the most, and the key players within this sub-category. For instance, you may be keen on working in a specific field (eco-tourism), or a particular region (the Kimberleys), or country (China) or activity (nature photography). You might feel more comfortable starting by working for a company already active in the field of your choice. On the other hand, you might wish to jump in the deep end by starting as a freelance, or with your own small business. Fill in the Finding a Job in Travel checklist in the Resources section, and then start contacting the specific organisations which service your areas of interest. If they cannot help you, ask who can, and continue the search. If you can afford it, go to the location where you wish to base yourself, and do your research on the spot. If you can't do this, then hit the phone, Internet, fax, or write letters. Persistence and passion will be your greatest allies here. And before you say, 'But I've left my run too late', consider the experience of Pam Dimond who began her travel career in her late forties.

Pam Dimond: The people person

My first travel adventure was to Bali in 1976 with my then husband and two-year-old son.

I was 22 and determined not to miss out on adventure just because we had had a child. We stayed for a few months and travelled the island on a motorbike. My career was in catering, which included running a café and catering business in Sydney, as well as enjoying the occasional classes with chefs in Italy and France.

When I was 46 I answered an Intrepid advertisement for a tour leader in China. I was older than all the other applicants (by a long way) and thought that my age might be a problem but I made it through the four interviews, happily based purely on suitability for the job.

My role is to accompany groups on tours around China, Central Asia and Vietnam, and organise transport, accommodation, meals and activities. I've also led tours to Russia. The leader can be required to be everything from counsellor to group entertainment. I didn't have any Chinese language when I started, but now speak a little Mandarin. The most important thing is that you are a people person and enjoy all different ages, backgrounds and nationalities. You also need to be well travelled, open-minded, experienced in managing money, and able to react well in crisis situations.

The best things about my job are people first, second and third: the people you meet leading trips in China, the strong friendships you form with other leaders, and the friendships with local operators and guides who introduce us to their culture and take us into their families and communities. I love travelling to many different interesting and fascinating places, and the freedom from routine. No Mondays or weekends, a different waking time every morning and never having to clean a room, make a bed or wash up.

The downsides include having to deal with difficult people who choose to go to China but expect it to be just like home and get extremely upset with the differences instead of accepting and enjoying them. I don't have a normal social life as I'm constantly travelling. My work doesn't end after eight hours but goes 24 hours a day, sometimes for four weeks straight. It's challenging to always be putting everyone else first, and hardest of all is getting close to people after spending an intense few weeks of your lives together and then having to say goodbye.

But I'd do it all over again tomorrow. This is the best job I've ever had. I would encourage anyone who is thinking of tour leading to just go for it. After three years in China, I now have a house in the south of China and plan to set up a small school in the countryside where Chinese cooking will be taught by a qualified cook. I hope to combine this with tour-leading part-time.

Finding a satisfying career in travel isn't necessarily easy. As with many of our life dreams, from the bottom of the mountain, the peak looks an awfully long way away. But seeing the tiny figures of those ahead, steadily trudging their way upward, reminds us that just about anything is possible if you want it badly enough.

I'd love to just take off somewhere exotic, but I never seem to have the money or the courage ...

WHAT'S STOPPING YOU?

So what's exotic? According to the dictionary, the definition includes strikingly unusual or colourful in appearance or effect, strange, exciting. This gives a lot of scope for those wishing to step out of their day-to-day existence with an adventure. The issue of money can be a challenge but, depending on how badly the travel bug has bitten, not insurmountable. After looking at your essential expenditure, work out what your truly disposable income is, and plan to have an automatic debit made from your pay packet, for a weekly contribution towards a dream trip in a year's time. (For those with budgeting issues, see money-saving ideas on page 315) Request the required leave from your employer now for that date one year in advance. Then invest the $25 or so necessary to purchase a Lonely Planet guide to the destination in mind. Resolve to read this as a form of research. Supplement this information with Internet research as well as contacting the regional tourism office. Stick a picture of the destination near your work station. Start reading about solo travellers who have taken on the world. Inspire yourself.

Chapter nineteen
THE EXPATRIATE EXPERIENCE: TRADING NATIONS

Expat.

If the very word sends a thrill to your marrow, you're a prime candidate for the long-term overseas adventure. For some, short trips will satisfy their wanderlust. For you, the visit just isn't enough. You want to experience other cultures as a resident, and anything less will be shortchanging yourself.

If expatriate life is something you've always wanted to try, it doesn't have to be as daunting a change as it may sound.

Currently more than 700 000 Australians are living in other countries. Per capita, this makes us one of the most adventurous nations in the world, no doubt influenced by our 'tyranny of distance'. Those who wish to travel to another country are forced to cover long distances, and so usually stay for a while. In the 1960s it became a rite of passage for many young Australians to travel to Europe or North America for a year or more. Now Australians of all ages and life stages are seeking an extended stay in another land.

If you are one, chances are you have already picked the country where you wish to stay, but the practicalities of lining up work and accommodation might be proving a little trickier.

The previously recommended strategy of trialling this move is probably out of the question – with the airfare and short-term accommodation prohibitively expensive. So most of your research will need to be done before you take the leap. If you are moving because of a job transfer, you may have employer support for initial accommodation, schooling if children are involved, household services, and moving your possessions. You may also have access to colleagues who've gone before you and can offer practical advice. If you are not supported in this way, your challenge is more demanding, but this is no reason why it can't be fun.

The best overview of the thorough preparation required for expats is in *The Expert Expatriate – Your guide to successful relocation abroad,* a book written by American authors Melissa Brayer Hess and Patricia Linderman, possessing more than 30 years of expatriate living experience between them. This compendium breaks the experience into manageable proportions: research, preparation, building cross-cultural skills, attitude and adjustment, being an expat spouse, and re-integrating upon your return to the home country. It also lists a wealth of useful resources to get you started. Its greatest value, however, lies in the realistic strategies suggested to assist with your psychological adjustment to the new environment. For those 'left behind' the life of the expat can seem extremely glamorous. But this view usually fails to take into account the frustrations of re-learning basics in a foreign environment, often hampered by less than perfect communication skills.

John and Enid Robinson: Starting again

In their early fifties, John and Enid Robinson decided to leave their three adult children and home in Melbourne and move to Dubai to develop John's recruitment business. They had previously lived in Kuwait, so were not strangers to the expat life, but they still found the first few months a trying time. John summarises their experience:

THE FIVE BEST THINGS ABOUT OUR CHANGE OF COUNTRY:

1. The chance to experience a different culture from the inside.
2. Having a fresh start, the excitement of organising a house, furniture, and making new friends.
3. The opportunity to do very well in business by bringing my international and Australian experience to a developing market.

4. The challenge of creating business in a completely different environment. Discovering what works and what doesn't in a unique market.
5. There is no income tax in the United Arab Emirates, therefore the individual is directly and fully rewarded for effort and success.

THE FIVE WORST ASPECTS:

1. Missing family and good friends left behind.
2. I miss Australia. It is a superb country with friendly, open people and is very well organised. By comparison, most other countries in the world are much more difficult and frustrating to live in.
3. However long we live in Dubai we will always be outsiders. We are part of sub-communities (Australians, recruitment industry, various societies, etc.) but not part of the national community.
4. The scarcity of good Australian wines.
5. The expense of starting again, sometimes doubling up on the things you have such as houses, cars, computers, etc.

WHAT I WISH I HAD KNOWN BEFORE THE MOVE:

1. The residency and work permit procedure. This time could have been halved if I had known in advance what was required and when.
2. Some of the local quirks that increase the frustration level for newcomers, for example, not being allowed to buy a car, open a bank account or sign a rental agreement until I have residency, which can take three months.
3. Those products which are not available in the local market, which I could have brought with me.
4. The cost of the major items to be purchased.
5. Who to talk to in the local Australian expat community for on-the-ground (invaluable) advice.

Getting started

There are eight main steps:

1. Gather information
2. Move from the general to the specific
3. Review your work/activity options
4. Do a realistic cost projection
5. Review income expectations
6. Set a timeline
7. Do an emotional checklist
8. Review a cultural readiness checklist

1. Gather information

Become a total zealot when it comes to information about your new location. Start with the Department of Foreign Affairs and Trade (DFAT) website, and download all the brochures on living and working overseas, as well as checking travel information and consular contact details for your intended country of residence. Find out the main newspaper in the area you will visit, and read it as much as possible either online or by a subscription. Often an English language newspaper is available as well. All the points about research in the earlier part of this chapter still apply to an international departure. Note all the specific resources in the *Expert Expatriate* which you can check out online. The SBS (Special Broadcasting Service) guides to the world are invaluable. Access from Dymocks Booksellers, or browse on the SBS web page under 'SBS store'. Highly recommended are the *SBS World Guide*, the language guides, and the individual 'Culture Smart' guides published by Explore Australia. Go to your library and grab every other book you can find that's relevant. Invest in a Lonely Planet guide to your new town or city or country – it will repay you many times with objective, current information and a great overview of the good, the bad and the ugly.

2. Move from the general to the specific

It's fine to dream about living in Tuscany, British Columbia or South-West England. But your dream will not progress while it's stuck in such general territory. Try to gain sufficient knowledge to move toward a more specific location. For instance, you may redefine the above regions into:

- Tuscany – a small village near Sienna, with possibilities for work nearby.
- British Columbia – a well-serviced town near a national park with opportunities for a hiking business, perhaps Clearwater.
- South-West England – a large town, with lots of cultural activities, well serviced by transport and within a two-hour drive to London on the motorway – maybe Bath.

As you refine these possibilities, your questions will become more specific to the area, and the answers more useful for the hard logistical and financial planning you need to do.

3. Review your work/activity options

If you've already got a job in the new location, fine. If not, it can be difficult to source one from another continent. It's time to acquaint yourself with international recruitment agencies and to check out newspapers from the area. There are many, many such recruitment agencies, and the best way to start is to research via a professional association representing your profession – for example a nursing association, teachers union or human resource managers association. Remain flexible regarding your skills and how you might use them. If you are not planning to enter paid employment, it is equally as important to plan how you might spend your time. It is possible to be bored, lonely or despondent even though you have relocated to the most romantic/exciting/thrilling city on Earth. Work out why you want to go, and what mix of activities will succeed in delivering the life balance which best suits you. For instance, you may leap at the suggestion of your partner's work promotion to Brussels. Define what it is about Brussels that really excites you (proximity to France and Spain, opportunity to use language skills, being in the centre of political Europe?) and consider activities associated with these positives (painting excursions to the South of France, ceramic classes in Seville, language classes in Brussels, the possibility of working for the Economic Union or volunteering for an overseas agency.

4. Do a realistic cost projection

Fares, accommodation and moving costs may be easy to ascertain, but what about the 'hidden' costs that seem manageable until they are printed on a frighteningly high credit card bill which prevents you going out and enjoying yourself after you've arrived? Consider the real costs of moving by talking to someone who has done it before. Pick their brains re items which should go on the list: visas, mail relocation, power connection, vaccinations, parking permits?

5. Review income expectations

This is easier to do if you have employment lined up, or a stable stream of income, perhaps a retirement pension. It becomes more difficult to project if you are searching for a job in the new country and have yet to ascertain when and if some income will kick in. In the absence of any better information, start with the income you have today, and run with two projections – one where you do not find a job for twelve months, and one where you find a job on a very low income. If you can still afford to go, a well-paying job will be a real bonus.

6. Set a timeline

Now your plans are firming up, set some deadlines. Write priority lists for six months before, four months, two months, one month and one week. Bear in mind that items such as visas, medical requirements, and banking changes always take longer than you think. See if that mountain of activity can comfortably fit into your timeline. No way? Then try to move departure date.

THE DAYS OF THE RAJ ARE OVER ...

A recent article in the *Straits Times* newspaper in Singapore noted the following significant changes in expatriate assignments abroad:

- Expatriates are no longer receiving generous compensation packages with school fees, golf club membership, housing, food, car, annual home leave and relocation expenses.
- The new breed of expat is more likely young, single and on a short-term assignment. Their salaries are more likely to be tied to local salaries, and only accommodation or modest living expenses are offered as extras.
- Many companies are also reducing expensive expat postings by using cheaper options including short-term technical transfer assignments, increased business travel, telecommuting, video conferencing and local hires.

So if one of the attractions of expat life is the cushy lifestyle, it might be time to think again.

7. Emotional checklist

How capable are you of saying goodbye to most of your family and friends, if not all? If they are going with you, are you all equally keen? How do you behave under pressure? Do you and your wife fight like cat and dog? Do you and your brother have days without speaking? Are you taking children? How do you plan to handle their adjustment process? How do you plan to resolve these differences without friends and family around to comfort or mediate? Are you a self-starter? Are you flexible? Consider some of the personal skills you may need to develop.

8. Cultural readiness checklist

If you are moving from suburban Australia to a suburb in North America, it is likely, apart from a few quirky differences, that your language skills will enable you to communicate immediately with most of the locals. If your move is to a safari park in Nairobi, you may find language just one of many hurdles you will face. Some things you would never imagine can cause real embarrassment and distress in other cultures. How much do you need to find out about a country or a region before you go? What do you know about the history, ancient and recent? The local people? The environment? The current political situation? The living conditions? The mix of racial groups? The issues of concern to locals? Rate your knowledge on all of the above, and then get moving to fill in the gaps. There are any number of resources available, but two good starting points are the SBS books (see above) and television programs, as well as specific Lonely Planet guides, which are up to date, informative and objective. The Culture Shock series (books on living in various locations) also provide insiders' knowledge on different destinations. Borrow videos, both documentaries and feature films, which feature your destination. Find out from consulates about associations for new chums such as chambers of commerce, sporting or special interest groups and friendship associations. See if you can locate an email pen pal before you leave home. Start language classes – don't wait for the taxi at the airport to test your Spanish.

WHY ARE YOU *REALLY* GOING?

Are you leaving Australia to pursue a life in a new country because of the opportunities offered?

  OR Are you running away from problems which will follow you anyway?

  OR Are you deliberately placing yourself in an unfamiliar environment to test your mettle?

  OR Are you escaping a cloistered family environment?

Think about the reasons why you are going, and if they seem more about escaping negatives than embracing a positive new path, maybe this move needs closer scrutiny?

Happy expats

The following characteristics of successful expats comes from John and Geraldine McGrath, veterans of six years in Hong Kong and fourteen years in Singapore.

Characteristics of successful expats

The employee (John)

1. Flexibility.
2. Knowing a local language helps, but in Asia this can mean learning many.
3. You often need a rapid understanding of local culture in terms of do's and don'ts.
4. Many expats and functions mean it requires work to get out and meet people.
5. It's good to remember that part of the adventure is discovery. There will always be some mistakes.
6. Australians as a group are adaptable, without the reserve that is often associated with the English or the brashness associated with Americans. This adaptability, a 'she'll be right' attitude, and a willingness to meet people as equals means Australians fit in very well, and better than others.

The spouse (Geraldine)

1. Open-minded, adaptable.
2. Willingness to befriend anybody and everybody.
3. Be prepared to attend many business functions.
4. A transposable occupation helps.
5. An interest in (not necessarily a love of) the new community/country.
6. A desire to look beyond your immediate environment of family and friends, even if you consider yourself totally satisfied with your life as it is ... should be Number One.

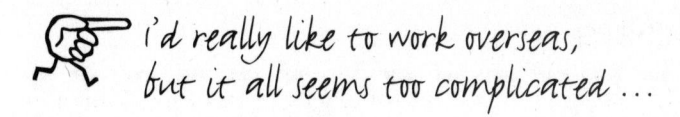

I'd really like to work overseas, but it all seems too complicated ...

WHAT'S STOPPING YOU?

When you stop to consider the vast number of possibilities for life as an expat, the decision-making process just gets harder. Don't let the limitless options daunt you. Until you go, you won't know which destination will work best. At some stage it may just be necessary to make some arbitrary decisions to narrow your scope, so you do not become paralysed by the wide variety of choices. Be led by your heart, and your passions. If you're a nurse who can get work in a wide range of countries and cultures, think hobbies, landscape, excitement. What really intrigues you about which destination? It could be the vast night skies in the Yukon, the teeming marketplaces of the Middle East, the humour and pub life in Dublin. Stick a pin in the map, commit to the locale, and get stuck into the research. Who knows what new life is awaiting you?

How Christine and Marius planned

Remember Christine and Marius from page 209? How did they get their planning right?

Dreams and objectives

- 'Just think of anything in the world you would really like to do and we'll work on a way to make it happen.'
- Living in Italy is the goal.
- Defining objectives associated with this goal, including more family time, personal expansion, language skills, painting — these cover the personal, the family and the creative.
- An agreed timeline (18 months).
- A method of financing the dream (renting home in Balmain).

Research

- Substantial research on the Internet.
- Language classes.
- Concerns including moving children, language challenges, official documentation, banking and health were noted up front and explored.

Expect the unexpected

- Death of Marius's father forces a rethink, change in location, and period of time to experience a different sea-change from the one they had planned.

Review periods

- Allow for an assessment and fine-tuning in line with original objectives.
- Allow for a period of adjustment by children in particular.

ON TAKING ALL FACTORS INTO CONSIDERATION:

Whenever we have come up to one of our review periods we have had some agonising moments as to whether the experience is working for him.

ON FITTING IN WITH THE LOCALS

I am also the de facto town photographer and so am continually called on when there is a communion or some such.

ON HOW IT HAS WORKED

We feel incredibly privileged to be here. It is wonderful.

Where are you going?

- What are the ways in which you'd like to change your life?
- Can you see ways these changes could be kick-started by changing location or going somewhere different, maybe on your own?
- Do you come home at night, and your house feels like a welcoming friend, or a cosy refuge from the troubles of the planet?
- Or are you merely existing in a home environment which is functional, but hardly friendly?
- Are you a confident traveller?
- If not, what worries you the most about going away? Getting out of your comfort zone? Fear of the unknown?
- Can you see ways to tackle these fears and gradually build your confidence?
- Is travelling alone a thrilling concept – or a totally worrisome chore?
- Can you recall a previous trip which caused you to come home, your soul singing, ready for new challenges and fresh adventures?
- Where was it? What created the magic?

ON YOUR WAY

No-one can time or measure or adjudicate your life changes – just when you get one bit right, another will go astray. Similarly, no one person can offer you all the wisdom you will need to navigate your way through the options, challenges and difficulties. But, like the Buddhist mantra of openness, the recognition that there is no one answer, resource or solution can free you up to see the many steps of wisdom on one of the many paths to one of the many possible solutions to your life changes.

This perception of change is not like reality TV shows when the experts come through the door, blow away your previous 'shabby' existence, and replace it with something new, exciting, glamorous, and totally foreign to your personality.

The reality of change is usually the exact opposite.

It lacks all the drama of the big makeover. It is not about experts who know more than you. It is about you as the expert in your own life journey, and slowly, step by laborious step, working your way towards something very rough around the edges, but with a core of substance. It is about finding your own intrinsic qualities and matching them to the people, the places and the activities which sing to your soul.

Where are you at?

By now you will have a good idea of the processes and stages of change and the qualities you already possess to get you where you hope to go.

The content of Part One describes how change comes, and how it works, whilst the actual mechanics of personal, vocational, or geographical change have been highlighted in Parts Two, Three and Four.

Throughout these sections, hearing how ordinary Australians have implemented and experienced their changes will have demystified some of these life events, and added insights and information.

So what have you learnt about changing your life? It's difficult. Sometimes it doesn't work. But even giving it a go can make a difference.

When it does work, it can offer you a second life, a whole new perspective, which is so much more than a token change for change's sake.

By defining your dreams, breaking them down into achievable plans, and putting these plans into actions, you create a truly positive shift in the way you live your life.

And what conclusions can be drawn?

Change is not mysterious

At any given time a broad range of your family, friends, and acquaintances are undergoing or creating significant life change. It is not to be feared, merely to be handled.

Change is manageable

You already know much more than you give yourself credit for to manage your life changes. The information you are lacking is not rocket science. It is accessible, and your previous experiences will equip you well for future change.

Change might seem overwhelming . . .

Until it is broken down into manageable chunks.

Remember Van Gogh's series of small steps? This is first stage of your new life planning. Integrate these steps with your toolkit of resources, and you will have all you need to get you on your way.

Change is continuous

Whether you embrace it, reject it or slump into denial, change will occur in your life. This is not about choice, but something from which you cannot escape. Ultimately you are the only one who can decide how you react to change, and whether it will represent a positive or negative life force.

Change is about taking responsibility

Achieving a different type of life for some will involve radical change, for others a fine-tuning of different aspects of their current existence. It starts when you take responsibility for your future, and refuse to drive along life's highways and byways with your eyes fixed firmly on the rear-view mirror. Yes, the past is what has created you, and, for this reason, needs to be acknowledged and honoured. But it doesn't have to create your future. Your dreams and goals should be the drivers of the rest of your life.

So what does it all come down to?

Self-belief

Loving yourself sufficiently to think you are worth the effort of a fulfilling life – and caring about yourself enough to take the time out to plan it. This is obviously about your self-esteem and self-belief, but not in a self-satisfied, 'I'm good enough for me' manner, rather a 'I deserve the best I can achieve' approach.

Dreams

Taking your dreams sufficiently seriously to actually believe they will happen. Why shouldn't they? Other people's have, and very few were about winning a lottery. Think of how seriously the Webbs took their possibilities – *Think of anything in the world you'd really like to do and we'll work out a way* . . .

Inspiration

It's also about not being envious of others who have made seemingly successful life changes, but allowing yourself to become inspired by their courage, energy and vision. Admiring their methods enough to copy them. Becoming infected by their enthusiasm.

Ideas

Being open to new ideas, different ways of approaching things, and new ways of thinking. Revitalising your outlook with different sights, sounds, people and places.

Perceptions

Training your mind to see the limitless possibilities of change instead of probabilities of failure. To see setbacks as a necessary part of life's sometimes circuitous route.

Self-discipline

Willingness to do the hard yards for something that matters enormously, and your ability to stick at it.

Key resources

This list is a mix of your attitude, personality and willingness to plan well and research thoroughly. It all comes back to the suggested programs in Chapter 4: taking stock, breaking your life goal into smaller tasks, and evaluating your personal toolkit. Remember the key resources in the toolkit?

Now fill in the checklist on the following pages, breaking each of these qualities into five you already have, and five you may require in order to implement your dream. This may require a lot of thinking, and if you struggle with five you *don't* have, this is good; don't try to dredge them up, just keep moving.

Note that attitude is on the top of the list, and money on the bottom. This is not by accident. As well as your own personal qualities, other people in your life will always beat money and qualifications in helping you on your way. This is not about flaky networking, but genuinely learning from other people who are generous enough to share their experiences. Why reinvent the wheel? If they've moved to South Africa and have a perspective on the expatriate experience in Cape Town, why would you start from scratch?

Remember also that information and resources can always be obtained. The funny thing is that we often locate it just after we've learnt the hard way. Do all the research you can, and more, but don't use your research as a delaying tactic which prevents you from making hard decisions – your change will be ongoing, as will be your research. Stick to decision-making deadlines wherever possible.

In asking useful questions, there are two key observations. It's not about finding the 'right' answers; it's all about the questions and the searching process. And it's not just about 'intelligent' questions, it's also about having the courage to ask the 'dumb' questions too – often the answers to these will be of much more value.

Finance is on the bottom of the list, but it's still there. Money does matter. Those who say it doesn't matter usually have too much. Ignore them. Very few people on limited incomes think it's of no consequence. But the degree to which money matters is the critical issue. If a lack of finance is forcing you to abandon your aims, it might be timely to look at the assumptions sitting behind this decision. Do more research on the amount you really need, and think about ways of adjusting your current expenditure, increasing your income, or extending the timeline for your plans.

	RESOURCES I HAVE ALREADY	RESOURCES I MIGHT NEED
Attitude	1. 2. 3. 4. 5.	
Personality	1. 2. 3. 4 5.	
Value system	1. 2 3 4 5	
Personal experience	1 2 3 4 5	
Educational qualifications	1 2 3 4 5	
Vocational experience	1 2 3 4 5	

	RESOURCES I HAVE ALREADY	RESOURCES I MIGHT NEED
Family	1 2 3 4 5	
Friends	1 2 3 4 5	
Work colleagues	1 2 3 4 5	
Financial assets	1 2 3 4 5	
Ability to access finance	1 2 3 4 5	

In short

What is your dream? Now commit to it as the major life goal you will work toward.

- Focus on it, and give this one major life goal priority over others.
- Define it, redefine it, redefine it again.
- Describe it, draw it, grab a photo which illustrates it, and put it somewhere you will see it every day.
- Write out the steps towards achieving this dream.
- Put deadlines against these steps.
- List five books you will read, five brains you will pick, five websites you will visit, five phone calls you will make to add to your knowledge.
- Put deadlines in your diary, and stick to them.
- Review your progress every week.

You can always modify these steps, but at least you've made a start.

No-one likes to be nagged, least of all those keen to get a new life. By now you will have worked out which strategies will suit you, and which resources might be useful. You either will have decided to keep an ideas book or journal and will be enjoying the dreaming and planning you do in these, or you won't. Some of the insights will have added value to your existence, or they won't. You know that no-one lives happily ever after. That life is just one damn thing after another. And as soon as one goal is achieved, someone will probably move the goalposts. But if this book has one purpose, it is to help remove some of the excuses you might have previously made as to why you've just never got around to it. Or provide some resources or examples which might encourage you to start. We all have dreams and most of them are not impossible.

> *The scariest moment is always just before you start. After that, things can only get better.*
>
> — STEPHEN KING

If the first step is to keep on dreaming,
And the second is to believe our dreams can come true,
Then the third must be to work out how.

ENDNOTES

FOREWORD

Interview with Peter O'Connor, *The Wisdom Interviews*, hosted by Peter Thompson, ABC Radio National, 12 May 2002.

CHAPTER 1

'the night during which…prepared for tomorrow's'. William Bridges, *Managing Transitions: Making the most of change*, Nicholas Brearly Publishing Ltd, London, 1991, 1995, p. 6.

'It is better to…where one is not'. Written on the wall of the *QE2*.

Elizabeth Kubler Ross, *On Death and Dying*, Touchstone, USA, 1969.

CHAPTER 4

The goal-setting, goal planning and goal pursuit categories are based on Dr Sylvie Lapierre, 'Positive Ageing and the Realisation of Personal Goals During Retirement', delivered at Maturity Matters, International Federation of Ageing, 6th Global Conference, Perth, Western Australia, October 2002.

Jill Ker Conway, *The Road from Coorain*, Mandarin Paperbooks, London, 1990.

CHAPTER 5

Survey on downshifting was obtained from Dr Clive Hamilton, *Growth Fetish*, Allen & Unwin, Sydney, 2003, pp. 205–7.

CHAPTER 7

'History, social class…or the devil'. Richard Bolles, *How to Do Life/Work Planning*, Keynote address, International Conference on Careers Guidance, Slovenia, 5.5.1999,
   <www.jobhuntersbible.com>.

CHAPTER 8

The concept of 'filling the well' was obtained from Julia Cameron, *The Artist's Way*, Pan Books, London, 1995, pp. 20–1, 'Stocking the Pond'.

CHAPTER 11

'The problem with…a guide to the guides'. Michael McGirr, 'The Good God Guide', Review of Rachael Kohn's book *The New Believers* in the *Age*, 19–20 December, 2003.

Statistics on religious affiliations was obtained from the Australian Bureau of Statistics, 2001 *Census of Population and Housing*, copyright Commonwealth of Australia, Canberra, 2001.

CHAPTER 13

'Retrenchment and redundancy facts' were obtained from *Retrenchment & Redundancy*, Catalogue 6266, Australian Bureau of Statistics, Canberra, July 2001.

Information on how to deal with your mortgage was obtained from Lyndell Fraser, General Manager, Mortgage Wealth, Retail Banking Services, Commonwealth Bank.

Redundancy experts: Locating such specialist advice can be difficult, but start with the larger financial services groups, and ask which of their advisers are best placed to help with redundancy issues, and whether they have information nights on this topic. Centrelink is also an excellent source of specific information on this topic.

CHAPTER 14

The quote from Faith Popcorn was obtained from *The Popcorn Report: Faith Popcorn on the future of your company, your world, your life* by Faith Popcorn (HarperBusiness, 1992).

Statistics on small businesses were obtained from *Small Business in Australia*, Catalogue 1321.0, Australian Bureau of Statistics, Canberra, 2001.

Statistics on the success of small businesses were obtained from Des Knight & Noel Whittaker, *Driving Small Business*, Simon & Schuster, East Roseville, 2002.

Estimates on the cost of a franchise were obtained from Lorelle Frazer & Scott Weaven, *Franchising Australia*, Griffith University, Queensland, 2002.

CHAPTER 15

Research from the Australian Institute of Family Studies was obtained from Ilene Wolcott, 'Dimensions of retirement', Working Paper no. 14, May 1998.
    <www.aifs.org.au>

CHAPTER 16

Information on levels of wellbeing for volunteers was obtained from The Australian Unity Wellbeing Index, in partnership with Deakin University, 4th survey, October 2002.

INTRODUCTION TO PART FOUR

Peter Mayle, *A Year in Provence*, Pan Books, London, 1990.

Frances Mayes, *Under the Tuscan Sun: At home in Italy*, Random House, New York, 1997.

Sarah Turnbull, *Almost French: A new life in Paris*, Bantam, Sydney, 2002.

CHAPTER 18

Statistics on the tourism industry were obtained from the Australian Tourism Commission website, <www.atc.com.au>, based on research for 2001–2.

CHAPTER 19

The *Straits Times* article on expatriates refers to Susan Long, 'Sunday Times' section, *The Straits Times*, 16 November 2003.

ON YOUR WAY

The quote was obtained from Stephen King, *On Writing: A memoir of the craft*, Hodder & Stoughton, London, 2000.

RESOURCES

CHAPTER 1

BOOKS

Managing Transitions: Making the most of change by William Bridges (Nicholas Brealey Publishing, London, 1991, 1995).
   Much lauded change-management handbook for human resource specialists, but also of great value (leaving American management terminology aside) to help individuals understand the nature of change and how they can make their change experience as positive as possible.

CHAPTER 2

BOOKS

Harvard Business Review on Managing Your Career by Richard Boyatzis, Annie McKee and Daniel Goleman (Harvard Business School Press).
   See 'Reawakening Your Passion for Work' – a great essay for burnt-out employees wishing to consider their options.

Making Time for Me by Penelope Ody (Kyle Cathie, London, 1999).
   A holistic approach to separating want from need, and moving away from life's 'overload'.

Oh, the Places You'll Go! by Dr Seuss (Collins, Great Britain, 1990).
   A wonderful children's classic with an enduring message for all ages.

Who Moved My Cheese? by Dr Spencer Johnson (Vermilion, U.K., 1999).
   An insightful short read that helps you to test your attitude to change.

ORGANISATIONS

Association of Career Professionals International
   The website contains useful information on the career services industry including personal and professional growth.
   <www.iacmp.org>

CHAPTER 3

BOOKS

Aligning Your Work and Purpose by Grace Johnston (Information Australia, 2000).
 As the title says – a thorough examination of work, purpose and the possible interaction between.

Authentic Happiness by Martin Seligman (Random House Australia, Sydney, 2002).
 By the author of *The Optomistic Child*, a very readable overview of creating and maintaining a positive attitude.
 <www.authentichappiness.org>

Be Your Own Life Coach by Fiona Harrold (Hodder & Stoughton, Great Britain, 2000).
 The ultimate in 'you can do it' books, but, once you get through the hyperbole, lots of fun suggestions for changing your life possibilities.

How Are We to Live? by Peter Singer (The Text Publishing Company, Melbourne, 1993).
 A comprehensive discussion of the nature of ethics, and how people can live an ethical life.

It's Only Too Late if You Don't Start Now by Barbara Sher (Hodder Headline Australia, Sydney, 1999).
 Described as 'self-actualisation' for middle-aged persons, it is actually a lively and engaging offering for those wishing to 'get over themselves' and get on with life. A good resource for confronting excuses as to why you can't do something you'd really like to.

Life Strategies: Doing what works, doing what matters by Dr Phillip C McGraw (Vermilion, London, 1999).
 A very North Atlantic 'cut the bullshit' personal development treatise that has some useful suggestions and insights.

The Real Meaning of Money by Dorothy Rowe (HarperCollins, London, 1997).
 Australian psychologist Dorothy Rowe explores the meanings we've created for ourselves about how money works and its place in our lives.

Understanding the Mid-Life Crisis by Dr Peter O'Connor (Pan Macmillan, Sydney, 1995).
 The Australian classic for those undergoing significant personal turmoil in midlife.

What Color Is Your Parachute? by Richard Bolles (Ten Speed Press, Berkeley, California, 2003).
 The standard by which all other career change handbooks are judged. For those who are confused about their vocational direction, simply the best book to read and ponder.

What Should I Do with My Life? by Po Bronson (Seker & Warburg, London, 2003). Subtitled 'The true story of people who answered the ultimate question', it sounds as though it will be about those who have given their lives for their country. Instead, it's a great read which canvasses the eternal search for meaning and purpose in our lives, and how some people go about it.
<www.pobronson.com>

You Can Change Your Life by Tim Laurence (Hodder Headline, Great Britain, 2003). Promising a 'future different from your past', Tim Laurence recommends the Hoffman process as a way of healing past hurts and moving into new territory, likened to a psychological 'detox'.

COMPANIES

The Centre for Worklife Counselling
Career development and life planning resources, as well as contacts for accredited career counsellors.
<www.worklife.com.au>
<worklife@ozemail.com.au>
(02) 9968 1588

ORGANISATIONS

Australian Association of Career Counsellors
The professional body for accredited Australian career counsellors.
<www.aacc.org.au>
1800 222 390

The Australian Counselling Association
National association for counsellors and psychotherapists. Website includes a code of conduct.
<www.theaca.net.au>
(07) 3857 8288

Australian Psychological Society
The largest professional association of psychologists in Australia. Website includes explanatory notes on the difference between psychologists and psychiatrists.
<www.psychsociety.com.au>
1800 333 497

Psychotherapy & Counselling Federation of Australia, Inc.
An umbrella association representing various psychotherapy and counselling associations across Australia.
<www.pacfa.org.au>
(03) 9639 8330

Values Journey
   A company that provides presentations and workshops to help those in the corporate sector identify and integrate their personal and company values.
   <www.valuesjourney.com>
   (03) 9804 7997

WEBSITES

Changing Course
   American website with stories of people who have made major life changes, and resources for people who are planning theirs.
   <www.changingcourse.com>

Cheryl Richardson
   Cheryl Richardson has written many books on life 'makeovers'. The website contains some of this content, encouraging online interaction.
   <www.cherylrichardson.com>

International Coach Federation
   A good starting point for an understanding of what coaches might offer, how they become accredited, what their ethics could be, and what you might reasonably expect from different types of coaches.
   <www.internationalcoachfederation.com>

CHAPTER 4

BOOKS

Change Your Thinking by Sarah Edelman (ABC Books, Sydney, 2002).
   A practical guide to understanding your thought processes and overcoming negativity.

Feeling Better: A guide to mood management by Antony Kidman (Biochemical & General Services, NSW, 1998).
   A guide to mood management, but also an overview of how cognitive behavioural therapy can help to implement positive changes in your life.

From Thought to Action by Antony Kidman (Biochemical & General Services, NSW, 2001, 2nd Edition).
   A clearly and simply written manual to help overcome self-defeating behaviours and institute a positive goal-setting regime.

Positively Fearless by Vera Peiffer (Thorsons, London, 1993).
   Easy-to-read overview of how fears are created and how they can be undone.

Re: Life by Dr John Lang (Prentice Hall, Frenchs Forest, 2002).
   A lively and useful overview of creating a balanced and healthy life.

CHAPTER 5

BOOKS

The Couples' Guide to Money: How to make the most of your financial power as a couple by Linda Gough (Allen & Unwin, Sydney, 2004).
> Although written from a twosome's point of view, it makes equally good sense for singles as an introduction to how to manage, invest and increase your money.

Don't Kiss Your Money Goodbye (jointly published by ASIC and the Financial Planning Assocation of Australia (FPA), revised March 2002).
> Plain English guide to removing the risk from investing your money. You can download a copy from the ASIC consumer website or request via phone or email.
> <infoline@asic.gov.au>
> <www.fido.asic.gov.au>
> 1300 300 630.

Growth Fetish by Clive Hamilton (Allen & Unwin, Sydney, 2003).
> A considered response to society's preoccupation with economic growth and affluence.

Making Life Rich without Any Money by Phil Callaway (Harvest House Publishers, Oregon, 1998).
> Humorous but sincere, Callaway takes on the real joys of life, starting with health, family and friends. A reminder of what really matters.

Making Money Made Simple by Noel Whittaker, (Simon & Schuster, Sydney, 1992).
> A starting point for those wishing to understand the basics of personal finance management.

Making Money: The keys to financial success by Paul Clitheroe (Viking, Camberwell, 2003).
> A great starting point for your personal financial planning. Covers all the basics you need to understand.

The 9 Steps to Financial Freedom by Suze Orman (Bantam Books, Sydney, 2000).
> Written by Oprah's resident finance guru, a surprisingly concise summary of financial commonsense and how to get your act together.

ORGANISATIONS

Australian Securities and Investments Commission (ASIC)
> Federal government organisaton which enforces and regulates company and financial services laws to protect consumers, investors and creditors.
> <www.asic.gov.au>

RESOURCES

Centrelink
  The best starting point for a free, objective financial planning overview – phone or visit the website to find out when a seminar will be held locally. Seminars are directed at all Australians, and not tailored for only those who are or will be seeking a full or part pension.
  <www.centrelink.com.au>
  <national.seminar.bookings@centrelink.gov.au>
  13 63 57

Financial Planning Association (FPA)
  The professional association for financial planners in Australia, which works to raise standards in the industry and to educate the public about the need for financial planning.
  <www.fpa.asn.au>
  1800 337 301 or 1800 626 343 (Victoria only)

NICRI (National Information Centre on Retirement Income)
  A free, independent and confidential service funded by the Federal Governement, with the aim of improving the level and quality of investment information for those with modest savings, iinvesting for retirement or facing redundancy. It offers leaflets, technical papers and a freecall information line.
  <www.nicri.org.au>
  <NICRI@nicri.org.au>
  1800 020 110

CHAPTER 7

BOOKS

Are You Needing Help after Someone Has Died? (Department of Family & Community Services, Canberra, 2003).
  A guide published by Centrelink to helping people prepare for and cope with bereavement.
  <www.centrelink.gov.au>

The Beginner's Guide to Retirement by Michael Longhurst (Hodder Headline Australia, Sydney, 2000).
  A thoughtful and thorough discussion of the key issues of retirement, and strategies to maximise your successful transition from the workplace. Particularly strong on relationships.

Caring for the Aged by Gordon Hammond & Rodney Jilek (*Australian Women's Weekly* Health Series, ACP Publishing, Sydney, 2003).
  Useful resources for those dealing with ageing friends and relatives.

Don't Sweat the Small Stuff … and it's all small stuff by Richard Carlson (Hyperion, New York, 1997).
  Useful reminders of how to keep the big picture in mind.

The Five Love Languages by Gary Chapman (Moody Press, Chicago, 1992).
An exploration of the different ways we love – and what we, often unfairly, expect from our loved ones.

The Fog Garden by Marion Halligan (Allen & Unwin, Sydney, 2001).
A work of fiction based on author Marion Halligan's experience of losing her husband to cancer. A celebration of marriage, and a moving perspective on loss.

Hannah's Gifts: Lessons from a life fully lived by Maria Housden (Thorsons, London, 2002).
A mother's response to the way her three-year-old daughter faced death. Simply told and full of the joy of existence.

I Could Do Anything if Only I Knew What It Was by Barbara Sher (Hodder Headline Australia, Sydney, 2003).
For those interested in making some life changes but are unsure what they really want, this gives practical tips on finding a direction. A terrific 'excuse remover'.

It's Never Too Late by Barbara and Dick Jarvis (Lothian Books, South Melbourne, 2003).
For those seeking strategies to reintroduce romance to their lives.

Learned Optimism by Martin Seligman (Random House Australia, Sydney, 2003).
A fascinating overview of how a 'glass half empty' personality can learn to become a true optimist.

Passionate Marriage: Keeping love & intimacy alive in committed relationships by David Schnarch (Scribe Publications, Melbourne, 1997).
Clinical psychologist David Schnarch shares his observations on and case studies of the enhancement of sexual intimacy in long-term relationships.

Power of the Plus Factor by Norman Vincent Peale (Ballantine Books, New York, 1978).
Very forceful, as only Norman Vincent Peale can be, but full of useful insights into the value of attitude and persistence.

Quest for Life by Petrea King (Random House Australia, Sydney, 1992).
Health, healing and meditation for those with life-threatening illness.
<www.petreaking.com>

The Road Less Traveled by M. Scott Peck (Arrow Books, London, 1990).
This book has sold six million copies. It's no wonder. First written in 1978, it is, quite simply, a manual on how to grow up and take responsibility for your own actions.

A Round Heeled Woman by Jane Juska (Chatto & Windus, London, 2003).
In her late sixties, Jane Juska writes of her adventures of lust and love after placing an ad for a man in the literary section of the *New York Times*. A robust assertion of the mature sexually active woman.

A Short Guide to a Happy Life by Anna Quindlen (Random House Australia, Sydney, 2000).
> A very short and visually rewarding summary of the triumph of attitude, and understanding what truly matters in your life.

Side by Side: How to think differently about your relationship by Jo Lamble and Sue Morris (Finch Publishing, Sydney, 2000).
> A guide to thinking clearly about relationships, what expectations you hold and how realistic these might be. Practical and informative, it should be required reading for all those contemplating a long-term relationship.

Sometimes Hearts Have to Break by Petrea King (Random House, Sydney, 1997).
> Twenty-five case studies of those who have found healing and peace through life-threatening illness.
> <www.petreaking.com>

The Successful Self: Freeing our hidden inner strengths by Dr Dorothy Rowe (Harper Collins Publishers, London 1993).

When Bad Things Happen to Good People by Harold Kushner (Avon Books, New York, 1981).
> For anyone who ever asked, 'Why Me?', an approach to understanding and weathering the vicissitudes of life.

When Things Fall Apart: Heart advice for difficult times by Pema Chödrön (Shambhala Classics, Boston, 2000).
> Based upon Tibetan Buddhist principles, it provides ways of reordering your existence in the wake of bad news.

Your Best Year Yet by Jinny Ditzler (Thorsons, London, 1994).
> A practical and useful guide to life planning, one step at a time.

The 7 Habits of Highly Effective People: Powerful Lessons in Personal Change by Stephen R. Covey (Fireside, New York, 1990).
> A clearly written and persuasive program for managing yourself with integrity and the flow-on effect it can have on your life.

ORGANISATIONS

Australian Funeral Directors' Association (AFDA)
> A professional association which provides support for the bereaved. See the website for information on 'What do I do when someone dies'.
> <www.afda.org.au>
> (03) 9859 9966

Beyond Blue
> Federal government-funded website for those wishing to learn more about depression and its treatment. Includes a 'Do I have depression' checklist.
> <www.beyondblue.org.au>

The Family Court of Australia
> Containing a step-by-step guide to proceedings for those undergoing separation, divorce or other family concerns. Individual courts offer dispute resolution and mediation services.
> <www.familycourt.gov.au>
> 1800 050 321

National Association for Loss and Grief (NALAG)
> Non-profit Australia-wide organisation that was started after the 1977 Granville train disaster in New South Wales. Offers information and referrals for each state.
> <www.griefaustralia.org>

Relationships Australia
> Non-profit community-based organisation providing professional services to support relationships. Available nationally, some services for a fee.
> <www.relationships.com.au>
> 1300 364 277

CHAPTER 8

BOOKS

The Artist's Way by Julia Cameron (Pan Books, London, 1995).
> Excellent 'how to' workbook for those wishing to get in touch with their creativity.

A Creative Companion: How to free your creative spirit by SARK (Celestial Arts, Berkeley, California, 1991).
> As the subtitle suggests, a fun collection of strategies for unlocking your creative nature.
> <www.campsark.com>

A Decent Proposal: How to sell your book to an Australian publisher by Rhonda Whitton & Sheila Hollingworth (Common Ground Publishing, Altona, Vic, 2001).
> You would be mad to consider writing your book proposal without reading this first. Invaluable, practical information for first-time authors.
> <www.booksonwriting.com>

Everything I Know about Writing by John Marsden (Mandarin, Port Melbourne, 1993).
> How to use language to convey meaning in the most effective way. Eminently readable, and highly useful for those who wish to write better.

Inspiration Sandwich by SARK (Celestial Arts, Berkeley, California, 1992).
> Described by the author as 'food for the soul', it's a colourful workbook of creative ideas.
> <www.campsark.com>

New Journalism by E.W. Johnson and Tom Wolfe (Picador, London, 1990).
> A compilation of the best of American literary non-fiction in the sixties and seventies, showing how lyrical non-fiction writing can become.

On Writing: A memoir of the craft by Stephen King (Hodder & Stoughton, London, 2000).
> Author Stephen King muses on writing and the creative process. Part biography, part writing manual, a very user-friendly introduction to the writer's life.

The Right to Write: An invitation and initiation into the writing life by Julia Cameron (Macmillan, London, 2000).
> Writing inspiration and exercises for those seeking some structure for their scribblings.

The Writing Book: A Workbook for Fiction Writers by Kate Grenville (Allen & Unwin, Sydney, 1990).
> One of the most practical and inspiring guides to the art of writing – both fiction and non-fiction. Full of useful exercises for those wishing to practise or polish their craft.

The Writing Life by Annie Dillard (Harper & Rowe, New York, 1989).
> Writer Annie Dillard shares her love affair with words.

ORGANISATIONS

Australian Society of Authors
> Professional, not-for-profit association which promotes and protects Australian illustrators and writers. Also offers mentoring and manuscript assessment services.
> <www.asauthors.org>
> <asa@asauthors.org>
> (02) 9318 0877

Fellowship of Australian Writers
> Not-for-profit association encouraging writers through promotion of writing opportunities and readings etc. Distributes to members a bi-monthly magazine listing writing competitions and awards.
> <www.writers.asn.au>
> (03) 9528 7088

CHAPTER 9

ORGANISATIONS

Adult Education
> Tasmanian adult-education provider of long and short courses. Also offers Book Groups Tasmania and Adventures Abroad.
> <www.tafe.tas.edu.au/ae>
> (03) 6233 7237

Council of Adult Education
> Try the website for online course search and booking, or phone for a catalogue.
> <www.cae.edu.au>
> (03) 9652 0611 or 1800 601 111

Open Learning Australia
> Internet portal for registering for distance education online. Contains 'Are you ready for distance learning?' quiz.
> <www.ola.edu.au>
> 1300 363 652

The Training & Adult Education Branch (ACT)
> Manages the vocational education and training system in the ACT.
> <www.decs.act.gov/services>
> (02) 6205 8555

WEA (Worker's Educational Association)
> Voluntary, independent not-for-profit adult education organisation, offering a full range of courses, including some available online. One of Australia's largest providers of adult and community education. The website is easy to navigate and full of great course options.
> South Australia: <www.sae-wea.com.au>
> (08) 8223 1272 or 1800 638 749
> Sydney: <www.weasydney.nsw.edu.au>
> (02) 9264 2781

WEBSITES

The Good Guides
> Supports the directories sold through newsagencies, which provide facts and ratings on all Australian Universities.
> <www.thegoodguides.com.au>

Universities of the Third Age
> A site where Universities of the Third Age, particularly those in Australia and New Zealand, share ideas, resources and information. The 'Resources' button takes you to a page containing links to many other sites which offer resources for U3As, U3A members and older people in general.
> <www.u3aonline.org.au>
> <info@u3aonline.org.au>

CHAPTER 10

BOOKS

Changing Habits, Changing Lives by Cyndi O'Meara (Penguin, Ringwood, 2000).
> A simple but effective nutritional program based on making small changes, incrementally, to the way you eat.

Everyman by Derek Llewellyn-Jones (Penguin, Ringwood, 1999).
> A manual for understanding how male bodies function and how men can maximise their health.

Everywoman: A gynacological guide for life by Derek Llewellyn-Jones (Penguin, Ringwood, 1998, 9th Edition).
> The definitive manual for women from 18 to 80, explaining how the female body functions at all ages and stages.

Fighting Spirit by Lauren Burns (Viking, Camberwell, 2003).
> Warm-hearted account of the focus and determination required to become an Olympic champion.

It's not about the Bike: My journey back to life by Lance Armstrong, with Sally Jenkins (Allen & Unwin, Sydney, 2002).
> *Tour de France* cyclist Lance Armstrong relates his tale of overcoming adversity to struggle against cancer, and to recover sufficiently to take out the top cycling prize in the world. A celebration of family and human spirit.

Power with Age by Dawn Hartigan (Brolga Publishing, Ringwood, 2004).
> For older athletes keen to maintain fitness and flexibility.

ORGANISATIONS

Active for Life
> An initiative of Fitness Australia to help those who wish to understand the balance between food and exercise. Website has handy calculators for weight, calorie needs and target heart rate.
> <www.activeforlife.com.au>

COTA
> 'Living Longer, Living Stronger' health program for older adults, subsidised by COTA, to be extended to a national program in 2004. Information available from Seniors Information Victoria.
> <www.cotavic.org.au>
> 1300 135 090

Fitness Australia
> The representative body for the fitness industry in Australia, responsible for establishing standards within the industry and ensuring its long-term viability. It is the organisation through which Government and other industries will communicate with and provide support to the fitness industry. Also helpful information on choosing an accredited fitness centre.
> <www.fitnessaustralia.com.au>

The Quest for Life Foundation
>Established by counsellor and cancer survivor Petrea King in 1990, it provides residential programs at the foundation's centre in Bundanoon, New South Wales, for those fighting serious illness.
>\<www.petreaking.com.au\>

WEBSITES

women.gov.au
>Provides women of Australia with easy-to-find information about government services of specific relevance to women, including health and wellbeing, and families and relationships. An excellent resource for fact sheets on specific health concerns.
>\<www.women.gov.au\>

VIDEOS

Home Yoga Practice by Adam Shostak.
>Videos for those wishing to pursue their yoga through home practice, including specific videos for seniors, and for lower back, and neck and shoulder problems.
>(02) 6684 5323

BOOKS

Buddhism without Beliefs: A contemporary guide to awakening by Stephen Batchelor (Bloomsbury, London, 1997).
>A simply written explanation of Buddhism as a way of living rather than a system of beliefs.

The Consolations of Philosophy by Alain de Botton (Penguin, Ringwood, 2001).
>An erudite but joyful roundup of the great philosophers' views on the trials of life and how one might endure them.

A History Of Western Philosophy by Bertrand Russell (Unwin Hyman Limited, London, 1987).
>The classic text for those wishing to understand philosophy within the context of different Western societies. First published in 1946, and regularly reprinted.

How to Practice: The way to a meaningful life by His Holiness the Dalai Lama (Simon & Schuster, New York, 2002).
>Basic steps to practising morality, meditation and wisdom.

An Introduction to Buddhism: An explanation of the Buddhist way of life by Geshe Kelsans Gyatso (Tharpa Publishing, Cumbria, England, 2002).
>Explains the essential principles of the Buddhist way of life.

The New Believers: Re-imagining God by Rachael Kohn (HarperCollins, Australia, 2003).
> Rachael Kohn has been presenting 'The Spirit of Things' on ABC radio since 1997. Her book is an exploration of trends in the search for the spiritual, and contemporary expressions of different faiths.

The New Buddhism: The Western transformation of an ancient tradition by James William Coleman (Oxford University Press, New York, 2001).
> Exactly as the title suggests, an exploration of Western manifestations of an ancient faith.

Sanctuaries: Spiritual and health retreats in Australia, New Zealand and the South Pacific by Barbara Hasslacher (Choice Books, Marrickville, NSW, 2000).
> A listing of the main Christian, Buddhist and Meditation sanctuaries and retreats in the South Pacific.

The Story of Philosophy by Bryan Magee (Dorling Kindersley, Great Britain, 2000).
> An invitation to question the fundamentals of our existence and experience – both erudite and visually stunning.

The Tibetan Book of Living and Dying by Sogyal Rinpoche (Random House Australia, Sydney, 2002).
> An introduction to Tibetan Buddhism for Western minds.

Understanding Judaism by Carl S. Ehrlich (Duncan Baird Publishing, London, 2004).
> An introduction to the key tenets of the Jewish faith.

The Wisdom of No Escape by Pema Chödrön (Element, London, 2003).
> A selection of talks given by this American Buddhist nun at the first Tibetan monastery in North America. Chödrön offers a way of accepting the joy and pain of life through a 'path of loving kindness' towards yourself as well as others.

The World from Islam: A journey of discovery through the Muslim heartland by George Negus (HarperCollins, Sydney, 2003).
> An accessible and engaging overview of the Muslim faith, its adherents and its effects on the modern world.

Zen Mind, Beginner's Mind: Informal talks on meditation and practice by Sunryu Suzuki Roshi (Weatherhill International, Trumbull, CT, USA, 1970).
> An 'Americanisation' of Zen Buddhism.

ORGANISATIONS

Tai Chi Academy
> Based in Woden, ACT, this tai chi academy also offers the services of Lama Choedak Rinpoche, founder and spiritual director of the Tibetan Buddhist Society of Canberra, in classes for meditation.
> 02 6296 1357
> <info@taichiacademy.com.au>
> <www.taichiacademy.com>

WEBSITES

<www.abc.net.au/compass>
> The website of ABC TV show Compass, offering essays and interviews on faith, values, ethics and religions across the world.

<www.abc.net.au/rn/relig/spirit/>
> The website of ABC Radio National program *The Spirit of Things*, which explores religion and contemporary spirituality.

CHAPTER 14

BOOKS

The Business of Bed and Breakfast by Sharron Dickman and May Maddock (Hospitality Press, Melbourne, 2000).
> A thorough grounding in the business of running a B&B, as opposed to just letting out the spare room.

Consulting, Contracting, & Freelancing: Be your own boss by Ian Benjamin (Allen & Unwin, Sydney, 2003).
> The definitive Australian guide on how to asses your suitability as a consultant and develop a realistic business plan to get you going.

Driving Small Business by Des Knight and Noel Whittaker (Simon & Schuster Australia, East Roseville, NSW, 2002).
> A practical discussion of the key issues confronting small-business owners, and the oh-so-critical break-even point.
> <www.noelwhittaker.com.au>

The Franchisee's Guide (Commonwealth of Australia, Canberra, 2001).
> Small business consumer information for people buying, extending or renewing a franchise. Only available as downloadable PDF from ACCC website.
> <www.accc.gov.au/content>

The Franchisee's Guide by Martin Mendelsohn (Franchise Council of Australia, Melbourne, 1998, 6th edition).
> Purchase via website – for $16.50 it's a small investment for a terrific overview.
> <www.franchise.org.au/shop>

Happy Mondays – Putting the pleasure back into work by Richard Reeves (Perseus Publishing, Cambridge, MA, 2002).
> A celebration of work and what it can add to your life.
> <www.yourmomentum.com>

I Need Balance in My Life by Dr James Cowley (Richmond Ventures, North Sydney, 2003).
> Rather than dreaming of a different life, Dr Cowley suggests practical adjustments to your current one, with the ultimate aim of more harmonious work–life balance.

Making Your Future Work by Marcus Letcher (Pan Macmillan Australia, Sydney, 1997).
> Highly readable overview of the changing workplace and how to stay flexible, to maximise your chances of finding and enjoying a fulfilling work life.

Minding Her Own Business by Gloria Meltzer (McGraw Hill Australia, North Ryde, 2003).
> Subtitled 'an insiders guide...', this is a must read for any women contemplating starting up their own business.

Minding Their Own Business by Gloria Meltzer (McGraw Hill Australia, Roseville, 2001).
> Fascinating stories of all types of people who took the leap of faith into small business. (A favourite is the lawyer who spent five years learning how to become a baker.)

Own Your Own Franchise by Garry Williamson (Allen & Unwin, Sydney, 2002).
> Of great assistance to those wishing to explore issues from the franchisee's point of view.

Start Me Up by Toney Fitzgerald (Simon & Schuster Australia, East Roseville, NSW, 2002).
> Written to assist those who wish to convert their business idea into a successful reality, the tone is racy but the content very useful, and the resource section is helpful for those starting their small-business research.

Taking Control of Your Own Career by Barbara Buffton (How To Books, Oxford, UK, 1999).
> Using neuro linguistic programming (NLP) to overcome obstacles to changing your vocation.
> <www.howtobooks.co.uk>

Tax for the Very Small Business by Susan Young and Kate Robinson (Penguin Books, Camberwell, 2003).
> A thorough explanation of taxation legislation and implications for small-business owners and operators.

Your Home Business: Insights, strategies and start-up advice for aspiring entrepreneurs by Helen Chryssides (Allen & Unwin, Sydney, 2004).
> A thorough overview for those wishing to take advantage of workplace flexibility and enjoy the benefits of a home office.

52 Strategies to Work Life Balance by Ian Hutchinson (Pearson Education Australia, Frenchs Forest, NSW, 2003).
> Weekly strategies for optimising the balance between your paid work and your leisure time.
> <www.lifebydesign.com.au>

MAGAZINES

Franchise Directory (Niche Media)
> Annual publication of the Franchise Council of Australia. Includes a directory and profile of all major franchise groups as well as a listing of new opportunities.

Franchising & Own Your Own Business (Niche Media, Melbourne).
> Bimonthly magazine published on behalf of the Franchise Council of Australia. An excellent starting point for would-be franchisees.
> 1800 804 160

Franchising & Own Your Own Business Yearbook, Pamela Oddy & Ros O'Sullivan (eds) (Niche Media).
> Good overview by a number of experts in the field on law, finance, marketing and management.

COMPANIES

Business Connect
> Source of educational seminars and information forums for small-business owners and managers. Provides links to online business resource centre.
> <www.businessconnect.net.au>
> <info@businessconnect.com.au>
> (02) 9437 9333

Entrepreneur Business Centre
> Includes question-and-answer service, online resources and archives of small-business queries.
> <www.ebc.com.au>
> <support@ebc.com.au>
> 1300 300 586

Franchise Relationships Institute
> Creates and distributes educational and management materials for the global franchising sector. The institute was founded by psychologist and author Greg Nathan and is based on the belief that a constructive relationship between franchisees and franchisors is essential for the success of both parties.
> <www.franchiserelationships.com>
> (07) 3217 7323

ORGANISATIONS

Australian Business
> More than an organisation or website: an invaluable resource centre for those contemplating starting, buying or running their own business. Includes archived articles on all facets of small business.
> <www.australianbusiness.com.au>

Australian Tax Office
Tax facts for new small-business owners. Includes a section specifically devoted to franchises.
<www.ato.gov.au/businesses>

Franchise Council of Australia
National association which represents the interests of franchisees, franchisors, and service providers nationally. The best starting point for anyone seriously considering a career in franchising or purchasing a franchise.
<www.franchise.org.au>
<info@franchise.org.au>
1300 669 030

Workingconnections
A registration-based employment service for both work-seekers and employers run by the Over-fifties Association.
<www.workingconnections.com>
<jobs@workingconnections.com>
(03) 9650 6144

WEBSITES

BEP/Franchise
Franchise section of the federal government BEP website. Go to the homepage and type 'franchising' into the search box for detailed information.
<www.business.gov.au>

Business Entry Point
All you need to know, from the government point of view, to setting up, managing and expanding your business.
<www.business.gov.au/BEP>

Franchise Central
Good repository of franchise knowledge, with free online magazine.
<www.franchisecentral.com.au>
1300 558 278

Melbourne IT
Visit this website to check out possible domain name registrations and to register (if your choice is still available). If .co or .com.au is taken, try .net or .biz.
<www.melbourneit.com.au>

CHAPTER 15

BOOKS

Ageing Well by George E Vaillant, M.D. (Scribe Publications, Melbourne, 2002).
A scientific evaluation of the effects of ageing and the indicators of factors which create successful ageing.

Are You Planning for or Needing Help in Retirement? (Department of Family & Community Services, Canberra, 2002).
>A guide to options and income from Centrelink for those who are planning or entering retirement.
><www.centrelink.gov.au>

Before and After Retirement by Peter Cerexhe (Choice Books, Marrickville, 1998).
>Overview of retirement planning issues, particularly funding.
><www.choice.com.au>

Changing course: How do I retire? by Kaye Healey (Choice Books, Marrickville, 2002).
>An overview of the issues affecting those who wish to cut back on their working life.
><www.choice.com.au>

Facing the Fifties: From denial to reflection by Peter A O'Connor (Allen & Unwin, Sydney, 2000)
>A wide-ranging discussion of the issues facing fifty-something Australians, including first-person interviews about a life stage which can be as potent as adolescence.

Living Well in Retirement by Noel Whittaker (Simon & Schuster Australia, East Roseville, 2000).
>Practical guide to managing and maximising retirement income.
><www.noelwhittaker.com.au>

Midlife: A manual by Steven Estrine Ph.D. and Judith Estrine (Element Books, Massachusetts, 1999).
>A practical and fun 'manual' for older readers, particulary useful on family dynamics.

Rethink, Relax, Retire: Financing your retirement when your super and savings aren't enough by David Upton (Pan Macmillan Australia, Sydney, 2002).
>One of the more useful approaches to funding the 'less work more play' years, based on practical strategies rather than the 'get rich quick' variety.

RetireBizzi by Jill & Owen Weeks (Lifestyle Info Services, Camberwell, Vic, 2001).
>A great source of ideas and practical information for those wishing to start a small or micro business.
><www.retirebizzi.com.au>

Retirement Income Streams by Dr Ed Koken and Barbara Smith (Taxpayers Association, Elsternwick, 2001, 2nd edition).
>Excellent explanation of the various income streams available for Australian retirees, and their comparative advantages and disadvantages.

Working & Living in Retirement by Kaye Healey (Choice Books, Marrickville, 2004).
>An exploration of the many options available to those who don't want to opt out.
><www.choice.com.au>

MAGAZINES

Your Life, Your Retirement (Retirement Publishing, Melbourne)
    Bi-annual national magazine for 40+ adults seeking information on life planning, finance, health, relationships and travel.
    <www.yourlifechoices.com.au>
    <publisher@yourlifechoices.com.au>
    (03) 9824 6211

ORGANISATIONS

Australian Association of Independent Retirees
    National membership organisation and advocacy group for those who are self-funding their retirements.
    <www.independentretirees.com>
    <info@independentretirees.com>
    1800 063 304

Australian Pensioners' and Superannuants' Federation
    Established nationally in 1956, AP&SF is a network of affiliated autonomous state, regional and national consumer organisations. It represents 44,000 individuals and membership includes pensioners, state superannuants, and retired unionists. It aims to promote older people's independence, opportunities and choices, by undertaking research from a consumer perspective, by providing information and resources, by lobbying governments, businesses and services
    (02) 9281 4566

Carelink
    Free and confidential information services for older Australians to support independent living within communities. Available at 'walk-in' shops in 65 locations nationally, or via telephone or website.
    <www.commcarelink.health.gov.au>
    1800 052 222

COTA National Seniors
    Independent consumer organisation for over-fifties offering advocacy, activities and a bi-monthly magazine.
    <www.cota.org.au> or <www.nationalseniors.com.au>
    1300 76 50 50

Older Persons Action Centre
    OPAC began in 1983 and is a lobby group representing the interests of older people, especially those living on low incomes. Full membership for those aged over fifty years, and those under fifty years old can join as associate members.
    (03) 9650 4709

Probus
> Association for retired or semi-retired Australians to promote active minds, expand interests and meet new friends.
> <www.probus.com.au>

Rotary Downunder
> The world's first service club now has more than one million members worldwide. Formed to encourage business people to give back to their communities, the website lists individual clubs' locations and meeting times.
> <www.rotary.org.au>
> (02) 9633 4888

WEBSITES

American Retired Persons Association (ARPA)
> With some 30 million members, this association is well placed to conduct extensive and useful research on the modern form of 'retirement'. The website offers many items of interest and resources for the over-fifties.
> <www.arpa.com>

Seniors Card
> ACT
> <www.cota-act.org.au/seniors_card/seniors_card_main.htm>
> <cversegi@cota-act.org.au>
> (02) 6282 3777
>
> Northern Territory
> <www.seniorscard.nt.gov.au>
> <ost@nt.gov.au>
> 1800 777 704
>
> NSW
> <www.seniorscard.nsw.gov.au>
> <info@seniorscard.nsw.gov.au>
> 1300 365 758
>
> Queensland
> <www.families.qld.gov.au/seniorscard>
> <seniorscard@families.qld.gov.au>
> (07) 3224 2788 or 1800 175 500
>
> South Australia
> <www.sacentral.sa.gov.au>
> (08) 8226 6852 or 1800 819 961
>
> Tasmania
> <www.dpac.tas.gov.au/divisions/seniors/card>
> <seniors.card@dpac.tas.gov.au>
> (03) 6233 4532 or 1800 678 174

Victoria
<www.dhs.vic.gov.au/seniorscard>
<seniors.card@dhs.vic.gov.au>
(03) 9616 8241

WA
<www.osi.wa.gov.au/seniors>
<judithan@dcd.wa.gov.au>
(08) 9220 1123

2Young2Retire
Stimulating US-based website for those with a lot of living to do. Subscribe for a free newsletter.
<www.2young2retire.com>

CHAPTER 16

ORGANISATIONS

Australian Volunteers International
Australia's largest international volunteer organisation, sending people to 68 different countries, including Australian indigenous communties.
<www.australianvolunteers.com>
1800 331 292

Conservation Volunteers Australia
Involves the community in conservation projects in urban, regional and remote areas of Australia in short-term projects, completing about 1500 every year.
<www.conservationvolunteers.com.au>
<info@conservationvolunteers.com.au>
1800 032 501

National Mentoring Association of Australia
An association for mentors, educators and researchers.
<www.dsf.org.au>
(08) 9360 2344

CHAPTER 17

BOOKS

Buying a Home in France by David Hampshire (Survival Books, United Kingdom, 1996). Can be purchased from the website, where books on buying a home in Spain, France, Florida and Italy are also available, as well as a series on living and working in just about all major European countries as well as Canada and United Arab Emirates. The website also offers brief reports on living, working, retiring, or home purchase in a broad range of destinations.
<www.survivalbooks.net>

Choosing the Best Mortgage for You by Glenn Daley (McGraw-Hill Australia, Sydney 2003).
> Assumes no prior knowledge of the market, so it is useful for those wishing to learn about different ways of financing property. Includes information on what mortgage brokers can offer.

Clear Your Clutter with Feng Shui by Karen Kingston (Judy Piatkus Ltd, London, 1998).
> A small gem of a book. Read it in an afternoon and then set to work to clear your clutter, organising your home and your life in the process.
> <www.piatkus.co.uk>

Get Organised: A practical guide to organising your home and office by Carol Posener (Lothian Books, South Melbourne, 2002).
> A useful guide to the philosophy and practicalities of organising your home and office. Also useful for establishing systems and maintaining order. Virgos will love it.

Property Smart by Terry Ryder (Wrightbooks, Qld, 2002).
> A full coverage of how the property market works and what you should know before making real estate decisions.

Smarter Property Improvement by Peter Cerexhe (Allen & Unwin, Sydney, 2004).
> Maximising your investment in real estate by adding value to your property.

Streets Ahead: How to make money from residential property by Monique and Richard Wakelin (Hodder Headline Australia, Sydney, 2003).
> Offers a good overview of key issues relating to property purchase and sale.

Where to Retire in Australia by Jill & Owen Weeks (Lifestyle Info-Services Pty Ltd, Camberwell, 2000).
> This book looks at 24 ideal destinations for those seeking a lifestyle change from city life. It has a broader application than its title suggests, with particularly useful criteria for assessing your potential sea-change.
> <www.where2retire.com.au>

Who's been sleeping in my bed? How to swap your home and enjoy free holiday accommodation worldwide by Jackie Hair (Exile Publications, South Perth, 2001).
> Founder of home exchange club, Latitudes Home Exchange, Jackie Hair shares 35 years of travel experience and home-swapping expertise. Includes a comprehensive, country-by-country home-swap directory.
> <www.iinet.net.au/~exile>

MAGAZINES

Australian Property Investor
> A useful guide to property values and helpful background for those considering purchasing property.
> <www.api.com.au>

Your Mortgage
A comprehensive bi-monthly magazine devoted to buying, selling and obtaining the best mortgage possible. The website is a resource-rich portal for those seeking loans or looking at refinancing.
<www.yourmortgage.com.au>
<info@yourmortgage.com.au>

COMPANIES

First National Real Estate
National Australian real estate group with excellent free guides outlining the major steps involved in buying and selling property.
<www.firstnational.com.au>
1800 032 332

ORGANISATIONS

Real Estate Institute of Australia
Start with the Real Estate Institute of Australia, and then go to individual state institutes (accessible from this home page) for objective information on property sale and purchase. For a quick summary of stamp duty in all states, use the calculator on the Victorian website.
<www.reiaustralia.com.au>
<reia@reiaustralia.com.au>
(02) 6282 4277

ACT
<www.reiact.com.au>
(02) 6282 4544

New South Wales
<www.reinsw.com.au>
(02) 9264 2343

Northern Territory
<www.reint.com.au>
(08) 8981 8905

Queensland
<www.reiq.com.au>
(07) 3891 5711

South Australia
<www.reisa.com.au>
(08) 8366 4300

Tasmania
<www.reit.com.au>
(03) 6223 4769

Victoria
<www.reiv.com.au>
(03) 9205 6666

Western Australia
<www.reiwa.com.au>
(08) 9380 8222

Retirement Village Association of Australia
National association for accredited retirement villages across Australia. Because the legislation can vary from state to state, see also state divisions of the RVA for specific state retirement-village requirements.
<www.rva.com.au>
1800 240 080

WEBSITES

Toll Transitions
For useful overview information and quotes on moving home.
(Formerly movinghome.com.au)
<www.tolltransitions.com.au>

Victorian Government's Valuer General website
For information on buying, selling and recent property prices.
<www.land.vic.gov.au>

CHAPTER 18

BOOKS

Art of Travel by Alain de Botton (Penguin Books, London, 2003)
About travel: why we go, and how to do it in a more fulfilling way.

Explore Australia by Caravan by John and Jan Tait (Explore Australia Publishing, Sydney, 2003).
A detailed and fascinating guide to travelling the continent in a caravan or motorhome. Well worth the outlay for those on extended 'grey nomad' style adventures. 'Author's choice' notes indicate quality accommodation.

Five Months in a Leaky Boat by Ben Kozel (Macmillan, Sydney, 2003).
Tale of epic proportions about a rowing journey through Mongolia and Siberia.

Full Tilt: Dunkirk to Delhi by bicycle by Dervla Murphy (Flamingo, London, 1964).
Irish writer, Dervla Murphy recounts her journey on her bicycle, Roz, across the highways and byways of central Europe and Asia.

Gutsy Women: Travel tips and wisdom for the road by Marybeth Bond (Travelers Tales Inc., San Francisco, 2001).
> Useful and practical advice for single female travellers, written with an American accent.
> <www.travelerstales.com>

The Handsomest Man in Cuba by Lynette Chiang (Bantam, Sydney, 2003).
> A charming and entertaining account of one woman's pedalling adventure on a folding bike.

A House Somewhere: Tales of life abroad, Don George & Anthony Sattin (eds) (Lonely Planet, Melbourne, 2002).
> An evocative anthology of some of the world's best travel writers sharing their thoughts on their homes abroad.
> <www.lonelyplanet.com>

Inspiring Adventures Overseas: Special interest travel by Kate Armstrong and contributors (Global Exchange, Newcastle, 2002).
> A potpourri of experiential travel options, from archaeology to genealogy to being a pilgrim. Includes a useful directory.
> <www.globalexchange.com.au>

Learning to Float: The journey of a woman, a dog and just enough men by Lili Wright (Bantam, Sydney, 2003).
> A whimsical road book about a 30-something who drives down the east coast of America seeking enlightenment.

Long Distance Information by Julie Welch (Pan Books, London, 1999).
> Julie Welch combines a whimsical memoir of marathon running, cycling, retrenchment and never giving up.

Slow Travel: Sell the house, buy the yacht and sail away by Mari Rhydwen (Allen & Unwin, Sydney, 2004).
> For those desperate for a sea-change, a book that will encourage you to 'take the impetuous decision' and just go for it.

Traveling Solo by Eleanor Berman (Globe Pequot Press, Connecticut, USA, 2003, 4th Edition).
> An inspiring book of advice, resources and commonsense for single travellers. Many resources focus on North American travel opportunities, but the listed websites are very useful.

Travel Photography by Richard l'Anson (Lonely Planet, Melbourne, 2000).
> An excellent starting point for those wishing to combine a love of photography with an urge to travel.
> <www.lonelyplanet.com>

Volunteer Work Overseas by Peter Hodge and contributors (Global Exchange, Newcastle, 2004, 2nd Edition).
    As specific as the title suggests, full of volunteering opportunities and advice on how to get started.
    <www.globalexchange.com.au>

MAGAZINES

Gourmet Traveller (ACP Publishing, Sydney).
    Food and travel magazine with classified advertising section featuring diverse travel options.
    <www.ninemsn.com.au/gourmettraveller>

National Geographic Adventure Magazine (National Geographic Society, Washington DC).
    American monthly magazine featuring stunning photography and inspirational articles on adventure locations around the globe. *National Geographic* also produce he monthly *Traveller* magazine for more mainstream destinations.
    <www.nationalgeographic.com/adventure>

Outdoor Australia Magazine (Emap Publications, Sydney).
    Bi-monthly Australian magazine for outdoor adventurers covering bushwalking, rock climbing, canoeing, mountaineering, sea kayaking and lightweight camping. Includes regular out-supplements *Climbing Australia*, *Paddling Australia* and *Camping and Travel*.
    <www.outdooraustralia.com>

COMPANIES

ATG Oxford / Outdoor Travel
    Based in Oxford, UK, this company specialises in walking tours in Europe. Bookings via Outdoor Travel Pty Ltd.
    <www.outdoortravel.com.au>
    <info@outdoortravel.com.au>
    (03) 5750 1441

Australian House Sitters
    A long-established (1993) Australian-based home-sitting company. Site includes testimonials from happy sitters.
    <www.housesitters.com.au>
    1800 502 002

Explore Worldwide
    UK-based small group travel company specialising in remote adventure experiences, including 75 trekking and hiking tours. Represented in Australia by Adventure World.
    <www.exploreworldwide.com>
    (02) 8913 0700

HomeLink
One of the longest-established domestic and international home-swap companies.
<www.homelink.com.au>
<info@homelink.com.au>
1800 643 558

InterNational Park Tours
Offering 30 different guided walking tours in national parks in Australia and overseas, from shorter camping tours to longer lodge-based ones.
<www.parktours.com.au>
info@parktours.com.au
(07) 5533 3583

Intrepid Travel
Offers independent travel experiences within a small-group environment, staying in special accommodation and travelling by bike, bus, train and more.
<www.intrepidtravel.com>
1300 360 887

Mary Rossi Travel
Boutique luxury travel agency for those seeking different experiences.
<www.maryrossitravel.com>
<rep@maryrossitravel.com>
(02) 9957 4511

Peregrine Adventures
Offers small group tours with local language guides, worldwide. Associated with Gecko tours, for the younger, budget-conscious traveller.
<www.peregrine.net.au>
(03) 9663 8611

Sherpa Expeditions
UK-based specialist walking and cycling travel company offering adventures worldwide.
<www.sherpaexpeditions.com> or <www.outdoortravel.com.au>

Travel Associates
Appointment-only travel agency for those in search of new experiences. Eight offices nationally.
<www.travel-associates.com.au>
1800 044 066

The Travellers Bookshop
A treasure house of experiential travel books. Great for those with the itch to go, but looking for inspiration on the how, when and where.
<book@thetravelstore.com.au>
(03) 9417 4179

Valentines Travel
Founded by Biddy Naylor, and specialising in small group walking tours in France and Italy for women only.
<www.valentinestravel.com.au>
(07) 5447 4406

ORGANISATIONS

AESOP
AESOP business volunteers use their skills and experience in the Pacific, South East Asia, and with Indigenous Australian businesses. Projects include eco-tourism, office management, legal training and human resource projects among many others. Upcoming projects are listed weekly on the website.
<www.aesop.org.au>
<info@aesop.org.au>
(02) 6285 1686

Australian Society of Genealogy
The Society of Australian Genealogists is a non-profit organisation established in 1932 to advance genealogical education. An excellent starting point for those researching family histories.
<www.sag.org.au>
<info@sag.org.au>
(02) 9247 3953

BIG 4 Holiday Parks
For single road travellers, the BIG 4 Holiday Park group provides 166 destinations nationally, offering camp sites, caravan and motorhome sites and cabin accommodation with strict standards of maintenance and hygiene. But the real bonus is the shared kitchen and barbecue facilities, and happy hour times which provide the opportunity for companionship. Members receive a 10 per cent discount on accommodation.
<www.big4.com.au>
<info@big4.com.au>
1800 632 444

Campervan & Motorhome Club Of Australia
A nationwide organisation with 36 000 members, which consists of regional chapters for those wishing to enjoy the recreational-vehicle lifestyle. A solo traveller network encourages travel opportunities and rallies with other singles. A monthly magazine, *The Wanderer,* and specially tailored motorhome insurance are part of $60.50 first-year membership (drops to $44 per annum thereafter).
<www.cmca.net.au>
<enquiries@cmca.net.au>
(02) 4965 4480

Earthwatch Institute
    Promotes the understanding and action necessary for a sustainable environment by engaging volunteers in scientific field research. You can donate, join and/or participate. Limited vacancies are available for unpaid twelve- and sixteen-week internships.
    <www.earthwatch.org> or <www.earthwatch.org/australia>

The Gawler Foundation
    Founded by cancer survivor Ian Gawler, the organisation offers integrated support for people affected by cancer and other illnesses. Also a source of wellbeing and meditation courses and retreats, as well as books and tapes.
    <www.gawler.org>
    (03) 5967 1730

Mosaic Association of Australia
    For experts, new chums, and all those in between.
    <www.mosaicmadness.com.au/mos-oz>

Willing Workers on Organic Farms
    Work all year round in exchange for food and board supplied by 1200 Australian hosts on organic farms, or 600 in other countries. Handbook costs $45 (single) or $50 (double).
    <www.wwoof.com.au>
    <wwoof@wwoof.com.au>
    (03) 5155 0218

World Wildlife Foundation
    Opportunities for travel with the WWF are listed on the website, and interested people can sign up for the regular travel newsletter.
    <www.worldwildlife.org>
    Or try <www.panda.org> and click on the 'how you can help' button.

WEBSITES

Bicycle Australia
    The most comprehensive listing of bicycling associations can be found on the Bicycle Australia website. This site links to most touring associations as well as state cycling bodies.
    <www.woa.com.au/ba/links/>

Escape Artist
    Comprehensive array of resources, information and links for those wishing to 'restart their lives overseas'. Don't be put off by the listing of expensive international real estate at the top of the homepage; keep scrolling down for the real information
    <www.escapeartist.com>

Headwater Holidays
: Another UK company offering worldwide destinations for 'off the beaten track' activity holidays including hiking, cycling and dining.
<www.headwater.com>

International Home Exchange Network
: Based in Florida, this home exchange company offers a members' service for listings, and free access to listings for non-members. Cost is US$29.95.
<www.ihen.com>

National Organisation for Adult Learning
: Based in the UK – a great starting point for summer school opportunities.
<www.niace.org.uk>

People Travel the World
: Want a yacht in the Virgin Islands? A sailboat in Denmark? A catamaran in Honolulu? Try this home exchange site for exhange or rental life on the ocean wave. See also 'planning & guides' for how to organise an exchange.
<www.peopletraveltheworld.com>

Sherpa Expeditions
: UK-based specialist walking and cycling travel company offering adventures worldwide.
<www.sherpaexpeditions.com.au>

Singles Home Exchange International
: US$30 charge per annum for singles, couples, single parents and small families seeking international home exchange. Browsing the listings is free.
<www.singleshomeexchange.com>

The Solo Traveller
: Information for those travelling alone in Australia.
<www.thesolotraveller.com>

Tales from a Small Planet
: This website has comprehensive links to websites regarding taxes, exchange rates, schools, expatriate life, travel abroad and mail order shopping, as well as tales from expats all over the globe. Inspire yourself about your next destination.
<www.talesmag.com>

Travel Alternatives
: Managed by David Sheehan, author of *Work Around Australia*, this site provides information on opportunities to work, study or volunteer abroad or locally.
<www.travelalternatives.com.au>

CHAPTER 19

BOOKS

Australian Expats: stories from abroad, Bryan Havenhand and Anne MacGregor (eds) (Global Exchange, Newcastle, 2003).
   Tales from Australian expats of all ages, in all countries.

Culture Shock! Surviving Overseas – A globe trotter's guide by Frederick Fisher (Graphic Arts Center Publishing Co., Portland, 1995).
   Suitable for adventure and activity seekers or business travellers looking to educate themselves on the more pragmatic aspects of world travel.
   <www.timesone.com.sg>

The Expert Expatriate: Your guide to successful relocation abroad by Melissa Brayer Hess and Patricia Linderman (Intercultural Press Inc., Maine, USA, 2002).
   A concise, well-organised plan of attack for those contemplating or living the expat life. Includes detail on holding your marriage together, organising for school-aged children and optimising your experience of other cultures.
   <www.expatguide.info>

Teaching English Abroad: Talk your way around the world by Susan Griffith (Vacation Work, Oxford UK, 2003, 6th edition).
   A comprehensive listing of opportunities for teaching English as a second language in just about every non-English speaking country in the world. From qualifications to preparation to skills to materials, it's thorough, detailed (includes more than 700 language schools), and very readable.

Work Around Australia by David Sheehan (Global Exchange, Newcastle, 2003, 2nd edition).
   A useful starting point for those with the urge for long-term travel but without a budget to match.
   <www.globalexchange.com.au>

COMPANIES

   Christine and Marius Webb offer a personal accommodation referral service in the Upper Tiber Valley between Arezzo and Sansepolcro in Italy. Email your tour details, length of stay and areas of interest and they will respond with several suggestions to consider. The range is Palazzo to B&B, single to large group, long or short stay.
   <mjwebb@technet.it>

Global Exchange
   Information for those who wish to work or learn overseas. Includes books, resources and a messageboard.
   <www.globalexchange.com.au>
   <info@globalexchange.com.au>
   (02) 4929 4688

WEBSITES

Department of Foreign Affairs and Trade
Initially hard to locate information for those planning on working abroad, but once you crack the code, it works well. Go to the website, select Travel Advice, then select (from the very bottom of the page) 'Other travellers' information', and click on 'View a list and download'. Only then will you be richly rewarded with information on assisting Australians overseas, backpacking, travelling seniors, women travellers etc.
<www.dfat.gov.au>

Vacation Work
Perhaps the most comprehensive holiday-work website available – includes a substantial list of books published by Vacation Work, as well as job vacancies, work exchange and links to other sites.
<www.vacationwork.co.uk>

Visit web page
www.getanewlife.com.au
to access all web addresses listed in the resource section from this site, as well as a full listing of books and organisations of interest to those seeking a new life.

CHECKLISTS

CHAPTER 3
Finding your crossover point

VALUES	SKILLS	PASSIONS	WOULD LIKE TO ...

EXAMPLE: MARY ANNE

Mary Anne is single, 52, with modest savings. She has worked as an administrative assistant in the Department of Health and Aged Care for 18 years. She would like a change, but apart from travelling overseas for a few months using long service leave, she is not sure what else to do. All she knows is that the idea of the morning train from Bankstown to central Sydney is no longer making her soul sing.

VALUES	SKILLS	PASSIONS	WOULD LIKE TO ...
Environment – clean/green	Word processing	Being on the coast	Meet new people
Honesty	Reading music	Singing	Stop commuting
Egalitarianism	Physically strong and fit	Being alone	Read more
Social equity	Office administration	Ceramics	Feel more involved in vocation
	Delegation	Gardening	Lose weight
	Thrifty		Live in a closer-knit community

FINDING THE CROSSOVER:

Because we are not as personally involved as Mary Anne is, we can see clearly some possible links. Her passion for the coast, environmental values and desire to live in a closer-knit community and stop commuting all seem to point to using her long-honed administrative skills in a job, perhaps with the Department of Natural Resources and Environment, but in a seaside town where she might consider relocating.

Read Mary Anne's example, then fill in the values, skills, passions and 'would like to ...' columns above.

What crossovers can you see? Circle complementary qualities and aims. Is a pattern emerging? Are new possibilities springing to mind?

CHAPTER 3
Goal planning: Creating achievable tasks

GOAL	COMPONENT TASKS	PRIORITY OF TASKS	NECESSARY ACTION	INFORMATION REQUIRED	POSSIBLE RESOURCES	POSSIBLE OBSTACLES	DEADLINE	DATE TASK COMPLETED
Example: Buy a formal-wear hire franchise business	• Talk to family	1	Make time	Nil		They may hate this idea	22.10.04	
	• Check finances	2	See accountant	Tax returns etc		Nil	29.10.04	
	• Check approx costings	3	Check classifieds	Local & interstate papers	Library, newsagents, websites	Nil	22.10.04	
	• Check legal requirements	6	Find lawyer	Ask colleagues		Difficult to find franchising lawyer?	5.11.04	
	• Learn about franchising from magazines, websites, books, owners	7	Assemble all resources	As listed		Time	12.12.04	
	• Learn about best areas	8	Talk to retailers	All they can offer		They may not share information	12.12.04	
	• Visit formal-wear hire stores	5	Phone Bob to see if he will help	Ditto		Ditto	19.12.04	
	• Do personal skills audit	4		Check small business books		Need to be objective	5.11.04	
	• Make final decision	9					Over Xmas	

CHAPTER 3
Orientation checklist:
Where have you been and where are you going?
Creating or responding to change

	10 YEARS AGO	5 YEARS AGO	NOW	CHANGES
YOUR SITUATION				
YOUR ROLE				
YOUR ATTRIBUTES				
USEFUL EXPERIENCES				
IDEAS				

CHAPTER 5

50 useful questions to ask a financial adviser

STARTING YOUR MEETING
1. What qualifications or experience do you have?
2. Are you licensed to give financial advice?
3. May I have a copy of your advisory services guide?
4. What can I expect from this meeting?
5. What fees do you charge?
6. Can you give tax advice?
7. What if I have concerns about the outcome of this interview?
8. What other information is held on my file and what do you do with it?

CHECKING YOUR INVESTMENT OPTIONS
9. How does a managed fund work?
10. For how long should I keep my money invested?
11. How much money do I need to start an investment portfolio?
12. When is the best time to start advertising?
13. How do I know what level of risk is suitable for me?
14. How can I reduce the risk of losing my money?
15. What is the long-term benefit of adding money regularly into my investments?
16. Is it better to put extra money into my home loan to pay it off, or into managed investments?
17. Can you show me the ways to pay my mortgage off sooner?
18. What is the difference between growth and income investments?
19. Will I be charged a fee if I withdraw money from a managed fund?
20. Do you have any capital-guaranteed investments?
21. Do you have any tax-effective investments?

22. How can I protect my investment portfolio from the effects of inflation?
23. Can I invest with other fund managers?

FINDING OTHER WAYS TO INVEST
24. I've paid off some or all of my home loan and have surplus income every month. Can I use this to build an investment portfolio?
25. What are the benefits and risks of gearing and would it be appropriate for me?
26. Apart from investments, what else do you provide advice on?
27. Where can I find information about alternative investment products?
28. Can you help me invest directly in shares?

PERFORMANCE AND TAKING RETURNS
29. How can I track the performance of my investments?
30. What ongoing information will be given to me about my investments?
31. How has the particular fund been performing over the medium to long term?
32. Can you tell me what types of investments the fund invests in?
33. Who manages the fund, how long has it been operating and how big is it?
34. Should I reinvest my returns or take the income from my investments?
35. How often would I receive income from the fund?

TAKING THE MYSTERY OUT OF SUPERANNUATION
36. What are the benefits of investing in super?
37. What ways can I contribute to my super?
38. Am I putting enough money into super?
39. How do I know that my super is invested wisely?
40. Why should I consolidate my super into one fund?

GETTING READY TO RETIRE

41. When should I start planning my retirement?
42. How do I know if I will have enough to retire on?
43. How can I structure my investments to make sure that I have enough income to live on in my retirement?
44. What happens if I die – who gets the money?
45. What tax will I have to pay when I remove funds from my super account?
46. How should I structure my retirement income so I can still receive social security entitlements?

MAKING SURE YOU'VE GOT THE RIGHT INSURANCE

47. Can you calculate and recommend how much cover I should have?
48. If I become sick or injured and cannot work, what type of insurance cover can replace my income to cover living expenses such as mortgage repayments?
49. Can you help me make provisions for my family if I become disabled, get sick or die?
50. How would I know if my superannuation includes insurance?

And the answers? They're not all set in stone. A good financial adviser may answer the same question differently for different people, depending on each client's individual circumstances.

© *Your Life, Your Retirement* magazine, Issue 17, 2003

What is your starting point? How much do you have? (see page 314)

It's important to understand how much you have in assets, what you may still owe, and which assets you are planning to use to assist fund your retirement. Completing this table will you give a snapshot of how much you already have to help fund your chosen lifestyle once you stop working.

When thinking about your individual items you may want to consider if there is a need to keep these long term. Please note that joint ownership refers to items you may own with your partner or associates.

Assets and Liabilities

VALUE OF ASSETS	You	Your Partner	Joint Ownership	Are You Planning to Sell this Asset?
Family Home	$	$	$	Y/N
Contents	$	$	$	Y/N
Motor Vehicle 1	$	$	$	Y/N
Motor Vehicle 2	$	$	$	Y/N
Boat/Caravan	$	$	$	Y/N
Other	$	$	$	Y/N
Other	$	$	$	Y/N
Total (A)	$	$	$	Y/N

VALUE OF EXISTING INVESTMENTS	You	Your Partner	Joint Ownership
Investment Property	$	$	$
Superannuation Funds	$	$	$
Annuities or Pensions	$	$	$
Term Deposit(s)	$	$	$
Shares	$	$	$
Managed Investments	$	$	$
Cash at Bank	$	$	$
Other	$	$	$
Total (B)	$	$	$
TOTAL ASSETS = (A) + (B)	$	$	$

TOTAL JOINT ASSETS (C) = $

VALUE OF LIABILITIES	You	Your Partner	Joint Ownership
Current Home Loan Balance	$	$	$
Current Investment Loan Balance	$	$	$
Current Personal Loan Balance	$	$	$
Combined Credit Card Limits	$	$	$
Lease/Hire Purchase Balance	$	$	$
Other	$	$	$
Other	$	$	$
Total (D)	$	$	$
Total Value of Assets = (C) − (D)	$	$	$

TOTAL VALUE OF ASSETS (E) = $

Income and Expenditure

ANNUAL INCOME DETAILS	You	Your Partner	
Salary/Wages	$	$	
Other Taxable Income	$	$	
Tax Free Income	$	$	
Centrelink/DVA Income	$	$	
Pensions	$	$	
* Other	$	$	
Reportable Fringe Benefits	$	$	
Total	$	$	$

* Please indicate all other income e.g. franked income, family trust distributions, etc.

ANNUAL EXPENDITURE

Item	Amount	Item	Amount
PERSONAL/FAMILY EXPENSES		**TRANSPORT**	
Food	$	Registration/Licensing	$
Clothing	$	Insurance	$
Gas, Water & Electricity	$	Petrol & Maintenance	$
Medical	$	Car Loan/Lease	$
Entertainment	$	Other	$
Phone, Post, Internet	$	*Sub-total*	$
Education	$	**GENERAL**	
Furnishings	$	Superannuation	$
Other	$	Life Insurance	$
Sub-total	$	Trauma/Disability Insurance	$
HOUSING		Personal Loan(s)	$
Rates & Taxes	$	Credit/Store Cards	$
Insurances	$	Gifts	$
Repairs & maintenance	$	Savings	$
Rent/Mortgage	$	Other	$
Other	$	*Sub-total*	$
Sub-total	$		
		TAX-DEDUCTIBLE EXPENDITURE	
		Income Protection Insurance	$
		Memberships	$
		Professional Taxes	$
		Other	$
		Sub-total	$
		TOTAL	$

CHAPTER 5
How can I reduce my spending?

BUDGET BONUSES

Item	Action	Possible saving per week	Possible saving per month	Possible saving per year
Daily coffee	Reduce by 3 per week	$8.00	$32.00	$384.00
Restaurant meals	Reduce by one per month		$60.00	$720.00
Grocery shopping	Shop at supermarket with a list	$10.00	$40.00	$480.00
Petrol	Use 'Shop-A-Dockets' for discounts	$2.50	$10.00	$120.00
Holidays	Use a house swap instead of paid accommodation	$600 x 2		$1200.00
Gifts	Buy discount cards or shop at sale times (not last minute)			$100.00
Phone	Avoid calls to mobile phones			$50.00
Entertainment	Only visit movies on a discount night			$80.00
Potential Total per Annum				**$3134.00 ****

HOW CAN THIS GROW?

** This doesn't merely represent $3134, but if it was compounded at a 5% increase on a yearly basis for 5 years it would be:

Year	Start amount	Plus principal	Plus interest	Potential total saved
One	3134		3290	3290
Two	3290	6424	6745	6745
Three	6745	9879	10373	10373
Four	10373	13507	14182	14182
Five	14182	17316	18181	18181

CHAPTER 16
Volunteer Checklist:
How can I make the best contribution?

WHAT SECTOR OF VOLUNTARY WORK REALLY INTERESTS ME?

Arts
Animals
Business
Children
Cultural
Educational
Environmental
International
Health
Heritage
Language Skills
Sporting
Other

WHAT ARE MY SKILLS?

Practical
Educational
Vocational
Positive personality traits
Other

REASONS WHY I WISH TO BECOME A VOLUNTEER:

Fill in spare time
Get out of the house
Help people
Get more structure in my life
Achieve more life balance
Meet people
Support a cause
Give something back

MY PREFERRED TIME COMMITMENT:

Annual
Monthly
Fortnightly
Weekly
Daily

CHAPTER 17
Costing your property: The real cost of buying a home

Item	Example	Amount
Approximate price of home (Hobart)	$375 000	
Stamp duty (Transfer of land)	$12 550	
Stamp duty (Mortgage)	$1164	
Fee for registration of property transfer	$1013	
Title search	$13	
Registration of mortgage	$59	
Valuation fee	$600	
Legal expenses	$2200	
Rates	$550	
Electricity connection	$100 (approx)	
Gas connection	$52.80 (cylinder rental)	
Other Power	$	
Telephone connection	$209	
Other (e.g. dog-proofing existing fence)	$300	
House insurance	$800	
Contents Insurance	$880	
Repairs	$1000	
Bridging finance	Not required	
Removalist	$4500	
Moving insurance	$650	
Subtotal (expenses)	$26 640	
TOTAL	**$401 640**	

Note how that affordable $375 000 house in suburban Tasmania has now blown out by $26 279 – costing more than $400 000 for the move.

Do your sums first. Of course you will be getting rebates on other insurance already in place, but normally this is not sufficient to cover new startup policies. The costs of selling an existing property (e.g. real estate agent commission/fees, advertising costs, auction fees) have not been included, but need to be if this is your situation.

CHAPTER 17
Is this the right home for me?

Fill in the second column, firstly with your own priorities, then, after consultation, those of family members. Rate your current home on these same criteria, and then do a similar assessment on a property in which you are interested. There is no score here, but hopefully this objective priority list will enable you to choose to stay or move with a great deal more self knowledge, as well as a degree of consensus amongst family members.

EXAMPLE	PRIORITIES	CURRENT HOME	NEW PROPERTY
MY PRIORITIES 1. Smaller town in rural NSW 2. Smaller house (only 2 bedrooms) 3. Home office capability 4. Low-maintenance garden, or ability to pave 5. No mortgage			
MY FAMILY'S PRIORITIES **– New partner** 1. Rural NSW, large or small town 2. Either flat or small house 3. Near to golf course 4. Good local library 5. Home we can live in for rest of our lives **– Teenage daughter** 1. Town with decent social scene 2. Good shopping 3. Decent secondary school nearby 4. Town must have swimming pool 5. Not too far out of town			
TEN NON-NEGOTIABLE FEATURES 1. Rural NSW 2. Two bedrooms 3. Low maintenance 4. Car parking space for 2 cars 5. Single storey 6. Rural views 7. Golf course accessible 8. Possibility of staying long time (not getting built out) 9. No major renovations needed 10. Room for a home office			

CHAPTER 17
Sea-change Checklist:
Asking the useful questions

	YES	NO
EMOTIONAL		
1. Do you have an 'ideal' location in mind?	☐	☐
2. Have you considered any others?	☐	☐
3. What are your reasons for choosing this location?	☐	☐
4. What are the reasons for your move?	☐	☐
5. Are they convincing?	☐	☐
6. What do you hope to achieve by this move?	☐	☐
7. Are your expectations realistic?	☐	☐
8. Is this a shared ambition, or are your cohabitants (flatmates, family members) against the idea?	☐	☐
PRACTICAL		
9. Are there ways of trialling this move without fully committing?	☐	☐
10. Have you thoroughly researched this area?	☐	☐
11. How do you plan to do this:		
Rent?	☐	☐
Sell?	☐	☐
Swap?	☐	☐
12. Are you seeking the same type of residence, or are you changing the nature of accommodation also?	☐	☐
13. Would redecorating or renovating be the best solution?	☐	☐

	YES	NO

FINANCIAL

14. Can you afford this? ☐ ☐
15. Have you considered less-expensive options? ☐ ☐
16. Will this move cost you money, or make money, or be cost neutral? ☐ ☐
17. Are you aware of all the costs involved? ☐ ☐
18. If you are purchasing property, or land, with the intention to build, have you researched the potential of this new property compared with the potential increase in value in your current home? ☐ ☐
19. Is this part of a retirement strategy? Will it still be a good location when you are older? ☐ ☐
20. Has a financial adviser or accountant checked your sums? ☐ ☐
21. Are you aware of all the taxation implications of buying and selling, including grants and capital gains tax which may be payable? ☐ ☐

There is no ideal score for this checklist – but if you have answered 'Yes' to questions 5, 7, 8, 10, 17, 20 and 22, you're well placed to make a sound decision.

CHAPTER 18
Finding a Job in Travel Checklist

Read the example of Terry who wants to set up a diving business in the Maldives, and then use this as a template against which to formulate your plan of attack for your travel career. Remember, no idea is too ludicrous — there are Australians in every corner of the globe enjoying highly fulfilling travel careers — and having a huge amount of fun. Go for it!

LOCATION	TYPE OF TOURISM	SELF-EMPLOYED OR WORK FOR COMPANY?	COMPANIES OFFERING THIS TYPE OF TRAVEL EXPERIENCE	OTHER RESOURCES I SHOULD EXPLORE
Where do you really want to go?	Is there a particular area of tourism you would like to work?	Which would suit you best?	Do you know of any?	What else is out there?
TERRY'S DREAM				
Maldives	Diving	Work for company with view to being self-employed in 2 years time	Will need to find out	Diving schools in Australia Professional diving associations Insurance needs Traveltrade magazine
YOUR DREAM				

GOVERNMENT ASSISTANCE IN THIS AREA	SKILLS I CAN BRING TO THIS CAREER	SKILLS I WILL REQUIRE	HOW WILL I ACQUIRE THESE SKILLS
Check local, state and federal levels in Australia, as well as international bodies.	List them all, both formal and informal	Do your own list, and then supplement after discussing with someone already working in the field you wish to pursue.	Break down into specific, and manageable steps
Maldives tourism ATO DFAT Government of India	Diving expertise Business maturity Accountancy experience People skills	Knowledge of location Local language skills Business requirements in Maldives Accommodation available for tour groups, and self Currency regulations	Go there, using frequent flyer points Start language classes Contact Indian government Search via Internet

ACKNOWLEDGEMENTS

A sincere thank you to people who agreed to be interviewed for the case studies. In many cases, this meant talking to a complete stranger, but all willingly shared details of how their life changes had evolved:

Adam Shostak, Adrian Morgan, Biddy Naylor, Bill Underwood, Brad Mander, Brandon Charlesworth, Charles Brass, Christine & Marius Webb, Enid & John Robinson, Christine Garth, Professor Jacques Miller, Grace Johnston, Ged Lawrence, Glenn & Andy, Greig Whittaker, Dianne & Mike Cecil, Geraldine & John McGrath, Laura Jennings, Liz Broome, Lottie, Mandy Chalmers, Maree Goodings, Nola Diamantopoulos, Pam Dimond, Reverend Noah Park, Rebecca Doyle Walker, Renee Shapero, Sally Polmear, Seena Samuel, Steve Funnell, Tony Dyer.

Thank you also to friends and colleagues who generously shared their specialist information, time, and ongoing support:

Tim Corcoran, Pamela Oddy, Shane Murray, Garry Bear, Don Hyde, Alison Manning, Anne Brooking, Rachael Pickworth, Anne Rady, Frances Menzies, Rebecca Gallagher, Allan Crompton, Judith Watkins, Jill Weeks, Melanie Claussen, Elizabeth Heussler, Elizabeth White, Chris & Deborah from Books in Print, Jen Bird, Marie Lugg, and Tim at Neillson Central Park.

And at Allen & Unwin:

A special thank you to Sue Hines who saw the bigger picture, Clare who shaped the rough material, Karen who cared about the detail, and Andrea who refused to rest until an unruly pile of paper looked, and felt, like a real book.